Christology in Context

What They Say...

"Vashum's announced project... was the development of an Indigenous Theology that would speak out of Naga culture to Naga people living the contemporary postcolonial (neo-colonial?) realities of greater Nagaland. While his direct topic here is the development of Christology in the Indigenous context of Naga Peoples, his greater goal is to generate the political, economic, theological and philosophical language that will help Indigenous Peoples in India establish their voice within the greater societal whole of India."

Tink Tinker, author, *Missionary Conquest: The Gospel and Native American Cultural Genocide*

"At the time when dominant society tries to suppress our indigenous culture and language and majority societies consider indigenous culture as inferior, this scholarly work of Vashum on *Christology in Context: A Tribal-Indigenous Appraisal of North East India* demonstrates how our cultural resources can enrich in understanding Christ in context. I hope this work will generate new theological thinking and perspective."

Wati Longchar, author, *Returning to Mother Earth: Theology, Christian Witness and Theological Education*

"This particular book is written in the context of the Naga Christians who had constructed the image of Christ from the Euro-American perspective which has hindered their perception of Christ and eventually affected their Christian commitment. Vashum pointedly raises questions such as who Jesus is and what might Jesus mean for the Naga community? This will help the tribal Christians in India to rightly perceive, confess and proclaim Jesus from their hearts, rather than reproducing the Chalcedonian formula without understanding it. The book offers a serious articulation on contextually relevant Christology and hence it is worth reading to engage ourselves for further reflection and exploration."

K. Thanzauva, author, *Theology of Community: Tribal Theology in the Making*

Christian Heritage Rediscovered - 49

Christology in Context

A Tribal-Indigenous Appraisal of North East India

Yangkahao Vashum

CWI

Christian World Imprints™

First Published in 2017 by

Christian World Imprints™
Christian Publishing & Books from India
H-12 Bali Nagar, **New Delhi-110015**
info@christianworldimprints.com
www.ChristianWorldImprints.com
Phone: +91 11 25465925

ISBN: 978-93-5148-171-3 (HB) ISBN: 978-93-5148-172-0 (PB)

Cataloging in Publication Data--DK

Courtesy: D.K. Agencies (P) Ltd. <docinfo@dkagencies.com>

Vashum, Yangkahao, author.
Christology in context : a tribal-indigenous appraisal of North East India / Yangkahao Vashum.
pages cm. -- (Christian heritage rediscovered ; 49)
ISBN 9789351481713 (HB)
ISBN 9789351481720 (PB)

1. Jesus Christ--History of doctrines. 2. Jesus Christ--Person and offices. 3. Indigenous peoples--India--Nāgāland--Religion. 4. Naga (South Asian people)--India--Nāgāland--Religion. 5. Nāgāland (India)--Religious life and customs. I. Title. II. Series: Christian heritage rediscovered ; 49.

BT198.V37 2016 DDC 232 23

Printed in India

Dedication

A father's dream was to go to college but could not attain his dream. But he did not give up dreaming. He instilled his passion and motivated his son to carry forward his dream.

This book is a fulfilment of a father's dream for his son....

***AVA* [Father]**
Thank You
For your sacrificial love, unwavering support
and for inspiring me become
who I am today.

MAP OF NAGALAND

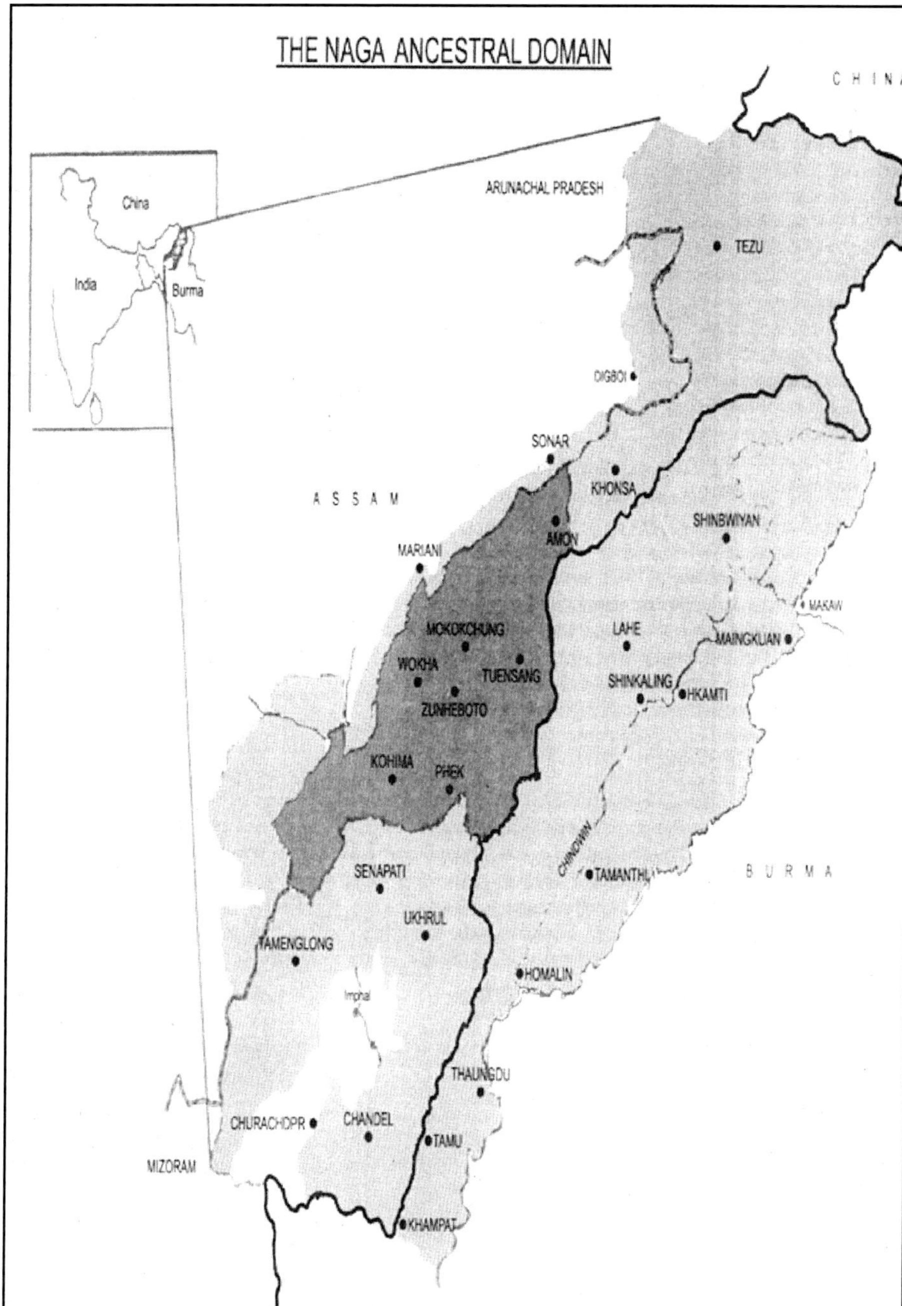

Map not to be scaled

Contents

Foreword-I

The euro-christian colonialist world has proclaimed its gospel to Indigenous Peoples now for more than a couple of centuries. We Indigenous People have longed to hear our own voices speaking back to the colonial missionaries, speaking in tones that make sense in our own cultures. In this book, Yangkahao Vashum takes a giant step towards accomplishing this goal. An Indigenous Naga from a predominantly Naga state in the northeast of India, Vashum has long attended to notions of Indigenous Theology—both as writer and as editor, particularly as editor of the *Journal of Tribal Studies*. He is a leader among an ever growing cadre of exceptionally strong Indigenous scholars who are rising to the postcolonial challenge of speaking back to the colonial masters in forceful and convincing fashion. His announced project, going back now several years, was the development of an Indigenous Theology that would speak out of Naga culture to Naga people living the contemporary postcolonial (neo-colonial?) realities of greater Nagaland. While his direct topic here is the development of Christology in the Indigenous context of Naga Peoples, his greater goal is to generate the political, economic, theological and philosophical language that will help Indigenous Peoples in India establish their voice within the greater societal whole of India.

Tink Tinker
Wazhazhe/Osage Nation, Denver

Foreword-II

With much joy and gratitude, I am writing the foreword for the book *Christology in Context: A Tribal-Indigenous Appraisal of North East India* by Yangkahao Vashum. In the effort for developing a tribal Christian theology, I have been waiting for a book on Christology from the tribal perspective.

I am very happy that Vashum took up this challenge and developed a contextual tribal Christology from a Naga perspective. Vashum has held the responsibility of the Dean of Tribal Study Centre, Editor of the Journal of Tribal Studies as well as the Dean of Post Graduate Studies of the Eastern Theological College for several years. Presently, he is the Head of Department of Christian Theology who has also edited and co-edited several books on Tribal Theology, and written and published several scholarly articles in reputed journals and books, nationally and internationally.

Tribal Theology is a contextual theology which was born out of the tribal people's struggles in India against discrimination, marginalization and identity crisis in religion as well as politics. This particular book is written in the context of the Naga Christians who had constructed the image of Christ from the Euro-American perspective which has hindered their perception of Christ and eventually effected their Christian commitment.

Responding to this problem, Vashum wrote this book and argued that any attempt to articulate a Naga-Indigenous Christology must begin by "defining Christology and the gospel for the Nagas in ways that might be more compelling and more culturally appropriate for them." He pointedly raises questions such as who Jesus is and what might Jesus mean for the Naga community? This will help the tribal Christians in India to rightly perceive, confess and proclaim Jesus from their hearts, rather than reproducing the Chalcedonian formula without understanding it.

He argues that "a Naga-Indigenous Christology will be a reflection of the people's experience of oppression, suffering; it will identify and express the concerns and longings that Nagas live with each day; and, it will embody their aspirations to be a sovereign people able to dream and shape their own future." Indeed, I believe that this affirming and liberating Christology will provide the substance for a Naga-Indigenous theology that Naga Christians can claim as their Christ.

In this effort, Vashum used cultural resources, then recaptured certain images familiar to the Nagas such as (1) Jesus as the Rooster (2) Jesus as Elder Brother and Ancestor (3) Jesus as Liberator, and (4) Jesus as Reconciler. These four images were chosen not only because each is widely known among the Nagas, but also because each metaphorical image offers specific but rich resources for the affirmation of Jesus Christ in the tribal people's context in North East India.

The book offers a serious articulation on contextually relevant Christology and hence it is worth reading to engage ourselves for further reflection and exploration.

K. Thanzauva
Aizawl, Mizoram

Foreword-III

Should Tribal/Indigenous people abandon our own culture and embrace western culture to follow Jesus? Yangkahao Vashum argues "NO". True, Christians are confused over the issue of Gospel and Culture. We often think that western culture is Christian culture. When it comes to western culture we do not question but just accept them as Christian culture. When we incorporate our cultural elements in our worship and theological reflection, we question and resist. I posted some pictures on facebook of the worship led by Paiwanese tribe in Taiwan a few months ago. One fellow wrote, "Is this worship or cultural performance?" I said we had a very meaningful worship. The fellow said, "No, pagan way of worship." We need to understand that Gospel is different from western culture. Christians often think that conversion to Christianity means one should abandon our rich traditional culture because they are pagan, evil and demonic. We should follow what western missionaries have taught us. What they said and taught are absolutely right, we should not change, or question but just follow. This is called colonized mindset or mentality. This is called distortion of gospel message and our rich cultural traditions.

St. Paul argued about the importance of culture in understanding Christ in Galatians 3:1-14. Galatians were not Jews, they were followers of Christ from Gentile background. (The ancient Galatian city is now the capital city of Turkey). They had their own rich cultural traditions. After they decided to follow Jesus they wanted to act like Jews, just as we want to act like westerners. They wanted to be circumcised, follow strict observance of Sabbath, and apply and follow Jewish laws and customs. This created conflict and misunderstanding among themselves and also spoiled their relationship with their fellow brothers and sisters who were not yet Christian. Just like the mentality of some of Asian Christians who think that by "adopting and following western culture, we become better Christians", those Galatians also thought that by observing Jewish law and practices they would become better follower of Christ. So, St. Paul is challenging them, saying "You foolish Galatians! Who misguided you?" He pushed several questions further - Did you receive the Spirit by observing law? Did you not receive the Spirit by faith? Do you think that by mere observance of Jewish laws will change your life?

Do you think that Jewish practices and customs will transform your life? Paul argued that mere observance of laws and rituals of somebody else's culture has nothing to do in following Jesus. It will rather uproot you from your own people and culture.

Paul connects his argument citing the "Spirit" and "Faith". They are the basis in following Jesus; not the observance of Jewish laws and ritual practices.

In OT, the `Spirit' is compared to `wind'. The wind blows wherever it wills. Nobody can control it. It does not make distinction between the Jewish and Gentiles, male or female, Christians or `non-Christians'. It does not make distinction between humans and non-humans. The wind is also compared with the breath of God which gives life to all. The Spirit was working even before Abraham. God's Spirit was at work even before Israel as a nation came into being. Here, St. Paul wants to affirm that the God as Spirit is present in all cultures from the very time of creation. Since, the Spirit is present in all cultures we should not abandon it. We must celebrate it. Galatian culture is also good and colourful because of the presence of Spirit. One must follow Jesus without forsaking one's own culture.

Diversity is God's structure of creation. It is like a rainbow. All colours are unique and different, and together with different colours make the rainbow beautiful. So, also God who created all whether minority or majority traditions all are beautiful and must be respected, protected and also nurtured. Not only western cultures, tribal cultures are also richly blessed by God. Not only majority culture, but also the smallest tribe tradition is blessed by God. The world will become richer when we celebrate together in different cultures and traditions with respect and love. Christian faith, worship and theology will be more colourful and meaningful when we incorporate our own indigenous traditions. It is indeed sad that many tribal/indigenous communities around the world have forgotten indigenous cultures thinking that it is inferior and demonic.

According to Paul, "Faith" in Christ makes our celebration of cultural diversity different and meaningful. Faith and action always go together. Faith in Christ leads us to transformed action. Observance of law and customs without faith will just make routine ritual observance, duty for the sake of duty, or celebration of Christian events for the sake of normal yearly celebration without any meaning. Work without faith leads a person to bondage and curtails one's freedom. But, faith makes our cultural diversity liberating and transforming. Faith leads us to respect others, but not condemnation. Faith leads us to value life more than mere ritualistic practices, like observance of Sabbath for the sake of ritual. We are not saying that all our tribal/indigenous cultural practices are good; we are not saying that we should go back to traditional customs and practices. Paul is urging that we should preserve and practice our customs and culture in a transformed or changed manner because of faith in Christ. Culture is dynamic. There is no fixed culture. Some cultures are destructive to life; misuse and manipulation of culture have led to domination and exploitation of many people. Faith in Christ leads us to discern human limitation and challenge us to transform, resist, and reject the oppressive elements in our culture for the sake of saving life. Faith in Christ leads to new action in love. Therefore, Paul is challenging Galatians not abandon their culture. Instead, transform them into what Jesus Christ taught us and celebrate the diversity in rainbow color to glorify God.

At the time when dominant society tries to suppress our indigenous culture and language and majority societies consider indigenous culture as inferior, this scholarly work of Vashum on *Christology in Context: A Tribal-Indigenous Appraisal of North East India* demonstrates, how our cultural resources can enrich in understanding Christ in context. I hope this work will generate new theological thinking and perspective.

Wati Longchar
Yushan Theological College & Seminary, Taiwan

Abstract

A Christology which is empowering and meaningful must not only be grounded in the socio-economic and political realities of the people, it must also incorporate the best of the peoples' values and traditions. Accordingly, a Naga-Indigenous Christology will be this sort of empowering theology and will likewise be informed and guided by Naga-Indigenous values and traditions. A significant component of a postcolonial theological methodology is the reclamation of the past stories and traditions which sustained the people for tens of generations. When these traditional resources are incorporated with the people's contemporary experience, it becomes possible to construct a relevant and meaningful Christology of culture and liberation.

The construction of a Naga-Indigenous Christology is an important dimension of dreaming the future in light of the Naga people's past and present experiences. In formulating this empowering Naga-Indigenous Christology, I have relied a great deal on certain concepts and models of non-Naga Indigenous peoples, but I have enlisted only the Naga resources in order to produce a contextual Christology using the following four cultural images: 1) Jesus as the Rooster, 2) Jesus as Elder Brother and Ancestor, 3) Jesus as Liberator, and 4) Jesus as Reconciler. I chose these particular images because they are widely known among the Nagas, the metaphorical image each is appropriate to the socio-economic and political exigencies, and each is comprised of its own set of multiple rich resources. The image of Jesus as the rooster conveys the significance of the sacrificial death of Jesus in a way that is culturally recognizable and relevant to the Naga people. Similarly, the portrayal of Jesus as the ancestor and elder brother enables Naga Christians to relate to Jesus in a familiar and meaningful way: Jesus as the ancestor is "God with us" who is there for the people in times of sorrows and joy; the past, present, and future come together in Christ; and Jesus as elder brother represents a much needed role model for all. The image of Jesus as the liberator resonates with considerable power in the lives of the Naga people as they strive to persevere in their struggle for political, social, and economic freedom. However, the significance of Jesus' liberative work goes far beyond human freedom; it encompasses the whole of Creation in which humanity and the rest of Creation constitute the community in need of liberation. My examination of two peacemaking traditions of the Naga people, the traditions of *Pukreila* and *Aksü*, demonstrates in direct contradiction of colonizer's insistence that Nagas were and are warmongering savages, they were and are a peace-loving people who place great value in friendship and harmonious co-existence. These traditions of peacemaking and reconciliation enrich our understanding of the significance of the role of Jesus as reconciler. Finally, the power of Christological belief insists that liberation, reconciliation, and healing must be understood as the necessary and inter-related components of one larger vision and as such cannot be addressed in isolation from each other.

Acknowledgments

This book is the outcome of my Ph.D. studies; originally undertaken as my dissertation and submitted to the Joint Ph.D. program of the Denver University/ Iliff School of Theology. Other than few addition and improvisation, the original content of the dissertation is produced as they are.

Reasearch is a collective effort. I have many people and organizations to thank for their invaluable help and support all through the course of my Ph. D. studies; and, while it will not be possible to acknowledge everyone by name, my work and this project will remain incomplete if I fail to give credit where credit is due. I am greatly indebted to the following persons and organizations for extending me the much needed financial support: the University of Denver and Iliff School of Theology Joint Ph. D. program under the direction of Dr. Frank Seeburger, and formerly directed by Dr. Sheila Davaney, for awarding me the Louis Iliff Doctoral Fellowship; Ben Chan and the International Ministries of the American Baptist Churches; the Calvary Baptist Church of Denver and Senior Pastor Mary Hulst, not only for their financial support but for embracing me and loving me as one of their own; the American Baptist Churches of the Rocky Mountains; and the Paterson International Fund of the University of Denver for helping make possible my research trip to Northeast India in Summer, 2003.

My heartfelt gratitude goes to my dissertation committee members, Dr. George E. "Tink" Tinker, Dr. Edward P. Antonio, and Dr. Haider A. Khan, for painstakingly going through draft after draft of my dissertation chapters and offering me with necessary and incisive comments. I am especially indebted to Tink, the chair of my committee, who exemplifies the ideal as a teacher and mentor. He has not only been unwavering in his support of my work, he has instilled in me the spirit of self confidence and the courage to stand up for who I am and what I believe. I also owe a great debt to my friend late Eric Larson, not only for giving the time and effort to proofread each of the chapters, but for his insightful comments and suggestions and the stimulating conversions in which we engaged in those years of our time together. I am deeply saddened by his demise. I have lost a true friend in him.

I am deeply grateful to the Board of Trustees of the Eastern Theological College, Jorhat, and the administration for allowing me to take an extended leave from the faculty and the administration's steadfast support and patience those years I have been away. I am also extremely grateful for the encouragement and vision of the late Dr. Renthy Keitzar, formerly Principal of ETC, which opened the way for me to accept the challenge of Doctoral studies.

I thank all those friends who helped during my research visit of Summer, 2003. My deep respect and gratitude go to my Naga Uncles and Aunties who were kind enough to share with me the very rich, profound stories and traditions of our people. It is through them that we are able to appreciate and make manifest the enduring wisdom of our ancestors.

I cannot thank adequately my parents, sisters and brothers, and all my relatives, without whose love and encouragement I would surely have been unable to come this far. I say thank you to all of them.

Last but not least, I thank Semmichon Shimrang Vashum, my wife and my best friend, for her steadfast love and support in bringing out this book and for taking care of our children Mangazan and Pemting.

Above all, I thank *Reisang Chonme*, the Creator, for the steadfast love and leading hands in my life!

Introduction

Christianity came to Nagaland about 145 years ago when American Baptist missionaries, entered Nagaland. Until then Nagas, practiced or more precisely they lived their traditional religion as did other Indigenous peoples.[1] The two essential elements of their religion were the belief of the Sacred Other, and the people's understanding of the presence and activities of spirits; indeed, the profound influence of each of elements is still evident today. However, with the propagation of Christianity that followed those first missionaries, the principles, rituals, and ceremonies of our traditional religion have been largely forgotten. It is thought that today nearly 95% of Nagas have become Christians.

Until quite recently, Naga Christians have adhered strictly to theology promulgated by the Baptist missionaries over one and a half centuries ago. These missionaries failed to understand or appreciate the religious and cultural ethos of the Naga people. Unfortunately, Naga Christians have assimilated Euro-american ideologies and prejudices embedded in the missionaries' message which denounces and condemns the traditional beliefs and religious values that had sustained for generation upon generation. To this day, most Naga Christians believe that to be authentically Christian they must shun everything from the past and embrace every idea and norm espoused by the Western Church; indeed they believe that the most important obligation of a Christian is to adhere strictly to the tenets of the Christian faith as promulgated by the Christian West. Very often when Naga

[1] I will be using the terms "Indigenous" and "Tribal" interchangeably in reference to the Naga people and other Indigenous peoples. While the Nagas and other Indigenous communities in India are commonly referred to as "Tribals," they are all integral members of the world's Indigenous community. My consistent use of Indigenous-Tribal/Tribe reference affirms that membership and its fundamental relationships. Additionally, I will be making use of certain concepts and ideas from non-Naga Indigenous peoples so my use of the terms interchangeably will reduce much confusion. Secondly, tribals in the Northeast India are themselves indigenous people, meaning they are the native people of the land. The term tribe or tribal is an imposed term given to the indigenous people of the region by the colonizers and western anthropologists and sociologists. Additionally, the Indian government for the administrative purposes, has simply categorized them as "Scheduled Tribe." The people never called themselves as tribals; they know each other by their own ethnic names such as Sumis, Khasis, Garos, Tangkhuls, Boros, Mizos, Adis, Wanchos etc.

Christian churches celebrate a jubilee, either silver or golden, the predominant theme adopted for the occasion has been, "From Darkness to Light,"[2] which reiterates the unequivocal distinction between the pre-Christian era and the Christian era, and thereby reminding the community and the world, that the Nagas lived in darkness before they were brought the "Light" of Christianity.

While the growth of Christianity has proved to be of profound significance to Naga peoples, they have also been struggling for political independence from India for nearly sixty years. They have experienced political oppression, economic exploitation, cultural alienation, physical violence and death on an alarming scale over the course of their struggle for sovereignty. One specific consequence of this conflict is that many Nagas today feel compelled to reconsider their faith in God. The churches are now seriously attempting to address the obvious need for a relevant and meaningful theology; that is, a theology that embodies the Naga cultural heritage and identity and allows them to regain respect for themselves as individuals and as a people.

One theological theme that requires serious consideration is a contextualized Christology. As of now there is no existing Naga-Indigenous theology that includes a serious systematic formulation of Christology which reflects the faith realities of Naga Christians. Too many Nagas envision Jesus in terms of the portrayals presented by the Euro-western and Amer-european missionaries.[3] The Naga people continue to imagine Jesus as fair skinned, blond or red-headed, and blue eyed.[4] My intention in addressing this problem is to begin discussions which must take place in constructing a Christology that is informed by Naga cultural values and priorities and, is therefore, distinctly and inherently Naga. I will demonstrate that a relevant Naga Christology of culture[5] and liberation must use and be

---

[2] "From Darkness to Light" was the theme chosen on the occasions of the celebration of the Centenary of Tangkhul Baptist Long in 1996 and 125 years of Christianity in Nagaland respectively. Nagaland Baptist Church Council, *From Darkness to Light: A Publication of the Nagaland Baptist Church Council in the celebration of the 125 years of Christianity in Nagaland* (Kohima: Nagaland Baptist Church Council, 1997); cf. A Yanang Konyak, *From Darkness to Light: A Story of the Baptist Work among the Konyak Nagas* (Guwahati: Christian Literature Center, 1986); Renthy Keitzar, *Triumph of Faith in Nagaland* (Kohima: NBCC, 1987).

[3] This is primarily a reference to the American Baptist missionaries who worked among the Naga people.

[4] While the majority of theologians and scholars are involved with ongoing discussion and debate surrounding historical Jesus, my project is concerned with the historic and cultural Jesus Christ. I use the names "Jesus" and "Christ" interchangeably for Jesus Christ making no distinction among them. Indeed, Naga Christians make no distinction between Jesus and Christ. For them Jesus is Christ and Christ is Jesus and it is simply unthinkable to make any distinction between the two.

[5] By Christology of culture I mean cultural Christology in the sense that it utilizes Indigenous cultural resources for constructing Christology.

informed by Naga cultural metaphors in order to respond to the contemporary socio-political context of the Naga people.[6]

Any attempt to articulate a Naga-Indigenous Christology must begin by "defining Christology and the gospel for ourselves in ways that might be more compelling and more culturally appropriate for us."[7] And we do this by asking who Jesus is and what might Jesus mean for the Naga community? How might we profess and proclaim Jesus in a manner that is genuinely derived from and centered in the Naga people's experience and cultural reality? Seen from another perspective we might ask, what should a genuinely Christian response be to tribal peoples and cultures, given the extant animosity historically directed at Naga cultures by both the Christian missionaries and Naga Christians themselves?

Limits of the Research

The ancestral homeland of the Naga people spans the states of Arunachal Pradesh, Assam, Nagaland and Manipur in India and certain parts of Myanmar. Logistical restrictions involving time and distance necessarily limited this research work in two ways; however, each limitation is mitigated by a significant qualification. First, the proposed research area was limited to the Nagas living within the states of Nagaland and Manipur; now, having said that, the majority of Naga population actually live in these two states. The research was also intended to include Naga Christians generally, but I have instead focused on Baptist Christians who compose nearly 85% of all Naga Christians. As I have attempted to make clear, the construction of a relevant Christology within a Naga-Indigenous theology as the main concern of this study; but, there are political, social, and economic implications and consequences which are not only pertinent, they are in fact inextricable from this project and therefore demand a good deal of attention.[8]

Theory Base for Research

Theological reflection based on the life experiences and cultural heritage of the Nagas is an urgent task in Nagaland today. The Nagas are endowed with rich historical cultural resources which have not been considered relevant to the task of theological reflection. I will argue that for the development and articulation of a meaningful theology it is imperative that we identify and retrieve the cultural

[6] The cultural metaphors include Jesus as the rooster, Jesus as the ancestor and elder brother, Jesus as the liberator, and Jesus as the reconciler.

[7] George E. Tinker, "Christology and Colonialism: Jesus, Corn Mother, and Conquest." TMs, 8.

[8] My primary project is to construct a Christology using Naga cultural resources and metaphors. I make use of the cultural resources because they serve as invaluable sources for theological construction of Christology. Secondly, my discussion/critique of the missionaries is crucial for establishing the problematic of my project: the need for new cultural Christology for the Nagas. Therefore, my project is neither a historical nor an ethnographic; it is a Christological construction drawing upon resources from historical and ethnographic studies.

values that, while forgotten and nearly lost by many, are known by certain Nagas to be life affirming, empowering, and liberating. Therefore, we must begin the process of recollection, remembering and sharing all that is best in Naga culture with a view to formulate a theology which will ultimately be inclusive, dialogical and liberative.

I will begin by demonstrating the importance of the following four cultural images: first, Jesus as the rooster,[9] that is, the sacrificial animal of the tribal people in their cultural past is one image; the second is Jesus as the ancestor[10] and elder brother who is regarded as the source of filial connections that encompasses the past, the present, and the future including the dead in the Naga family and community. Third, is the image of Jesus as liberator. In the context of Nagas' liberation struggle from and against the state of India and now against the added forces of globalization of capital and the concomitant social evils that have invaded the people, the image of Jesus as liberator becomes critically important for the Nagas.

Last, but certainly not least, I will also examine the image of Jesus as reconciler in the context of contemporary Naga society which has unfortunately fallen into parochial quarrelling and factional clashes among a certain national freedom movement groups/factions. Sadly, these are the results desired by a few unscrupulous and self-important individuals and the consequences of this internecine fighting have left the Naga society more divided than ever before. There are two of the many widely known traditions of peacemaking in Nagas that I will discuss. The first is *Pukreila* as the peacemaker, a tradition associated with a woman *(Pukreila)* married to a man from another village. When there was a dispute between two villages *Pukreila* acted as mediator and helped resolve the dispute amicably. The second tradition is the *Aksü*, which is known for giving or sacrificing pigs between or among the villages as a symbol of goodwill and friendship. *Aksü* was also appropriate when opposing parties came to an amicable settlement between or among themselves; a pig is sacrificed as a symbol of their reconciliation and a pledge to maintain the peace and harmony among themselves.

My theoretical assumptions are based on Indigenous ways of knowing which in turn are based on and informed by the Indigenous worldview which is predicated on the view that everything, all of Creation, is related. I will follow the lead of Vine Deloria Jr.(Standing Rock Sioux) who argues for doing research according to

---

9 In addition to being a sacrificial animal, the rooster was also a mythic figure. According to Naga myth, the rooster was responsible for persuading the Sacred Other to provide light (sun light) to the world and the rooster was also the animal to whom the Sacred Other gave the responsibility of maintaining the duration of day and night.

10 Ancestors were also regarded as a source of life for the living and they represent the mystery of the invisible. Cf. M. Horam, *Nagas Old Ways New Trends* (New Delhi: Cosmo Publications, 1988), 19.

and following Indigenous ways of knowing. Deloria has very eloquently explained how the principle of relatedness of all Creation can be an effective methodological foundation for gathering information.

> "We are all relatives" when taken as a methodological tool for obtaining knowledge means that we observe the natural world by looking for relationships between various things in it. That is to say, everything in the natural world has relationships with every other thing and the total set of relationships makes up the natural world as we experience it. This concept is simply the relativity concept as applied to a universe that people experience as alive and not as dead or inert.[11]

Indigenous theologians such as, Tink Tinker(Osage), Wati Longchar and K. Thanzauva have argued from the perspective of Indigenous worldview that the starting point for Indigenous theology must be Creation, not human beings.[12]

My project of theologically constructing a Christology for Naga Christians will be guided by my understanding of the inter-relatedness of everything; in other words, I will construct a contextualized Christology that affirms the Creation centered worldview of the Indigenous people. It should also be noted that I begin with an intentional assumption that all Christian theology is inherently rooted in and informed by a particular cultural reality.[13] Accordingly, there is nothing intrinsically unchristian in the Nagas' efforts to recover and reclaim historically empowering cultural resources and values for purposes of formulating an expression of faith that will be meaningful and relevant.[14]

Review of the Literature

In *Jesus Through the Centuries: His Place in the History of Culture*, Jaroslav Pelikan offers a series of images in order to illustrate the place of Jesus in the history of culture, including: King of Kings, Cosmic Christ, Christ Crucified, Prince of Peace, Teacher of common sense, Liberator, and Man who belongs to the World. Similarly, John F. O'Grady has observed different models of Jesus, such as: the mythological Christ, Jesus the Ethical Liberator, the Human Face of God, the Man for Others, and Jesus as Personal Savior.[15] Walter Kasper has offered us

---

[11] Vine Deloria, Jr, *Spirit and Reason: The Vine Deloria Reader*, ed. Barbara Deloria, Kristen Foesten, and Sam Scinta (Golden: Fulcrum Publishing, 1999), 34.

[12] Both K. Thanzauva and Wati Longchar are prominent Indigenous theologians from Northeast India. Thanzauva belongs to the Mizo nation and Longchar belongs to the Naga nation.

[13] See Jaroslav Pelikan, *Jesus through the Centuries: His Place in the History of Culture* (New Haven and London: Yale University Press, 1985).

[14] Without being consciously aware of the fact Nagas have already incorporated certain traditional cultural and religious values in the expressions and practices of their Christian faith in the celebration of Christmas and other important Christian festivals.

[15] John F. O'Grady, *Models of Jesus* (Garden City: Images Books, 1982).

larger frameworks within which many of the images and models are conceived by identifying three major approaches in contemporary Christology:[16] Christ in a cosmological perspective, Christ in anthropological perspective, and Christ in the perspective of universal history. According to Kasper then, Pierre Teilhard de Chardin and Jürgen Moltmann represent the first approach; Karl Rahner is the best known proponent of anthropological perspective; Jürgen Moltmann and W. Pannenberg work from the universal history perspective. Also worth consideration is John P. Meier[17] development of a cultural Christology, and Richard Horsley's[18] examination of Christology in relation to politics.

When considered in the context of cultures of the so-called the Two-Thirds World, Christology assumes a much more urgent and practical clarity. This urgency is apparent in a Latin American Christology centered in socio-political liberation with Jesus as the Liberator.[19] Asian and African theologians also portray Jesus as the liberator but they have expanded this rather limited conception by infusing their Christology with familiar, traditional cultural images. In the case of Africa Christians, the cultural images chosen to empower their Christology include: Jesus as Master of Initiation,[20] Christ as Chief,[21] Christ as Ancestor and Elder Brother,[22] and Jesus as Healer.[23] Charles Nyamiti has identified two general types of Christologies which continue to develop in Africa: Christologies of inculturation and liberation.[24] Asian theologians understand that relevant Christology is done in the context of competing religious traditions in the sense

---

[16] Walter Kasper, *Jesus the Christ* (London: Burns and Oates, 1976), 17-18.

[17] John P. Meier, *A Marginal Jew: Rethinking the Historical Jesus*: Volume One. The Roots of the Problem and the Person. (The Anchor Bible Reference Library). (New York: Doubleday, a Division of Doubleday Dell Publishing Group, Inc. 1991).

[18] Richard Horsley A, *Hearing the Whole Story: The Politics of Plot in Mark's Gospel* (Louisville: Westminster John Knox Press, 2001).

[19] Jon Sobrino, *Jesus the Liberator: A Historical-Theological View*, trans. by Paul Burns and Francis McDonagh (Maryknoll: Orbis Books, 1993), José Míguez Bonino, ed., *Faces of Jesus: Latin American Christologies,* trans. by Robert R. Barr (Maryknoll: Orbis Books, 1977), Gustavo Gutierrez, *A Theology of Liberation: History, Politics and Salvation,* Revised ed. with a new introduction by the author. Trans. and edited by Sister Caridad Inda and John Eagleson (Maryknoll: Orbis Books, 1988).

[20] Ansleme T, Sanon, "Jesus, Master of Initiation," in *Faces of Jesus in Africa,* edited by Robert Schreiter (Maryknoll: Orbis Books, 1991), 85-102.

[21] François Kabasélé, "Christ as Chief," in *Faces of Jesus in Africa*, edited by Robert Schreiter (Maryknoll: Orbis Books, 1991), 103-115.

[22] François Kabasélé, "Christ as Ancestor and Elder Brother," in *Faces of Jesus in Africa*, edited by Robert Schreiter (Maryknoll: Orbis Books, 1991), 116-127.

[23] CéCé Kolié, "Jesus as Healer?," in Faces of Jesus in Africa, edited by Robert Schreiter (Maryknoll: Orbis Books, 1991), 128-151.

[24] Charles Nyamiti, "African Christologies Today," in *Jesus in African Christianity: Experimentation and Diversity in African Christology*, edited by J. N. K. Mugambi and Laurenti Magesa (Nairobi: Initiatives Ltd., 1989), 17-39.

that Jesus has rivals in the "saviors" of at least three other extant Asian religions such as, Krishna,[25] Buddha,[26] and Muhammad. M. Thomas Thangaraj has developed a Christology of Crucified Guru based on the Hindu concept of Guru as an exercise in cross-cultural Christology,[27] and Sathiananthan Clarke conceives a Christology by drawing upon the "theological explications of the symbol of the drum" from the Dalit religious traditions of India.[28]

Various culturally relevant Christologies have been and continue to be developed in particular regions of the world through the recognition and appropriation of traditional values and cultural realities. This sort of profound theological contextualizing has yet to develop in Northeast India. While Wati Longchar and K. Thanzauva, the leading theologians of the Northeast India, have been working diligently toward articulating Indigenous theology by reclaiming past cultural resources, they have not addressed Christology which is arguably the most important component of any Christian theology. While both have been consistent in arguing for formulating an Indigenous theology which is rooted in the authentic cultural soil of the people, each has chosen his own contextual starting point. Thanzauva has gone so far as to propose that the relevant method for doing Indigenous theology must combine synthesis and praxis model, or what is referred to as the synthetic-praxis method.[29] In addition to his insistence for recovering the cultural traditions of the people his theological discourse calls for social transformation that is guided by the vision of the Kingdom of God.

Longchar argues that a methodology that truly facilitates Indigenous theological articulation must come from within the matrix of Indigenous worldview.[30] In other words, the starting point for Indigenous theology must be Creation, not human beings. As I noted above, the Indigenous worldview acknowledges and affirms the inter-relatedness of all things, and recognizes and values the intrinsic harmony between humanity and nature. The entire reality of

---

[25] Ovey N. Mohammed, "Jesus and Krishna," in *Asian Faces of Jesus*, edited by R. S. Sugirtharajah (Maryknoll: Orbis Books 1993), 9-24.

[26] Aloysius Pieris, "The Buddha and the Christ: Mediators of Liberation," in *Asian Faces of Jesus,* edited by R. S. Sugirtharajah (Maryknoll: Orbis Books, 1993), 46-61.

[27] M. Thomas Thangaraj, *The Crucified Guru: An Experiment in Cross-Cultural Christology*, foreword by Gordon D. Kaufman (Nashville: Abingdon Press, 1994).

[28] Sathiananthan Clarke, *Dalits and Christianity: Subaltern Religion and Liberation Theology in India* (Oxford and Delhi: Oxford University Press, 1998), 5.

[29] K. Thanzauva, *Theology of Community: Tribal Theology in the Making*. Aizawl: Mizo Theological Conference, 1997. "Issues in Tribal Theology" in *Tribal Theology: A Reader*. Tribal Study Series No. 12. edited by Shimreingam Shimray. (Jorhat: Tribal Study Center Eastern Theological College, 2003), 17-36.

[30] Wati Longchar, "The Need for Doing Tribal Theology" in *Tribal Theology: A Reader*. Tribal Study Series no. 12. edited by Shimreingam Shimray. (Jorhat: Tribal Study Center Eastern Theological College, 2004), 1-16. "Doing Creation Theology with Tribal Culture of India" in *PTCA Bulletin* 13, no. 1 & 2 (June & December 2000), 37-43.

life, including our understanding of God and spirituality must be seen within the wider perspective of our relatedness with all Creation.

Significance and Contribution

The significance of this research lies in moving beyond existing Indigenous theological work by providing a comprehensive and in-depth treatment of the identified theological theme. In particular this research, will provide a significant treatment of the issues of Jesus' relevance as the cultural and spiritual liberator, hitherto not considered in Naga-Indigenous theology. The goal then is to address the profound need for a relevant and meaningful theological identity among the Naga Christians. An additional contribution will be to give a Naga-Indigenous Christology that is informed by people's experience and cultural reality.

Research Methodologies

My approach is multi-disciplinary. Historical and sociological analysis will be applied to gain understanding of the socio-economic and political situation of the Naga society. I will also employ historical and theological analyses of the work and influence of the Christian missionaries. Each of these is essential for underscoring the importance of socio-political context which will give life to the Indigenous theology I have proposed. By situating Naga Christianity in its socio-economic and political milieu, and by enlisting theories of postcolonial discourse, I will analyze the significance of the interaction between Christianity and Naga culture and Naga culture's influence, if any, in shaping existing Naga Christianity. More specifically, I will examine the ways Nagas have been influenced in how they understand the presence of Jesus Christ in their lives, and in the process, will locate the Naga situation within the wider context of postcolonial discourse.

Since, the purpose of research is to construct a Naga-Indigenous Christology informed by Naga cultural values and images it is imperative that the cultural values we recover and employ are life affirming and liberating. This project will therefore involve a process of re-collection and remembering. Primary resources include re-reading the history of religion, especially Naga-Indigenous religious and oral traditions and critically analyzing Naga people's experiences. In certain cases, I will use information obtained by interviews,[31] in order to illustrate and support my arguments.

Finally, I am proposing a theological construction of Christology. I will build on the extensive and very helpful work of Indigenous/Native theologians such as, Tink Tinker, Wati Longchar, K. Thanzauva and other liberation theologians

[31] I completed the process of the Institutional Review Board (IRB) of the University of Denver.

whose theological approaches take seriously the Indigenous worldview and cultural significance of the people.[32]

General Outline

Chapter one, presents a critical review of the works of the missionaries who worked among the Naga people. It examines the relations between colonialism and Christian mission in Northeast India with special reference to Naga people. This is critical for identifying and locating the theological context out of which a construction of Naga-Indigenous Christology must occur. Chapter two discusses and analyzes the socio-economic and political situations of the Naga people, situating Naga Christianity in its socio-economic and cultural-political milieu with a view to constructing a Naga-indigenous Christology that will be relevant to the people.

To provide a broader perspective on the author's treatment of Christology, chapter 3 offers an overview of Christological traditions and approaches as these are historically embedded in culture. In the history of Christianity, numerous images of Jesus have been significant and special attention will be given to how Jesus has been interpreted and portrayed in different cultures and contexts.

Chapter four addresses the methodological issues of Indigenous theology. First, it situates Indigenous theology within the wider context of postcolonial discourse and informed by its discourse, the whole category of Indigenous situation/theology has been theorized. Second, it delineates and analyzes its sources which consist of past cultural and religious traditions and values, myths and folktales, people's history and experiences of contemporary Naga society.

Finally, chapter five focuses on the constructive aspect of theology employing historical, political, and cultural resources that were identified in the preceding chapters to construct a Christology that will be meaningful and relevant to the experiences and cultural realities of the Naga people.

[32] The task of theology includes critical reflection and construction. My theological method includes appropriating critically cultural values and resources for purposes of constructing a relevant and meaningful Christology. And my project falls within the so-called contextual-liberation theology that advocates and takes seriously the Creation as well as human situatedness as the starting point for theology.

Chapter 1

Colonialism, Missionaries, and Indigenous A Critical Appraisal

The thesis of my research is to construct a Christology which is informed by Naga cultural values and images, and in a manner that is genuinely born out of Naga people's experience and reality. I will be approaching this research through the perspective of theories of postcolonial discourse. And as part of this approach, this chapter will examine the relations between colonialism and Christian mission in Northeast India with special reference to Naga people. This examination is key to unraveling the history of colonialism and its responsibilities for the subjugation of Naga people, politically, socially, culturally and religiously. Contrary to the widely held view that missionaries functioned independent of colonial powers, I will argue that there were close relations between colonial powers and missionaries and that however good their intentions might have been the missionaries participated in the colonial projects.

Colonialism and Christian Mission: A General Overview

The history of modernity is characterized both by colonial extension and missionary expansion in the non-European world. In the words of David J. Bosch the colonial period "precipitated an unparalleled era of mission."[33] When the European colonial forces had established control over non-European countries such as in Asia, Africa, Latin America and Pacific Islands, this consequently provided opportunities for Christian missionaries to follow suit with their missionary adventurism.[34] In general, wherever the colonial powers were planted

[33] David J. Bosch, *Transforming Mission: Paradigm Shifts in Theology of Mission* (Maryknoll: Orbis Books, 1991), 227.

[34] Edmund J. Dunn, *Missionary Theology: Foundations in Development.* Foreword by Richard P. McBrien (Washington, D.C.: University Press of America, 1980), 9.

there inevitably followed Christian missions. Historically, the general assumption was that colonial expansion to the non-Christian world was believed to be God's providence; it was regarded as opportunities for propagating the Gospel to the "heathen" world. At the time when the debate was raging in Britain on Christian missionary activities in colonies in general and India in particular, Wellesley argued that:

> It would not only be impolitic but highly immoral to suppose that Providence has admitted of the establishment of British power over the finest provinces of India, with any other view than of its being conducive to the happiness of the people, as well as to our national advantage.[35]

Penny Carson asserts that Wellesley's statement was consistent with the views of the Christian Evangelicals who were the major force behind the modern missionary movement. According to Carson, Evangelicals

> Saw no inconsistency between their conviction that Providence had given India to Britain for a higher purpose... and their belief that possession of India should also contribute to the national wealth. However, they were also increasingly concerned about the state of Indian society and its spiritual and moral welfare. Evangelicals argued that only through the inculcation of Christianity could Britain improve not only the spiritual but also the moral and material condition of the people.[36]

Of course, the history of colonialism and Christian missions go way back to the fifteenth and sixteenth centuries as a result of the expansion of Western Europe, the period often referred to as the "age of discovery and expansion." "During this age of discovery and expansion" wrote Richard P. Dunn, "the church sent forth missionaries steeped in European culture that was Christian and a Christianity that was intimately bound to European culture."[37] There was no doubt about the close connections between colonialism and Christian mission; they went hand in hand. For example, the kings of Spain and Portugal enjoyed the papal privileges granted to them for both colonial and missionary enterprises:[38] the Spaniards in Central and South America and the Portuguese in the western of Africa and

---

[35] Quoted in Penny Carson, "The British Raj and the Awakening of the Evangelical Conscience: The Ambiguities of Religious Establishment and Toleration, 1698-1833" in Brian Stanley, ed., *Christian Mission and the Enlightenment* (Grand Rapids: William B. Eerdmans Publishing Company, 2001), 46.

[36] Ibid., 46.

[37] Dunn, *Missionary Theology*, 10.

[38] Dunn, *Missionary Theology*, 11; Cf., Bosch, *Transforming Mission*, 228.

Brazil. Both were known for imposing Catholicism, their state religion, on the nations they colonized, "asserting the state's duty to further the progress of the *Corpus Christianum*."[39] In fact, "The propagation of the faith and colonial policies became so intertwined that it was often hard to distinguish the one from the other."[40] Winona LaDuke, an American Indian scholar and activist, an Ashinaabeg (Ojibwe) by tribal affiliation, said it best:

> Papal law was the foundation of colonialism; the Church served as handmaiden to military, economic, and spiritual genocide and domination. Centuries of papal bulls posited the supremacy of Christendom over all other beliefs, sanctified manifest destiny, and authorized even the most brutal practices of colonialism.[41]

Both the colonial powers and missions held the "civilizing responsibility" which is also known as the "white man's burden" as their shared goal. "The mutual binding between missions and colonial politics was at its strongest where the two accepted the 'white man's burden' as a genuine responsibility which some anti-imperialist missionaries referred to as Christian imperialism."[42] It might rather be more appropriate to call these missionaries liberal missionaries than "anti-imperialist" missionaries, after all, none of the missionaries were anti-imperialist in a true sense.

The Scottish debate on mission methods in the eighteenth and nineteenth centuries further underscored this point. The debate centered on whether civilizing or Christianizing should come first.[43] While some argued for civilizing the people first others argued for the latter. Those in favor of the latter argued that Christianizing itself was a means of civilizing and the two went together inevitably anyway. This view was represented by James Montgomery when he wrote:

> The wisdom of man says, "First *civilize*, and then *Christianize* barbarians;" but the wisdom of man has proved itself foolishness in every experiment of the kind . . . . The counsel of God is the reverse; 'Go and preach the gospel to the Gentiles . . . you will civilize them by Christianizing them.[44]

---

[39] Carson, "The British Raj and the Awakening of the Evangelical Conscience," 47.

[40] Bosch, *Transforming Mission*, 228.

[41] Winona LaDuke, *Recovering the Sacred: The Power of Naming and Claiming* (Cambridge: South End Press, 2005), 11-12.

[42] Ibid., 7.

[43] Ian Douglas Maxwell, "Civilization or Christianity? The Scottish Debate on Mission Methods, 1750-1835," in Brian Stanley, ed., *Christian Missions and the Enlightenment* (Grand Rapids: William B. Eerdmans Publishing Company, 2001), 123-140.

[44] Ibid., 123.

The view was that Christianizing and civilizing are two sides of the same coin; in other words, they were inseparably linked.

The most potent weapon behind the civilizing mission was the philosophy that not only entertained but created the idea of superiority over the native race. The idea of the civilizing mission originated in the French *mission civilistrice* which was itself rooted in the "idea of mastery."[45] This idea of mastery was further based on twin fundamental assumptions "of the superiority of French culture and the perfectibility of humankind." Note, this French cultural superiority became the imperial ideology of the British colonizers from the late eighteenth century. The civilizing mission subsumed what the English had been referring as "improvement" or "betterment" or "moral and material progress." According to Michael Mann:

> Basically, the *mission civilistrice* rested upon the idea of mastery – or, in other words, "to be civilized was to be free from specific forms of tyranny: the tyranny of the elements over men, of disease over health, of instinct over reason, of ignorance over knowledge and despotism over liberty." However, in spite of this 'enlightening agenda,' the concept of the *mission civilistrice* was used above all for the self-legitimation of colonial rule.[46]

Colonialism, Missionaries, and Nagaland (Northeast India)

The British colonization of India in the eighteenth century and the eventual British control over the northeast region in the nineteenth century – the region inhabited basically by the indigenous peoples – served to open doors to the region for the missionaries. The pioneer missionaries who came to Northeast India in the nineteenth century belonged to the American Baptist Foreign Mission and Welsh Presbyterian Mission.[47] Though the Roman Catholic missionaries did cross the path on their way to Tibet and China prior to the protestant missionaries as early as 1626, they did not start any mission work in the Northeast region.[48]

---

[45] Michael Mann, "'Torch Bearers Upon the Path of Progress': Britains Ideology of a 'Moral and Material Progress' in India: An Introductory Essay," in Harald Fischer-Tine and Michael Mann, ed., *Colonialism as Civilizing Mission: Cultural Ideology in British India* (London: Wimbledon Publishing Company, 2004), 4.

[46] Ibid.

[47] Prior to the American Baptist Missionaries, the British Baptist and Serampore Missions were already in lower Assam but their mission did not last for long and the BMS rather decided to donate its Gauhati property to American Baptist missionaries. F. S. Downs, *The Mighty Works of God: A Brief History of the Council of Baptist Churches in North East India: The Mission Period 1836-1950* (Guwahati: Christian Literature Center, 1971), 10-13.

[48] Jesuit missionaries, Frs. Stephen Cacella and John Cabral were said to have traveled to Goalpara and Kamrup in Assam looking for a passage to Tibet and China. Milton S. Sangma, *History of American Baptist Mission in North-East India (1836-1950)*, vol. 1 (Delhi: Mittal Publications,

They began their mission work in the region only in the early middle part of the twentieth century.

It was a known fact that there was a working relation between the British colonial powers and Christian missions in Northeast India. Although the British government maintained the existence of their policy of neutrality,[49] this policy did not stop some of the individual government officers from indulging in religious activities by way of either helping Christian missionaries or the native people. While the British government denied its involvement officially, the irony was that the government went on to justify its support of the missionaries.

The British India offered two reasons to justify their involvement in religious activities, particularly their support of the missionaries. First, the British administration justified their encouragement and funding of the Christian missions on the grounds that the hill people did not have any religion.[50] Of course the Nagas and other peoples in the region did have their ceremonies and religious culture but the English chose deliberately to ignore them even when they plainly saw. Secondly, they argued that the Christian mission schools were providing "secular" services rather than religious instructions.[51] On these grounds the government justified its activities and maintained that religious neutrality was not being violated. However, it was quite obvious that the missionaries were using education for the advancement of the Christian gospel and for the building of Christian community.[52] The British knew very well that education was a means of missionizing adopted by the missionaries, and as such its claim to justify on the ground of secular service proved to be simply untrue. Schools were also set up in the Assam plains for the evangelistic purpose although they were less successful.

1987), 14; cf. Sebastian Karotemprel, ed., *The Catholic Church in North East India, 1890-1990* (Shillong: Vandrame Institute, 1993), 25ff.

[49] The directives of the Court of Directors in London on their policy pf Religious neutrality read as follows: "It was well known that we would not engage in schemes for attempting to propagate Christianity among the natives; it is a matter of surprise to us that an active part in the prosecution of this plan should have been taken by a Member of the Government, and neither the plan itself nor the very extra-ordinary mode in which it came to be recommended to your notice should have appeared to you unobjectionable." Quoted in Downs, *North East India,* 37.

[50] Ibid., 53. According to Tinker, this is exactly what the English colonizers said about the American Indians in the Northeast (New England) some two centuries earlier (1620s, 1930s).

[51] Ibid., 53.

[52] As early as 1886, E. G. Philip, in a Jubilee report reiterated the following objectives of education: "In aim and plan, the great thing ever before the Mission has been evangelization. The Garos were ruined by sin. The Gospel alone can restore them. But the Gospel must be communicated. Almost of necessity the written page needs follow the preached Word. Such has been God's plan in all history. Hence, the absolute necessity of education among savages, as a chief handmaid to religion. Little call would there be, by a people who cannot read, for Scriptures and Christian Literature the foundation through them revealed Christ of Christian civilization." E. G. Philip, *Educational Work among the Garos, Jubilee Report*, 1886, 67.

The co-operation between the government and Christian missionaries (mission) existed in the following areas: First, in most cases the missionaries were invited by the British administration to initiate mission works among the people in Northeast region.[53] The first mission also known as the Shan mission was started at Sadya as part of an ambitious Asian mission which would eventually cover upper Burma and China besides Northeast India.[54] The missionaries thought that Sadya's proximity to Burma and China made it an ideal place from which to launch their mission activities. Although, the plan failed due to a number of circumstantial factors, it was certainly significant in that the doors for mission activities were thrown wide open.

British officials David Scott and Scott's successor Francis Jenkins are known to have contributed the most to the missionary endeavors in Northeast India.[55] Both Scott and Jenkins served as Commissioners of Assam and both came from an evangelical Christian background. Scott took keen interest in the Garo people and most of his service was focused there. He opened a school with the goal to convert the Garos to Christianity and in return it "would serve the interests of government insofar as stabilizing influence."[56] This was another clear example of a commitment on the part of the mission effort and the clear connection envisioned by the colonial governing officials.

Jenkins helped the missionaries in every possible way in his capacity as the Commissioner of Assam. He even:

[53] British magistrate of Sylhet invited William Carey of Serampore to initiate mission work among the Garos which led Carey to send Krishna Chandra Pal, the first Serampore convert to Garo areas. David Scott, the Chief Commissioner of Assam suggested the Calcutta council to invite missionaries to begin humanitarian activities among the hill tribes of Assam. In compliance with the joint appeals of the British officers Francis Jenkins (successor of David Scott), Charles Travelyan (prominent Company officer at Calcutta), and William H. Pearce (Baptist Missionary Society at Calcutta), the American Baptist mission in Myanmar (erstwhile Burma) opened a mission station at Sadya, the extreme eastern end of the Brahmaputra valley, the upper Assam. Sangma, *History of American Baptist Mission in North-East India*; Downs, *The Mighty Works,* 16-17; Dena, *Christian Mission and Colonialism*, 24f. Similarly, A Porteous granted permission for William Pettigrew to enter into Manipur state in 1894 and for missionary entry in Lushai hills, now Mizoram state.

[54] The first missionaries to arrive were Nathan and Eliza Brown accompanied by Oliver and Harriet Cutter.

[55] For a detailed information and discussion on Scott and Jenkins and their contributions to Christian missions refer to Downs, *North East India*. 33-52. Downs has given an extensive studies about them. Cf. Lalsangkima Pachuau, *Ethnic Identity and Christianity: A Socio-Historical and Missiological Study of Christianity in Northeast India with Special Reference to Mizoram* (Frankfurt and Maim: Peter Lang, 2002), 62-66.

[56] Ibid., 36. Jenkins was also interested in the educational work of the missionaries to the tribals. In several occasions, he wrote letters to British Authorities in Calcutta and the Mission home boards stating them the needs for mission works and requesting more missionaries in Northeast region.

> Made an annual contribution to the mission of Rs. 500 throughout his life (he remained in Assam following his retirement in 1861, settling in Guwahati) and secured government grants for a new press, for Assamese type for the press, and for some of its educational and literary work.[57]

It was a common practice among the colonizers to decide to settle down in the colonies rather than return to their home countries. As Albert Memmi notes in *The Colonizer and the Colonized,* it is hard for the colonizer to go home again because in his own country his standard of living would have to be significantly lowered.[58] So, he decided to stay in order to continue to live at the colonized's expense. And because the liberal colonizer felt some guilt about that, he had to devise ways to give back, that is, to justify his role as a "usurper" in the colony.

In recognition of the invaluable services rendered to the Christian missions the American Baptist Mission's home board in its official organ, the *Baptist Missionary Magazine*, published their words of appreciation and recognition to the British officials.[59] While this appears to be a normal circumstance in which due appreciations were expressed upon someone in return for the invaluable help received, in this case, in advancing the missionizing project, it also underscored the deep connection that existed between the missionaries and the colonial governing officials. Even if this was a case of relationship entered out of necessity as often argued by some, for advancing their respective projects, what mattered was that they worked together. The missionaries did receive help and in return contributed toward the colonial projects regardless of their good intention.[60]

The motive behind the British administration to invite missionaries was not far to seek – it was primarily for political expediency. The missionary efforts to further the civilizing mission were seen by the administration to be enhancing their efforts toward better administration among the native people. F. S. Downs

---

[57] For a detailed information and discussion on Scott and Jenkins and their contributions to Christian missions refer to Downs, *North East India*. 33-52. Downs has given an extensive studies about them. Cf. Lalsangkima Pachuau, *Ethnic Identity and Christianity: A Socio-Historical and Missiological Study of Christianity in Northeast India with Special Reference to Mizoram* (Frankfurt and Maim: Peter Lang, 2002), 42.

[58] Albert Memmi, *The colonizer and the Colonized.* Expanded ed. intro. Jean-Paul Sartre (Boston: Beacon press, 1965), 60-61.

[59] Downs, *North East India*, 42.

[60] Of course, the help and favor extended to the Christian mission was not limited to the Protestants only. The Roman Catholic missionaries were also extended similar help and support. In fact, Jenkins had not only warmly welcomed the Roman Catholic missionaries of Paris Mission – Fr. Rabin, Fr. Bernard and Fr. Krick – when they arrived in Guwahati in 1850 but also provided accommodations for them. Downs, *North East India*, 48; Cf. S. K. Barpuraji, "Early Christian Missions in the Naga Hills: An Assessment of their Activities," in *Journal of Indian History*, vol. 48, no.143, 1970, 427-435.

uses the term "pacification" – to describe how the British meant to pacify the hills people, without the expensive imposition of direct administration the British government sought the help of the missionaries.[61] This was reaffirmed in Jenkins' support of the missionary work in the hills areas.

The word "pacification" is an important colonial invention. It was used in U.S. Indian policy-making and implementation: "pacifying the war-like tribes" or "hostiles". George E. Tinker, an American Indian scholar and theologian in "Missions and Missionaries," speaks of pacification as both political and missionary objective over against American Indians.

> Christian missionaries began their work of converting the native peoples of the Americas soon after the beginnings of European invasion, both in the north and in the south. Indeed, the missionization of the native peoples in the Americas was the foundation for one of the primary European conquest strategies. In both mission and political-military documents this strategy was referred to as *pacification.*[62]

Then as recently as the early 1970s it was widely used in the U.S. war in Vietnam as part of the on-going narrative to justify U.S. invasion and control of Vietnam.[63]

The second motive was a social and administrative one – the British saw an opportunity to extend its administration that would minimize greatly the state's treasury working through the missionaries among the native people.

> When the tribes had been pacified through the use of military force, the missionary education system was simply a convenient and cheap way of rendering a service that would otherwise have been the responsibility of the government.[64]

One of the primary tasks of the missionaries was to open schools for the native people. Ministry through education became one of the most effective means of evangelizing among the people. In most places the missionaries were the first to introduce modern education system among the native peoples.[65] Whereas the government assistance generally came in the form of funding such

[61] Downs, *Northeast India*, 56.

[62] Tinker, "Missions and Missionaries," available from http://college.hmco.com/history/readerscomp/naind/html/na_022700_missionsandm.htm

[63] "The American Experience with Pacification in Vietnam," available from http://www.carrscompendiums.com/web_PAC1.html

[64] Downs, *North East India*. 60.

[65] The missionaries were responsible in introducing modern education among most tribals in Northeast India – while the Baptist mission worked among the Nagas, Kukis and Garos, the Welsh Presbyterians worked among the Mizos and Khasis.

as grants in aid, the missionaries ran and supervised the schools.[66] By inculcating modern education in schools the missionaries worked toward changing the habits and life styles of the Naga peoples.[67] Children were taught to abandon their traditional hairstyles and to adopt the style of the English and the missionaries. It should be noted that the American Indians had very similar experiences. In *Kill the Indian, Save the Man*, Ward Churchill discusses in great length how the churches and federal governments of the United States and Canada established education systems with residential schools for native children as one part of their assimilationist programs.[68] "Every single aboriginal child would be removed from his/her home, family, community and culture at the earliest possible age and held for years in state sponsored 'educational' facilities, systematically decultured, and simultaneously indoctrinated . . . ."[69] While the degree of measures adopted in terms of facilitating such assimilationist programs may vary, the goal of education in general remained the same for Nagas and American Indians; to strip them off their cultures and ways of life.

Of all the missionaries regardless of affiliation working in Northeast India, William Pettigrew's role was unique. He was a government appointed school inspector while at the same time working as a missionary in Manipur state.[70] In his first year in Manipur he was limited to providing "private tuition for the children of Government officers." He was prohibited from initiating any evangelizing activity among the Meiteis in the valley for fear that such activities could trigger social unrest and civil disobedience among the predominantly Hindu Meiteis. Consequently, Pettigrew was more a state official than missionary during this time.

Additionally, the colonial government having become aware of Pettigrew's growing reputation among the hill people, sought for his help in the recruitment

---

[66] William Pettigrew, "Report for the Years 1907-1909," in Champhang Jajo, ed. *Rev. William Pettigrew's Mission Reports and Letters, 1891-1932* (Ukhrul: Mrs. Phila Jajo, n. d.), 23. For the initial experience of introducing education among the Nagas refer to Tuisem A. Shishak, "The Impact of Pettigrew's Educational Ministry Upon the Tangkhul Naga Society," in *Souvenir: TBL Centenary* (Ukhrul: TBL Centenary, 1996), 32f.

[67] Downs, The Mighty Works, 41. In fact, the whole book deals with missionary education in Assam, Nagaland, Manipur, and Meghalaya states. Cf. Milton S. Sangma, *A History of American Baptist Mission in North East India*, vol. 2 (New Delhi: Mittal Publications, 1992), 2-4.

[68] Ward Churchill, *Kill the Indian, Save the Man: The Genocidal Impact of American Indian Residential Schools* (San Francisco: City Lights Books, 2004), 12-43.

[69] Ibid., 13.

[70] Pettigrew was an honorary Inspector of schools for the entire state (Manipur). Downs, *The Mighty Works*, 79. Of course, this was true in the case of William Dowd an educational missionary who worked among the Ao Nagas. In 1906, the Lieut. Governor appointed him as the honorary inspector of the Naga Hills. A. Bendangyabang Ao, *History of Christianity in Nagaland: The Ao Naga Tribal Christian Mission Enterprise,* 1872-1972 (Mokokchung: Shalom Ministry Publication, 2002), 36.

process and he did oblige with the request. Pettigrew was instrumental in recruiting many hill people to serve in the Labor Corps for the Allied forces during the First World War.[71] In recognition of the services rendered by the mission the British administration granted the mission a plot of land for starting a new mission station in Kangpokpi area along with Rs. 2000 earmarked annually in the state budget.[72] Thus administration lending hands in securing sites for mission station was another significant help the missionaries received from the government.[73] And still another area of co-operation was in the medical work.[74] In health services government assistance ranged from funding and grants in aid to providing free medicines and, at times, even personnel resources. It must be noted that medical aid and education always were and continue to be fundamental components in building the colonial infrastructure such as highways, railroads, and ports; ultimately indeed, all aid serves the purposes of the colonizer.

British Colonial Power and Christian Mission: An Evaluation

We will now consider whether the co-operation that existed between the colonial government and the missionaries amounted to actual collaboration and thereby determine if the missionaries were mostly innocent, or other wise. Different views abound and I would like to categorize them under three groups. The first group maintains the view that missionaries were a distinct element in the larger projects of colonialism. Among the scholars, S. P. Sinha is quite critical of the missionary activities in Northeast India and he maintains that Western missionaries were in close league with the colonial British power and their activities constituted colonial engagement. His comment that, "In fact Christian missionaries are there not for advocating a faith but for keeping imperialism alive"[75] represents the strongest criticism leveled against these missionaries.

---

[71] Shishak, "The Impact of Pettigrew's Educational Ministry," 33.

[72] Although, the clearing and construction work began in 1919, only in 1921 that the Croziers moved to the center followed by Pettigrews after their return from furlough. Pettigrew states, "the headquarters of our Baptist Mission in Manipur were removed in December, 1919, to Kangpokpi." in *Rev. William Pettigrew's Mission Reports and Letters, 1891-1932,* 34.

[73] Such relationship was also evidenced in Khasi hills and Mizo hills. O. L. Snaithang writing about the Khasi hills says, "Lieutenant Lewin of Cherrapunji...have been instrumental in securing a site for a mission station in the Jaintia area in 1842. This pattern of relationship had been first established by David Scott and Francis Jenkins who both were evangelical Christians and both helped the missionaries in many ways." O. L. Snaithang, *Christianity and Social Change in Northeast India: A Study of the Role of Christianity in Social Change among the Khasi-Jaintia Hill Tribes of Meghalaya* (Shillong: Vendrame Institue, 1993), 52.

[74] Milton Sangma talks about how the government assisted the missionaries in providing medical helps in Nagaland – Mokokchung and Wokha areas – free of cost. American Baptist Mission, vol. 2, 204 -205. Cf.

[75] Quoted in K. Suresh Singh, ed., *The Tribal Situation in India* (Shimla: Indian Institute of Advanced Study, 1972), 620.

The second group of scholars of which F.S. Downs[76] and Milton Sangma[77] are representative argue that the missionaries were not guilty of colonial engagement because they had their own goals and objectives and these were quite different from those of the colonial British administration. The missionaries' co-operation with the administration was prompted by necessity. Further, these scholars contend that this co-operation was limited to education and health services which were part of the humanitarian services rendered to native peoples. While this might be the case, and yet it must be noted that education and medical works were part of the colonial projects. Even if the missionaries did not consider themselves agents of colonial power, they participated, wittingly or not, in advancing the colonial projects.[78]

The third group argues that Christian missionaries however good their intentions might have been, contributed towards the colonial establishment in North East India. In the words of Niharranjan Ray:

> Naturally, these missionaries, some of them very well-meaning and pious souls determined to save these communities of people from everlasting damnation, as they saw it, were all part of great establishment of the foreign rulers, and consciously or unconsciously their mission was directed towards upholding and strengthening that establishment.[79]

This is very similar to the view of George E. Tinker, who argued in the context of American Indians that:

> The Christian missionaries – of all denominations working among American Indian nations – were partners in genocide. Unwittingly no doubt, and always with the best of intensions, nevertheless the missionaries were guilty of complicity in the destruction of

[76] In a number of his works Downs cites the good works of the missionaries among the tribal people in Northeast India. Downs, "Christianity as a Tribal Response to Change in Northeast India," in *Missiology: An International Review* 8 (October 1980), 407-416; "Identity: The Integrative Principle," in *Asian Journal of Theology* 6 (1992), 238-249; "Tribal Ecumenism in Northeast India: The Christian Role in Solidarity Movements," in Renthy Keitzar, ed., *Good News for North East India: A Theological Reader* (Guwahati: Christian Literature Center, 1995), 8-21.

[77] Sangma, *History of American Baptist Mission.* V; cf. Lal Dena, *Christian Missions and Colonialism: A Study of Missionary Movement in Northeast India with Particular reference to Manipur and Lushai Hills,* 1894-1947 (Shillong: Vendrame Institute, 1988).

[78] The Indians were suspicious of the missionaries and tribal Christians in Northeast India of aiding the British imperial rule. Downs, *North East India*, 61.

[79] Niharranjan Ray "Introductory Address," in K. Suresh Singh, *Tribal Situation*, 19.

> Indian cultures and social structures – complicity in devastating impoverishment and death of the people to whom they preached.[80]

I concur with the arguments of Tinker and Ray but with one exception. I agree with the premise that the missionaries, however good their intentions might have been, consciously and unconsciously contributed to the colonial project. However, I prefer to use the term 'contributed' rather than 'directed' which was used by Ray. To me the word 'directed' suggests intentionality – that this was intentionally willed from the beginning rather than unintended outcome. I believe the missionaries did come to Northeast region with the intention to propagate the gospel and they meant it to be good. At the same time, I also include the word 'consciously' to the 'civilizing' mission of the missionaries whether it be argued by some that it was the natural outcome of the preaching of the gospel - or part of the "White man's burden." The fact of the matter is that Christian missionaries did perceive civilizing the native people to be one of their objectives as is evidenced by their comments about and reactions to the native people. My reasoning for this will become evident in the discussion which follows.

There is an implicit assumption in the argument of those who claim that the missionaries came solely for the good of the native people; it is the assumption that these missionaries knew what was best for the native people and therefore they were virtually immune to any wrong doing. There is an obvious and profound element of uncritical acceptance of everything connected with the missionaries and Christian missions. Unfortunately, such arguments are still based largely on the dominant paradigm of analysis which perpetuates the validity of cultural elitism and precludes any attempts to see the other side of the experience - the stories of the victims. Even if they – including the Nagas themselves - profess to be studying from the perspectives of the natives they have clearly failed to critically challenge the assumptions of the dominant paradigm.

The case of modern education system will provide an adequate example. The missionaries were responsible for the introduction of modern education, literacy and literature to the native people whose own learning system and means for the transmission of knowledge were oral. The missionaries were responsible for reducing what were life-giving oral traditions down to stagnant written languages,[81] and remarkably they are to this day lauded for their "accomplishments"

---

[80] George E. Tinker, *Missionary Conquest: The Gospel and Native American Cultural Genocide* (Minneapolis: Fortress Press, 1993), 4.

[81] Missionaries like William Pettigrew, E. W. Clark, C. D. King and others were among the noted ones who reduced Naga dialects into written languages. While Pettigrew did for the Tangkhul Nagas, Clark and King did for the Aos and Angamis respectively.

in education.[82] Modern education, with all the wonders it brought to native peoples was at the same time responsible for undermining and unraveling the native peoples' cultures and ways of knowing, in many cases it even brought about their demise. What Albert Memmi said about the effects of the introduction of English language in Africa rings true for the Naga people.

> ...The colonized's mother tongue, that which is sustained by his feelings, emotions and dreams, that in which tenderness and wonder are expressed, thus that which holds the greatest emotional impact, is precisely the one which is the least valued. It has no stature in the country or in the concert of his peoples. If he wants to obtain a job, make a place for himself, exist in the community and the world, he must first bow to the language of his masters.[83]

In a similar manner, Ngũgĩ wa Thiong'o, a fellow African scholar asserts that if, "The bullet was the means of the physical subjugation, language was the means of the spiritual subjugation."[84]

Today Naga people, like any other indigenous people around the world, are faced with the question of the survival of their identity due to the loss of their life-sustaining traditions and cultures. According to Linda Tuhiwai Smith, such undermining of native knowledge systems is part of the mission of the imperial powers. Smith notes:

> Imperialism tends to be used in at least four different ways when describing the form of European imperialism which 'started' in the fifteenth century: (1) imperialism as economic expansion; (2) imperialism as the subjugation of "others"; (3) imperialism as an idea or spirit with many forms of realization; and (4) *imperialism as a discursive field of knowledge* (emphasis is mine).[85]

This leads us to the second function of modern education which is that of an indispensable tool of Western imperialism. Allan Bishop, in his essay "Western

---

[82] For a detailed discussion on the role of missionaries on modern education among the Nagas refer to the following works. Tuisem A. Shishak, "The Impact of Pettirew's Educational Ministry," 30-37; Bendangyabang Ao, *History of Christianity in Nagaland*, 34-37; For current issues in Christian education see Akheto Sema, "Current Issues in Christian Education and their Relevance for Theological Education: A North East India Perspective," in *Advancing with Christ: Souvenir of the Eastern Theological College Centenary Celebration* 2005 (Jorhat: Eastern Theological College, 2005), 77-102.

[83] Memmi, *The Colonizer and the Colonized*, 107.

[84] Ngũgĩ wa Thiong'o, *Decolonizing the Mind: The Politics of Language in African Literature* (Oxford: James Currey Ltd., 1986), 9.

[85] Linda Tuhiwai Smith, *Decolonizing Methodologies: Research and Indigenous Peoples* (London & New York: Zed Books Ltd. 1999), 21.

Mathematics: The Secret Weapon of Cultural Imperialism', debunks the myth of Western mathematics' cultural neutrality - the idea that Western mathematics is value free.[86] The conventional wisdom is that mathematical truths are universally valid. They are in a way. But Bishop goes on to ask:

> But where do 'degrees' come from? Why is the total 180? Why not 200, or 100? Indeed, why are we interested in triangles and their properties at all? The answer is, essentially, 'because some people determined that it should be that way'. Mathematical ideas, like any other ideas, are humanly constructed. They have a cultural history.[87]

There were and are many other valid ways of knowing including mathematical systems in non-European cultures. But these are demeaned and relegated to the category of 'ethno-mathematics', localized and specific mathematical ideas that are not part of or compatible with 'mainstream' mathematics; in other words they are inferior to Western mathematics.

Regarding the question of how Western mathematics can be seen as an instrument of imperialism, Bishop identifies three major mediating agents in the process of cultural invasion of the colonized countries by Western mathematics: trade, public and private administration and education. In the field of trade and commerce, the Western concepts of length, area, volume, weight, time and money were imposed on the Indigenous societies. Likewise, in administration Western numerical formulas and procedures were used "for keeping track of large numbers of people and commodities."[88] The third major medium for cultural invasion was education. "It was part of a deliberate strategy of acculturation – international in its efforts to instruct in the 'best of the West', and convinced of its superiority to any indigenous mathematical systems and cultures."[89]

Western mathematics as a product of Western culture is further associated with a particular set of values which Bishop identifies as rationalism, objectism, and power and control.[90] The rationalizing process and objectification of the world, coupled with science and technology understood as ways to control the physical and social environment, represent the values associated with Western mathematics. In a similar vein Gangmumei Kamei, a Naga statesman and scholar argues that modern education was "designed to inculcate European liberal ideas,

[86] Allan J. Bishop. "Western Mathematics: The Secret Weapons of Cultural Imperialism," in Bill Aschroft, et al, ed., *The Post-Colonial Studies Reader* (London and New York: Routledge, 1995), 71-76.

[87] Ibid., 71-72.

[88] Ibid., 73.

[89] Ibid.

[90] Ibid., 74.

literature, and science in the Indian mind, and to produce educated persons who could be conveniently employed to run the colonial administration."[91]

The uncritical acceptance of this modern education system has had a lasting affect on the way education is viewed and pursued in Nagaland. The critical question before us is this: Whose values, histories, stories, and knowledge are we to learn? Unfortunately, to this day almost all the courses/subjects, histories and knowledge taught in the schools and colleges are based on dominant Western and Indian education paradigms. Students read and learn more of Euro-American and Indian history and philosophy than their own. Very little of Indigenous history and culture are incorporated into the school experience. As a result, educated people in the region know more about Euro-American and dominant Indian histories.

The consequence is that the education introduced in Nagaland by missionaries and British colonizers, and continued by the Indian state, has been instrumental in not only perpetuating cultural dominance over the Naga people but also coercing Nagas to participate in their own colonization for over a century. What we must acknowledge is that this has been and is still a process of colonizing the minds of the Naga people through education. Dolly Kikon rightly argues that:

> ...The introduction of an 'approved' syllabus by the Indian state, can be seen as a process that 'recolonized' the Naga mind, to an extent where the Naga have lost the ability to construct their own past objectively and critically. This has resulted in misinterpretation and misappropriation of the Naga indigenous knowledge and perspectives.[92]

Ashis Nandy asserts that the colonization of the mind is no less debilitating a form of colonization than the material/geographical form. He offers this succinct summary of the psychological impact of such colonization:

> This colonialism colonizes minds in addition to bodies and it releases forces within the colonized societies to alter their cultural priorities once for all. In the process, it helps the concept of the modern West from a geographical and temporal entity to a psychological category. The West is now everywhere, within the West and outside; in structures and in minds.[93]

---

[91] Gangmumei Kamei, *Ethnicity and Social Change: An Anthology of Essays* (Lilong: Smt. Poungalu Gangmei, 2002), 138.

[92] Dolly Kikon, "Destroying Differences, Schooling Consent: A Critical Analysis of Education Policy in Indian-Administered Nagaland," in http://www.nscnonline.org/webpage/Articles/dolly_kikon.htm

[93] Ashis Nandy, *The Intimate Enemy: Loss and Recovery of Self under Colonialism* (Delhi: Oxford University Press, 1983), xi.

In a similar manner, Marie Battiste, a Mi'kmaq educator of Potlo'tek American Indian Nation, calls this colonizing of the mind a "Cognitive imperialism" which is a "form of cognitive manipulations used to disclaim other knowledge bases and values."[94] The far reaching impact of such cognitive imperialism is that, "Cultural minorities have been led to believe that their poverty and impotence are a result of their race."[95] True to this analysis, having internalized such negative views about themselves, the Naga people grow up blaming themselves for their unfortunate fate and condition. The Indian state fully armed with an education system coupled with repressive laws and a dominant visible military, has aggressively pursued a plan to rewrite and negate Naga people's history and cultural priorities. In this sense, education and educational institutions become instruments for control and hegemony.

Education and educational institutions were not the only mediums used to expand colonial controls over Naga people, Western medical practices, medicines, and hospitals were equally powerful modes of control. It has been often argued that European medicines and hospitals were instrumental in saving lives and improving the living qualities of the people. What is never acknowledged is the displacement of traditional Indigenous medicines and medicine persons and the cultural role these played. According to Michael Mann, "Colonial medicine was also considered a useful tool for ruling the country in its potential for *colonizing and civilizing* the bodies of the people [italics mine]."[96]

All the talk about improving the lives of the people through advanced modern education and medicines serves to affirm the broader Western idea of progress as this is measured in terms of technological advancement, medical advancement and development. Indeed, 'development' became the modern term for 'civilizing', but it still operates on the principle of imagined differences and constructed hierarchies.[97]

Naming of the Native: Who Calls the Shot?

Collusion among state, missionaries and Western trained anthropologists at least at the level of perception and perpetuating the colonial naming of the native people was obvious in many instances. After all, most of the so-called ethnographers and anthropologists who had written so much about the Nagas were also colonial administrators who compiled Naga ethnographies while serving the colonial state

[94] Marie Battiste, "Maintaining Aboriginal Identity, Language, and Culture in Modern Society," in Marie Battiste, ed., *Reclaiming Indigenous Voice and Vision* (Vancouver: UBS Press, 2000), 198.

[95] Ibid.

[96] Michael Mann, "'Torchbearers Upon the Path of Progress,'" 14.

[97] Ibid., 16.

in their official capacity.[98] The comments made regarding the Nagas who had gone to France during the WWI as part of the Labor-Corps is quite intriguing:

> One wonders what impressions remain with them from their sudden contact with *higher civilizations* at war. Possibly, they are reflecting that what they have seen, the White Man's condemnation of the relatively innocuous head-hunting of the Nagas savours of hypocrisy. Or does their *sang-froid* save them from being critical and endeavoring to analyse the seemingly inconsequent habits of the *leading peoples* of *culturedom?* Now that they are back in their own hills, will they settle down to the indigenous simple life and revert to the *primitive* conditions which were temporarily disturbed? [Emphasis mine][99]

In the light of this we may ask what do we mean by primitive? Balfour implies that when the so-called "civilized" nations wage war on one another this is an activity of higher civilizations? Whereas, "the relatively innocuous head-hunting of the Nagas" was an activity of people of lower civilizations and so it is primitive?

My intent here is to bring to light the crucial question of who defines who is primitive, and who is civilized? Who determines what qualifies as "higher" or "lower" civilizations? Throughout Western modern history and to this very day, the arbiter has always been the Western world, that is, Europe and the U.S. To be a bit more specific it has been England, France, Netherlands, Germany and the U.S. who have had militaristic and economic powers have been assuming this patronizing responsibility of naming and categorizing of all other peoples. They follow a simple yet very exclusive exemplar that of Euro-american culture as the "universal culture." Gramsci described such a claim as "an audacious heretics of modern age." Other cultures are significant "only in so far as they have become constitutive elements in European culture."[100] Any beliefs, practices, or traditions which were different and could not conform to this culture's norms and practices was considered at best inferior and in some cases demeaned to the extent of not even qualifying as a culture. Further, by extension, diversity and difference are qualities they do not tolerate easily; this imagined ideal that is Euro-american culture makes it extremely difficult to accept anything that is non-Euro Americans.

---

[98] For example, J. H. Hutton and J. P. Mills who have extensively written on Nagas were both senior officers in the British Administration.

[99] Henry Balfour, "Foreword," in J. H. Hutton, *The Sema Nagas* (London: Macmillan and Co, Ltd., 1921), xvi.

[100] Quoted in Suresh Sharma, *Tribal Identity and Modern World* (New Delhi: Sage Publications, 1994), 37.

But obviously, the world is populated with many peoples of different colors who possess their own cultures; they know the world does not revolve around Europe and America, as the earth revolves around the sun. At the heart of the issue is the claim for European superiority. Edward Said stated that the, "Idea of European identity as a superior one in comparison with all the non-European peoples and cultures"[101] was an idea that was aggressively advanced and an indispensable tool for world domination. Said calls this whole process of European bent on hegemonic drives over non-Europeans as a process of Orientalism. For Said, Orientalism is:

> ...produced and exists in an uneven exchange with various kinds of power, shaped to a degree by the exchange with power political (as with a colonial or imperial establishment), power intellectual (as with reigning sciences like comparative linguistics or anatomy, or any of the modern policy sciences), power cultural (as with orthodoxies and canons of taste, texts, values), power moral (as with ideas about what 'we' do and what 'they' cannot do or understand as 'we' do).[102]

This idea of superiority encompasses all aspects of life including political, cultural, social, intellectual, and moral.

According to Tinker, the European's belief in their superiority over against the indigenous peoples goes back at least to 1492 when Columbus first blundered into the islands of the Caribbean sea. Tinker quotes from an entry in Columbus' own diary as evidence.

> [October 12, 1492] They ought to make good and skilled servants, for they repeat very quickly whatever we say to them. I think they can be made Christians, for they seem to have no religion. If it pleases Our Lord, I will take six of them to Your Highnesses when I depart.... [October 14] ... these people are very unskilled in arms. Your Highnesses will see this for yourselves when I bring to you the seven that I have taken. After they learn our language I shall return them, unless Your Highnesses order that the entire populations be taken to Castile, or held captive here. With 50 men you could subject everyone and make them do what you wished.[103]

Colonialsim, Ethnographers, and Nagas

The attitude of Western colonizers and ethnographers regarding the Naga people was primarily negative and was constituted by colonial naming and exoticizing

---

[101] Edward Said, *Orientalism* (New York: Vintage Books, 1979), 7.

[102] Ibid., 12.

[103] Tinker, *Missionary Conquest*, 8.

such as primitive, uncivilized and people with no character, etc. Much of what has been written, including *The Naked Nagas,* makes crystal clear the views held by Western anthropologists and writers.[104] When describing the Sema Nagas, an ethnographer stated that "in treachery and lying they were and are quite unsurpassed, even among Nagas." He went on to add, "A Sema oath is worth less than the oath of any other Naga tribe."[105] Another colonial ethnographer described the Lotha Nagas as "a sullen race" and they "are alike filthy in their persons and habits, and have a pompous mode of addressing one which might in some cases be interpreted as insolent."[106] Similarly another colonial writer denigrated them as "uninteresting people with dirty persons and villages."[107] On the other hand, a more realistic and unbiased view about the Lotha tribe is presented in the following comments:

> Though the tribe contains a few habitual criminals, on the whole, very honest. Petty theft is rare, and a man can leave his spear and cloth by the side of a village path knowing that he will find his property untouched when comes to pick it up on his way home.[108]

The component of Naga culture on which critics have come down so heavily is their practice of "head-hunting." Most writers, past and present, have depicted Nagas as war mongers and savages whose daily lives were consumed by wagging war against each other and taking enemy heads. Here again, the most realistic assessment comes from the following comments. "War between Lhota villages was rare, and a powerful village surrounded by friends would regard defenses as unnecessary." [109] After all, if wagging war had been the daily order of their lives the Naga race would have been reduced to few survivors or already extinct and there would not even be any Naga today.

There is no denying the history of Naga war making. But then, was the near constant state of war in the period from the tenth through the seventeenth centuries in Europe, the so called "holy crusade" against Muslims fought in the name of religion, and the European conquest of American Indians of America and the aboriginals of Australia. They were as barbaric and gruesome as could be imagined yet the people who denounced the Nagas for their "head-hunting"

---

[104] Christopher von Fürer-Haimendorf wrote extensively about/on the Nagas and two of them he named The Naked Nagas and Return to the Naked Nagas respectively. Cf. H. H. Presler, *Primitive Religions of India* (Madras: Christian Literature Society, 1971).

[105] Davis, *Census of Assam*, 1891, part II, 247.

[106] Quoted in J. P. Mills, *The Lhota Nagas: With an Introduction and Supplementary Notes by J. H. Hutton* (London: Macmillan and Co., Ltd., 1922), 2.

[107] L. W. Shakespear, *History of Upper Assam, Upper Burma and North-Eastern Frontier*. 202.

[108] Mills, *The Lhota Nagas,* 19.

[109] Ibid., 22.

practices had traveled miles and miles to wage a war of conquest against them. It was the Europeans who enlisted the Nagas in the Labor Corps for war being waged in Europe twice in the first half of the twentieth century and, these were European wars, fought between and among European nations, with the exception of Japan in WWII, and so did not in fact encompass the whole world as was claimed.

I am quite critical of the way detractors have portrayed the Nagas, particularly the "holier than thou" attitude they assumed toward the Nagas and the double standard they applied as they passed judgment on them. The self-critical observation rendered by a British army officer who served in Northeast region particularly in the so-called NEFA (North East Frontier Area) which is now Arunachal Pradesh state, echo the concern of many people. He said, "In our indignation at the Naga for taking a few heads in battle, we gloss over the shortcomings of modern culture as manifested in the barbarities of gas chamber and germ warfare."[110] In a similar vein, a British administrator also called attention to European hypocrisy. "So-called civilized countries, which can destroy whole populations with a single atom bomb, can hardly afford to look down on a method of ritual warfare which, at the most, involved the loss of a few hundreds of lives every year."[111] Further, what is more damaging and also highlights the double standard is the perpetuation of the stereotype of Nagas as "head hunters" when there is no such stereotyping of the Europeans and Americans as holy crusaders, slave traders, or even perpetrators of genocide!

Reacting to the continued labeling of the Nagas as "former head-hunters" by powerful press agencies such as BBC, CNN, Reuters and others, the Naga International Support Center (NISC) in its press release November 15, 2004 offered these scathing remarks:

> First of all head hunting as a term has been used by the colonial powers. It was invented by colonialists to denounce tribal peoples. And, through its implicit appeal (connotation) on understanding these tribes, rather than peoples, as barbarians, they were thus described as lower kind. Similar to people living in caves that bash each other heads with clubs, head hunters are seen as people of a lower kind. Although only partially true, may be you don't call your people Dutch former slave drivers or slave dealers. Is it okay to describe Americans as former slave drivers or, the Dutch as former slave traders, or the Germans as former Jew exterminators, etc. How would you feel if CNN becomes popularly nicknamed as former slave drivers, now trying to dictate the

[110] Nari Rustomji, *Imperilled Frontiers: India's North-Eastern Borderlands* (Delhi: Oxford University Press, 1983), 4.

[111] Verrier Elwin, *Nagaland* (Shillong: Adviser's Secretariat, 1961), 11. Of course, even "a loss of few hundreds of lives" is quite exaggerated.

world in journalism? Also considering the term head-hunting to be factual, if only from the European perspectives, seems to be ridiculous because if people were really out to be hunting heads, they would be already extinct, for having exterminated both others and the last others themselves.[112]

Missionaries in Nagaland: Their Attitude, Intention, and Impact

The modern missionary movement and colonial expansion almost coincided with each other. While the goals of the colonial powers were political and economic, the missionaries' goal primarily was religious conversion, that is, converting heathens to Christian faith. However, both projects were predicated on the notion that Europeans are superior to all the natives and as such shared the belief that they had the responsibility to civilize the primitive.

Christian missionaries saw the Nagas and other tribals of the region as primitive, uncultured, uncivilized savages. Their description of the Nagas ranged from a people with no culture at all to a people with inferior culture, life styles and ways of life. Naga religion was denigrated as superstitious, demonic, and evil.[113] The peoples' character and virtue were severely criticized and they were held in very low esteem. Such negative portrayals of the native people is just part of the larger essentializing process or "othering of the other" that is necessarily employed by the colonial powers. It has been and continues to be experienced by Indians, Africans, the aborigines in Australia, the American Indians in North and South America and many, many more.[114]

Unfortunately, despite their good intentions and the positive work they did, the missionaries failed to understand or, more importantly, appreciate the religious and cultural ethos of the tribal people. What is even more unfortunate is that tribal Christians have bought into the stereotypes maintained and propounded by the missionaries, which necessarily negated and despised tribals' own traditional cultural and religious values. This way of thinking is so deeply embedded in the tribal Christians' beliefs that they consider their most important obligation as Christians to be unwavering adherence to the tenets of Christianity that were introduced to them by the missionaries. The Naga people's understanding of "God" is greatly influenced by the theologies of the early missionaries. People continue to view "God" in terms of the traditional attributes, such as "God"

---

[112] Naga International Support Center (NISC), Amsterdam. Press Release November 15, 2004.

[113] M. M. Clark, *A Corner in India* (Guwahati: Christian Literature Center, 1978), 1; Pettigrew's Mission Reports and Letters, 35-36; Gordon Jones, "Good News for North-East India", in Renthy Keitzar, *Good News for North East India* (Guwahati: Christian Literature Center, 1995), 4ff.

[114] Refer to Nandy, *The Intimate Enemy;* Franz Fanon, *The Wreched of the Earth* (New York: Grove Press, 1963); Memmi, *The Colonizer and the Colonized.*

the Omnipotent, the Omnipresent, and so on. Their understanding of Jesus Christ ranges from the traditional image of Jesus as suffering servant and savior to the image of Jesus as Lord of Lords, and King of Kings. Further, they have a very individualistic view of Jesus; Jesus is generally portrayed as "my" savior and redeemer. Such an individualistic conception of Jesus regrettably limits the salvific activity of Jesus Christ to the salvation of the individual soul; correspondingly, sin and salvation are thus understood in this narrow sense. To this day, most tribal Christians think that to be a true Christian means they must shun everything that is of the past and embrace uncritically whatever comes from the Christian West.

Very often when Churches celebrate a Jubilee, either silver or golden, the predominant theme for the occasion is "From darkness to Light,"[115] to draw an unequivocal distinction between the pre-Christian era and the Christian era, and thereby reminding the Nagas, and the world, that they were in darkness before they were brought the "Light" of Christianity. Such unmistakable reiteration serves to compound and reify for everyone this despicable and baseless contention that their traditions and ways of the past were nothing but evil and damned. It surely conveys the idea that their forefathers and foremothers were without the presence of God and must have suffered greatly for the lack.

Such understanding has led them to undermine and /or reject nearly all their cultural values and traditions. This is reflected clearly by the prevailing patterns and styles of worship as these are expressed in the hymns and songs[116] they sing and the preferred style and form of preaching. Except for the language, every facet of worship is meant to be an exact imitation of Western Christian style and tradition as they know it. This obsession with imitating the West is even plainly evident in the church buildings which are designed to replicate the gothic architectural style of the West.

Ultimately, however, the most critical problems engendered by tribal Christianity is the uncompromising deprecation and negation of the tribal worldview and the uncritical acceptance of "Western Christian worldview" brought to them by the missionaries. Tribal worldview which is characterized by its recognition of the undifferentiated unity between the sacred and the secular, the worldly and the heavenly, the physical and the spiritual was replaced by the Western Christian view which maintains that there are sharply delineated distinctions between all these oppositional binaries.[117] The traditional worldview

---

[115] "From Darkness to Light" was the theme chosen on the occasion of the celebration of 125 years of Christianity in Nagaland. This was also the theme of the Tangkhul Baptist Churches for its Centenary celebration in 1996.

[116] In recent years people have begun to adapt their traditional folk music into Christian worship and singing. The Mizos, Kukis, and Zeliangrongs have done the most in this regards.

[117] A number of Tribal scholars including Jonathan H. Thumra bemoan the loss of tribal worldview. Jonathan H. Thumra, "Impact of Christianity on the Socio-cultural Ethos of the

of tribal communities was overwhelmed by the view of humanity which valorizes the individual and that individual's salvation, which flatly contradicts the essence of tribal worldview as the inter-relatedness of all beings in creation.

Arguably, the most detrimental effect of the uncritical acceptance of a Western Christian worldview is its requisite compartmentalization, exemplified by the need to construct and maintain the separate designations of secular and sacred. There is clearly a disconnect in tribal Christian life today between, on one hand, the orthodoxy of the Church's doctrines and teaching, and the way tasks and responsibilities of daily life are carried out on the other. Traditionally, Nagas view religion as the entirety of one's interaction with the world rather than a propositional statement of faith; in other words, each action and all activity are considered religious. This is both explained and confirmed by their understanding that there is nothing in creation that isn't permeated by the presence of God, so one must live in the constant consciousness of divine Presence. Because of their reverence for all Creation and their belief in the primacy of the community rather than the individual, the tribals were demeaned and denigrated by the Western missionaries and colonizers as people without religion or God.

Additionally, the strong emphasis on the primacy of the individual has contributed a great deal to the gradual erosion of communitarian spirit and values which are the hall-mark of tribal community life. The missionaries "felt every ceremony should be abolished . . . . The tendency was to abolish the old things and substitute individualism for the strong community feeling . . . The result was a conflict not necessarily of arms but of culture . . . . "[118] Correspondingly, whereas the Western ideas of sin and salvation must be understood at the level of the individual, the social and corporate dimensions of sin and salvation lose all significance and are for the most part ignored.

The condemnation of tribal histories and ways of life has had far reaching psychological consequences for tribal people which manifests in self abasement and feelings of inferiority. People develop a sense of insecurity and inadequacy because of the repeated negation of their way of life.[119] In addition, an attitude of distrust and disdain develops regarding everything that was or is of their own culture. In his book *Black Skin and White Mask*,[120] Franzt Fanon tells how the Indigenous people in Algeria were faced with just such an identity crisis as a

---

Tangkhul Nagas," in *Souvenir: TBL Centenary*, 49-50; Panger Imchen, *Ancient Ao Naga Religion* (Delhi: Har-Anand Publication, 1993), 15.

[118] M. Alemchiba, "Problems of Readjustment to New Situation with Special Reference to Naga Tribes," in *Highlander*, vol. 4, 1 & 2 (March-April, 1973), 3.

[119] For a detailed study on the psychological impact of religion on the tribal people in Northeast India see Murry, Ezamo, *Tribal Spirituality Reconsidered: A Psychological Study of Religion* (Delhi: ISPCK, 1995).

[120] Franzt Fanon, *Black Skin, White Masks* (New York: Grove Press, 1967), 147f; Nandy in his *The Intimate Enemy,* talks about the psychological effects the colonial rule had upon Indians, 1-15.

result of French colonization. He explained that many Blacks developed a self-hatred and negative image of themselves and attempted to imitate the white colonizers in order to earn acceptance and status in the society. Fanon argues that the process started very early in the lives of the colonized, beginning in childhood and continuing throughout the person's entire life.

For many decades, tribals in Northeast India have demonstrated this identity crisis through their demeanor of self defeat. This psychological effect underscores a critical implication that concerns the liberative dimension of the human mind. So long as the tribal people suffer from the inferiority complex, and self deprecation which are the result of decades of internalizing an inferior self-image, liberation of the whole person can not be realized. In other words, tribal people's experience of liberation remains incomplete because their freedom is constricted either physically or psychologically. The Gospel of Jesus Christ proclaims liberation for all dimensions of life: the spiritual, physical, mental and emotional.

In recent years, at least outside the church people have begun to realize the value and necessity of rediscovering their cultural roots in order to redefine their identity as a Naga, Mizo, Khasi or Kuki. Student groups and other political and cultural organizations have taken various initiatives aimed at redeeming and promoting their traditional cultures and values. However, such awareness and the subsequent attempts have so far not been assimilated at the religious/church level. When there are certain initiatives at the church level, the concerns and contents of cultures are treated as social affairs and considered outside the purview of Christian worship life. In general, as previously noted, the churches continue to affirm traditional theology, worship and expressions of faith. In other words, Christianity has yet to set roots in our tribal cultural soil so that it remains totally alien to the tribals despite the fact that Christianity was introduced over one hundred forty five years ago.

Colonialism, Missionaries, and Indigenous Christology

The analytical study of the connections between the colonial project and missionaries is crucial to problematizing the theological context of the Naga people vis-à-vis the influences of colonization and missionization. The examination of colonization and missionization must be accompanied by the processes of decolonizing and de-missionizing to provide a necessary context from which an efficacious Naga Indigenous Christology can be realized. This examination has demonstrated how colonization and missionization resulted in the shaping and development of a distinct and highly Westernized form of Christianity in Nagaland. The combination of these two overwhelming forces has led to the near obliteration of Naga Indigenous culture and values. And, if somehow that is not enough, the Western worldview which informs and animates the civilizing and missionizing projects made inevitable the destruction of Naga Indigenous worldview and traditional ways in which the Nagas understood themselves and their place in the world. Their theological outlook including their understanding of "God" and Jesus Christ, has been and continues to be dictated by the missionary teachings. As I noted earlier too many Nagas imagine Jesus in terms of the image and descriptions presented by the Euro-western and Amer-european missionaries. A Christology derived from and centered in the Naga people's historical experience and cultural reality is a pressing task confronting Naga Christians; so, by addressing this problem I mean to begin the work of looking seriously at the possibilities of formulating a Naga-Indigenous Christology.

Chapter 2

Situating Indigenous Theology Historical, Socio-Economic and Political Setting of Nagaland

In my attempt to construct a Christology of culture and liberation, from the perspective of the Naga people it is critically important to locate the Nagas as a distinct population in a particular area of Asia over a certain period of time. In the preceding chapter, I have dealt with the history of colonization and missionization by way of locating the theological context out of which a construction of Naga-Indigenous Christology must occur. This chapter will examine the historical, political, and socio-economic situations of the Naga people. Tribal theology as a contextual theology must begin with the situatedness of the people; therefore I will begin by addressing the critical issue of who the Naga people are.

In Search of Identity: Who are the Nagas?

Very often the name Naga triggers in the minds of many outsiders different things. Some non-Naga people believe when Nagas are spoken of the reference is to either a sect of Hinduism known as Naga (snake) worshippers or the Naga dynasties of the Puranas and Epics.[121] There is no connection between these groups and the Naga people. Nonetheless the history and identity of the Nagas as a people has been the single most enduring site of contention between the Indian state and Nagas. Are the Nagas a distinct people with their own unique history, or are they Indians as claimed by India? For decades the Nagas have been defending their identity as a people in the face of Indian imperialistic rule and this struggle continues still today. Given the nature of their particular historical struggle with

[121] Gangmumei Kamei, *Ethnicity and Social Change: An Anthology of Essays* (Imphal: Smt. Pounganglu Gangmumei, 2002), 11-14.

Indian imperialism, all that Nagas have experienced and endured, it is critically important to re-examine the history of Naga origin.

Ethnologically and linguistically the Nagas belong to the Tibeto-Burman language as are some of the neighboring tribes in Northeast India, including the Kuki-chins, Mizos, Bodos, and Khasis.[122] The name "Naga" is actually a misnomer; the people never referred to themselves as "Naga." They knew themselves by their own distinct tribal names, such as: the Ao, the Mao, the Tangkhul, the Angami, the Sema, and the Lotha. While the etymology of the name is uncertain, there is a consensus among a number of scholars that the name "Naga" originated outside Nagaland with as of now unknown non-Naga people and was subsequently picked up and popularized by the British. Different theories have been put forward by Naga scholars and British colonial scholars as to the derivation of the name Naga;[123] not one of the theories – each theories based on conjectures and speculations – could establish with any certainty its derivation, and further, none of the theories enjoy a consensus of acceptance with the people. The fact is, the issue is of concern only to the purposes of the imperialist project of the Indian state.

Indeed, it is immaterial to the Naga people how they came to be called or named. What is important is that the name Naga functions as the collective signifier for the Naga people vis-à-vis the respective tribal names by which they are known. What ultimately matters to them is that they know they are a people with a common ancestry, distinct history and culture and they belong right where they are.

Origin of the Nagas

Nagas have a number of origin stories and related myths, most of which involved either emerging out of the earth or stone or cave. The Lhotas, like many other

---

[122] Gangmumei Kamei, *Ethnicity and Social Change: An Anthology of Essays* (Imphal: Smt. Pounganglu Gangmumei, 2002), 18f; Verrier Elwin, *Nagaland* (Shillong: Adviser's Secretariat, 1961), 2; Walter Thomas French, "Northern Naga: A Tibeto-Burman Mesolanguage," vol. 1 and 2 (Ph. D. diss., City University of New York, 1983), 5. Nagas resemble with the Dyaks and Kanyans of Broneo an Sarawak (now Indonesia and Malaysia respectively) Bataks of Sumatra, the Igorots of Philippines and others in their physical appearance and life style.

[123] Some of the well known ones include Nag and Nanga theories, the Nok theory, the Nokhar theory, and the Naka theory. Nag and Nanga are Sanskrit terms which means snake and naked respectively and the proponents of these theories argue Naga derived out of these names. Nok in certain Tibeto language including Ao, Nocte and Garo means people and the proponents argue that's the origin of the name Naga. Gangmumei and others rather argue Naga derived from Kachari Nokhar which means warrior. For R. R. Shimray, Naga derived from Burmese naka which means pierced ears. Seeing the people with pierced ears, the Burmese started calling them Naka. As stated, all these theories have flaws and problems. Cf. Verrier Elwin, ed., *The Nagas in nineteenth Centuries* (Bombay: Oxford University Press, 1969), 6, 83-84; Gangmumei Kamei, "Origin of Nagas," in R. Vashum et al, ed., *Nagas at Work* (New Delhi: Naga Students' Union Delhi, 1999), 7-9; R. R Shimray, *Origin and Culture of the Nagas* (Imphal: Mrs. Pamleiphy Shimray, 1985), 41ff.

tribes, believed their ancestors emerged out of a hole in the earth;[124] The Aos believed their ancestors emerged from six stones which they called *Long terok.* According to the mythology of the Maring, the Nagas lived and cultivated rice underground before they discovered the existence of a new world above.[125] They made their way out to the surface but only after killing a huge tiger that guarded the gate. The Tangkhul Nagas traced their origin to a legendary leader named Phungshoka who led his people out of the bowels of the earth.[126] Such stories of emergence from the earth have been widely interpreted by Nagas as the mother earth giving birth to the people. Some of these stories identify their origin location within the present Naga hills; the Aos' six stones for example are believed to be located in what is today Chungliyimti village in Sangtam Naga.

For years most scholars have followed the work of Western colonial writers who popularized the notion the Nagas must have migrated to the lands they now occupy from either China or Southeast Asia. Most scholars, including Nagas such as: M. Horam, R.R. Shimray, Alemchiba, and Gangmumei, speculate that Nagas were among those "Mongoloid" groups who had migrated from China and Mongolia to Southeast Asia and South Asia at different times and stages[127] while also conceding that their theories are based on nothing more than speculations and imagination; in the words of M. Horam, they are nothing but "figments of human imaginations." In my view the migration theories are merely a Western colonial invention meant to dislodge the Indigenous people from their status as the original inhabitants of the lands.[128] These theories are therefore not only

---

[124] The three brothers, Limhachan, Izumontse, and Rankhanda who were considered the ancestors of the three phratries of the tribe were said to have come out of a hole in the earth near the miraculous stone at Kezakennoma. Another tradition points to Mao areas as the common origin place for Lothas, Rengmas and Southern Sangtams. J. P. Mills, *The Lhota Nagas*, introduction and supplementary notes by J. H. Hutton, reprint (New York: AMS Press, 1979), 3-4. Hutton has a similar story but with a slight variation. The three brothers referred to were the Angamis, the Lhotas and the Rengmas – these three tribes are seen as having a common origin and ancestry. J. H. Hutton, *The Angami Nagas, with Some Notes on Neighboring Tribes*, 2nd ed. (London: Oxford University Press, 1969), 21.

[125] Shimray, *Origin and Cultures of Nagas*, 17-18.

[126] Their folk songs and legends are replete with such stories. T. Luikham, *Wung (Tangkhul) Naga Okthot Mayonza: Wung (Tangkhul) Naga Traditional Laws* (Ukhrul: By the Author, 1961), 24.

[127] M. Horam, *Nagas Old Ways and New Trends* (New Delhi: Cosmo Publications, 1988), 8-9; M. Alemmchiba, *A Brief Historical Accounts of Nagaland* (Kohima: Naga Institute of Culture, 1970), 19f; Kamei, "Origin of Nagas", 19f; Shimray, *Origin and Culture of Nagas*, 12-15.

[128] A number of American Indian scholars including Vine Deloria, Jr., George E. "Tink" Tinker, Ward Churchill, Glen Morris, have effectively challenged the traditionally held Baring Strait theory which holds that American Indians' ancestors migrated to North America from Siberia and points west via Baring Strait. They argue that the theory has no basis in fact and that it was/is a colonial ploy to lay claim to the homeland of the American Indians who are the original inhabitants of the lands. See Vine Deloria, Jr, *Red Earth White Lies: Native Americas and the Myth of Scientific*

fraught with guesses and speculations, they are also a serious distraction to the legitimate identity of the Nagas as a people. Accordingly then, rather than engage in another speculative exercise, I will simply reiterate the known facts about the origin of the Naga people.

There is sufficient evidence to corroborate that most Nagas came to their present-day settlements via Burma (Myanmar); and most Nagas, including the Tangkhuls, trace their origin to Thangtud, (or Samsok in Tangkhul) in Burma which lies on the west bank of Chindwin river.[129] Once the Nagas established themselves in the Naga hills, Makhel, approximately ten kilometers from Kohima which is the capital of Nagaland state, is believed to be the place from where most Naga tribes were scattered to their respective places. In fact, the Angami name for Makhel, *Makhoromia* means 'the place of departure'. There are a number of historical facts such as stone monoliths and sacred trees, besides the rich oral history that support the Makhel origin of dispersal of the Nagas.[130] Makhel is thus believed to be the oldest village of the Nagas.

O.K. Singh believes the recent discovery of pre-historic cave sites and other archaeological relics in Naga areas in recent years are representative of the palaeolithic culture.[131] Additionally, Singh is of the opinion that none of these archaeological finds and relics have any affinity with the rest of mainland India; rather they are found to be more akin with the Island South East Asia. And, "If the first settlers of these palaeolithic sites in the Naga Hills are assumed as the Nagas . . . then we can draw the conclusion that the Nagas have arrived at their homeland sometime around or before 10,000 B.C." concludes R. Vashum.[132] The Nagas have lived and been living in their homeland from time immemorial and there can be little doubt that they are the original inhabitants of these lands.

To reiterate, the Nagas are not and have never been Indians; they have their own distinct history and identity as a nation. The Nagas were autonomous and free and never conquered until the nineteenth century when the British forced the

---

Fact (Golden: *Fulcrum Publishing, 1997); Evolution, Creationism, and Other Modern Myths: A Critical Inquiry* (Golden: Fulcrum Publishing, 2002).

[129] A Tangkhul folk song called Miwurla (Origin song) tells of Samsok (Burma) as their place of origin. Here is the significant line:

Kachili tunglu....

Āvā *Samsokli tungthuiya*

(Whence thou cometh? O come I through Samsok, Burma).

Luikham, *Wung (Tangkhul) Naga Okthot Mayonza*, 169.

[130] For a detailed discussion see Shimray, Origin and Cultures of Nagas, 26-28; M. Horam, *Social and Cultural Life of Nagas* (Delhi: Low Price Publications, 1992), 22-23; and V. K Nuh, *Origin of Naga* (Kohima: Vision Press, 2002), 23-27.

[131] Quoted in Vashum, Nagas' Right to Self Determination. 21. Some of the prehistoric sites include Khangkhui cave in Ukhrul district, Songbu cave in Chandel district and Nongpok Keithelmanbi in Senapati district.

[132] Ibid., 22.

Nagas into the control of the British India administration. Visier Sanyu is right when he emphasizes the fact of Naga sovereignty before the arrival of the British:

> It needs to be stressed that before the arrival of the British the Nagas were politically independent. They did not share any of the governmental systems of India or Burma. It was purely a non-state society with peculiar polity where society functioned in a pure democratic form.[133]

Nagas and their Neighbors before British Contact

Given the fact that the Nagas lived a life of isolation, it could not be easily established to what extent the Nagas had interactions with her neighbors before the arrival of the British colonial forces. However, there is some historical evidence that suggests Nagas did have interaction with the people on the plains below in what is now Assam and Manipur. One of the close neighbors are the Kacharis of Assam and so the possibility of the Nagas coming into contact with them is quite high. Indeed, the "legends of the Kachari King Bhim are still current among the Kacha Nagas and the Angamis of Khonoma."[134] According to these legends, king Bhim would some day return to rule the people once more.

There is clear evidence which points to relationships between the Nagas and the Ahom rulers of Assam because it is known that the two groups engaged in a number of military and political confrontations and negotiations. Some even suggest that the Nagas had to pay taxes to the Ahom king in return for his allowing them to live independently. The Ahom kings were more than satisfied so long as the Nagas stopped attacking the Assamese who lived near the Nagas. There were also instances where the Ahom kings enlisted Nagas along with other tribes such as the Singphos and Khakhos into their military.[135]

The relations of Nagas with the neighboring Manipuris was marked both by fierce enmity on the one hand and uneasy but relatively peaceful coexistence on the other. In 1833 the Manipuris raided in Angami region as far as Kohima with the result that many houses were burnt and many lives were lost.[136] There were also occasions in which the Nagas – Tangkhul and Mao in particular – attacked and inflicted severe injuries on the Manipuris. Interestingly, there are stories that suggest Nagas and Manipuris are much closer to each other than it appears to be. According to one of the well known stories, the Tangkhuls and the Manipuris

---

[133] Visier Sanyu, *A History of Nagas and Nagaland: Dynamics of Oral Tradition in Village Formation* (New Delhi: Commonwealth Publishers, 1996), 127. Sanyu is a historian and a Naga of Angami nation.

[134] Hutton, *The Angami Nagas*, 13.

[135] Ibid.

[136] Ibid.

were brothers – the Tangkhuls as the elder brother and the Manipuris as the younger.[137]

There is also historical and cultural evidence to support the close connections between the two communities. The Manipuris, to this day continue with the practice of wearing Tangkhul Naga dresses on the concluding day of the celebration of *Laiharaoba* festivals. Furthermore, during the enthronement ceremony, the king and queen of Manipur would attire in the Tangkhul costumes.[138]

Both the communities have openly acknowledged and even attempted to strengthen their relationships such that significant interactions through exchange of visits and gifts have been going on between the chief of the Hundung village and the royal family of the Manipuris to this day. Unfortunately, the relationship between the two communities has never been as strained as it is today; the political and social tensions between the Nagas and Manipuris are at the boiling point.

Nagas and the British: A Brief Overview

The first British contact with the Nagas happened in 1832 when the British illegally entered the Angami region with the help of 700 Manipuri troops and 800 forced Manipuri laborers.[139] They came under heavy attacks by the Angamis who perceived any outsiders trespassing on their land as a serious threat to their freedom and sovereignty. The British made a number of raids on the Nagas during the years of 1839-1850 and these attacks were met with fierce and heroic resistance from the Nagas, at times leading to heavy loses on both sides. As much as the British forces were determined to exact surrender from the Nagas, the Nagas were equally, if not, even more so determined to defend their homeland by every means available. For the Nagas it was a matter of life and death. With each fierce battle the casualties multiplied on both sides but it was the Nagas who suffered the most. In addition to the loss of many lives, a number of villages were burned down, and also many granaries and domestic animals were destroyed.[140] Finally, in 1881 the British took full control of the Nagas.[141] Until then the Nagas mounted

---

[137] Yangkahao Vashum, *Tangkhul Naga-Christian Theology of Human Rights*, M. Th. Thesis, Gurukul Lutheran Theological College and Research Institute, 1994, 5.

[138] M. Horam, *Social and Cultural life of Nagas: The Tangkhul Nagas* (Delhi: B. R. Publishing Corporation, 1977), 236; Khayaipam Khamrang, *Towards an Eco-Theology: Resources in the Primal Religion of the Tangkhul Nagas*, M. Th. Thesis, Gurukul Lutheran Theological College and Research Institute, 1992, 7.

[139] Jenkins and Pamberton, British and Manipuri officers respectively led the troops.

[140] Cf. Sanjib Baruah, *Durable Disorder: Understanding the Politics of Northeast India* (New Delhi: Oxford University Press, 2005), 109.

[141] In 1866, the British for the first time established the Naga Hills District with Samaguting (Chumukedima) as the Deputy Commissioner's Headquarters. In 1875, the headquarters was moved from Samaguting to Wokha and not long after the Headquarters was shifted to Kohima in 1878. It must be noted that the British control was limited to only a certain portion of the Naga territory, especially the southwestern part of the Naga territory. The larger portion of the Naga

frequent attacks on the British camps located in the Assam valley and succeeded in inflicting heavy casualties on the British. During the period from 1854 to 1865 the Angami people attacked the British nineteen times, "in which 232 British subjects were killed, wounded, or carried off."[142]

The British control of the Nagas continued and ended with the transfer of power in 1947; unfortunately, for the Nagas this change only signaled the beginning of another chapter of foreign rule with India as the master. The British administration included special policies for the Nagas and other Northeast hill tribes which afforded them wide-ranging autonomies and protection not granted to the rest of India. Following its Forward Policy the administration introduced Inner Line Regulation in 1873 which initially had dual but undifferentiated foci "to protect plainsmen from Nagas and Nagas from plainsmen."[143] But later the scope of the Inner Line Regulations shifted to primarily protecting the Nagas and their land from encroachments and exploitation by the dominant Indian population. The Government of India Act of 1919 declared the Naga Hills District as a "Backward Tract" and treated it as distinct and separate from the rest of British India Empire. But following strong objections from many including members of British officers[144] to the use of the term "backward," the administration was forced eventually to replace it with a different name. Accordingly, in April 1937, the "Naga Hill Districts along with the North-East Frontier Tract, and the Lushai and North Cachar Hills were declared 'Excluded Areas' of the province of Assam."[145] The reason behind this different administrative system was the simple recognition of the distinctiveness of the Nagas from the rest of India. The Nagas were allowed their traditional authority, the village council to manage most administrative and judicatory work.[146] Throughout the entirety of British rule,

territory remained unconquered and unadministered for a long time. Later on, of course, the whole Naga areas came under British control.

[142] Alexander Mackenzie, *The North-East Frontier of Assam* (Delhi: Mittal Publications, 1979), 118.

[143] Alemchiba, *A Brief Historical Account of Nagaland,* 150.

[144] Simon Commission members, John Simon and Cadogan, who visited Nagaland in 1929 to ascertain the views of the Naga people, John Simon and Cadogan objected to the description of the Nagas as backward. Simon described it "nauseating' and Cadogan "misleading." Cadogan spoke of his displeasure in the house of Commons: "It is true that some of these tribesmen eat food which if you or I eat it, would give us ptomaine poisoning at once, but you and I have no right to say that because a third person can digest food which we cannot digest the person is, therefore backward. It might be that his inside had reached a more advanced state of evolution than your's or mine, but it is a mistake to imagine - and I am speaking seriously – that, because their customs are different from our's they are backward." Instead they favored Excluded and Partially Excluded Areas. Quoted in Elwin, Nagaland, 36.

[145] M. Horam, *Naga Polity* (Delhi: B. R. Publishing Corporation, 1975), 15.

[146] Luingam Luithui and Nandita Haksar, *Nagaland File: A Question of Human Rights* (New Delhi: Lancer International, 1984), 16.

with the one exception being the introduction of Euro-western administrative system at the district level, the Nagas were the most part on their own.

British Legacy: The Most Dangerous Legacy

Recent studies describe the British legacy for the Naga people to be the most dangerous legacy.

> The swift transfer of power from British to India effectively legitimized the boundaries and control despite the protest from the people. The British legacy of alleged borders and control has become fixed, creating an apparent permanent instability while there is no acceptance of re-thinking the imaginary geography.[147]

The British invented political borders to set apart India and Myanmar but in so doing they split in two the homeland of the Naga people. This was done, not surprisingly, without the prior knowledge or consent of the people. And, when the British were forced to leave India, they did so without solving the mess they had created including the border issue. Indeed it is the most dangerous legacy inherited by the Nagas from the British as the bloody years of struggle for independence has gone by decades. It has been seventy years since the Nagas declared their independence, one day ahead before India's own declaration, and to this day the Nagas have not attained their long cherished freedom. The Nagas were left to fence off on their own in the face of the mighty and powerful Indian armies. In spite of the repeated representations that the Nagas did not want to be part of India or any other outside power for that matter, the British government unfortunately chose to turn a blind eye on the Naga people. Instead they swiftly transferred the power to India and in the process the desire of the Naga people was deliberately and completely ignored. In the process, several innocent Naga lives have been lost and still the woes of the people continue unabatedly on daily basis.

To this day, the British government has not taken any responsibility for the historic blunder it committed, nor has it come forward to clarify its position on this long-standing Naga problem. The Naga people are vexed and bewildered at the deafening silence the British government maintained to this point.[148] Under

---

[147] Andrew West, *The Most Dangerous Legacy: The Development of Identity, Power and Marginality in the Transfer to India and the Nagas* (Hull: Center for South-East Asian Studies, 1999) (Occasional Paper no. 34), 54.

[148] In May 11, 2006, for the first time, Parliamentarians of the United Kingdom organized a conference of the Parliamentarians for National Self Determination (PNSD) in which nationalist leaders "including those from the Naga, Kashmiri, Kosovar, Palestinian, Sikh, Tamil, Chenchen, Kurd, Manipuri and other nations" were present. Part of the Draft Resolutions of the PNSD reads, "The PNSD calls upon the UK Govt. EU and UN and other international Institutions to create conditions for the peaceful exercise of self determination on the basis that this is the only just and

the auspicious leadership of the NSCN (National Socialist Council of Nagaland) the Naga people have repeatedly demanded the British government clarify its position, but to no avail.

One might ask whether there was ever any support for Naga independence from the British administration. The record shows no such support other than a few officers who voiced their support for a considerable autonomy for the Nagas. One such was J.P. Mills, the senior administrator in the late 1930s and as a result "he fell out of favor with the Congress party and the British administration had to move him out of the Naga hills because of his outspokenness."[149]

In regards to British contributions to Naga people, many cite building of infrastructure such as roads, schools, and hospitals, opening up the Nagas to the wider world from the other wise age-old village republic system of the people. I would be very cautious in claiming these as benefits of colonialism. For the Nagas each village was its own republic and their life revolved around the village. There was no national state that encompassed all the tribes despite the fact that they knew they belonged together as a people. As the Naga Hoho *White Paper* aptly states:

> The existence of sovereign Naga villages with their own territory, their system and population from time immemorial to this day is the living proof of Naga Sovereignty because the Naga nation is made up of sovereign Naga villages.[150]

The infrastructure built by the British was designed to enhance primarily their control, not help Nagas. And the creation of a national state is only significant because of the colonial invasion of Nagaland. It was during the British rule that the Naga political identity was born and developed but only as an act of resistance!

> The concept of "Nagas" was given an administrative form by the British and retained by them in that form. The British isolated the hill area and called it the Naga Hills District . . . . Through their organizing, the British gave a perception of Nagas to outsiders . . . .

effective means of conflict resolution in many of the world's current conflict zones . . . . PNSD calls on State Governments to engage in unconditional talks with national groups, such as the ongoing talks between the Indo-Naga talks, in order to resolve outstanding disputes involving national self determination." "Draft Resolutions – Parliamentarians for National Self Determination – PNSD 11th May 2006," accessed 16 May 2006; available from http://www.nagalim.nl/naga/index-2.html

[149] West, *The Most Dangerous Legacy*, 30.

[150] *White Paper on Naga Integration*. Compiled by the Naga Hoho and adopted at its 7th General Assembly held on May 20-22, 2002 at Senapati, vii. Similar view is expressed by Hokishe Sema. "The lack of unity and the absence of a single political system amongst the Nagas at that time proved to be advantageous for maintaining their independence." *Emergence of Nagaland* (New Delhi: Vikas Publishing House Pvt. Ltd., 1986), 17.

> The administrators-cum-anthropologists were several, wrote copiously, collected furiously (for museums) and put the Nagas firmly in the ethnographic museum and on anthropological maps."[151]

While it may seem as doing a favor to the Nagas through writings and collections, one must not lose sight of the fact that museums are colonial devices for describing and signifying the colonized Other. The spirit of nationalism and the desire for an independent nation burned in the hearts and souls of the Naga people even before the British transferred power to India in 1947. Accordingly, the Naga leaders expressed time and again their desire to be left alone whenever the British decided to leave India and Nagaland. They urged the British administration to do something that would ensure Naga independence but unfortunately nothing was done.

It is ironic that while the British helped raise the national consciousness and a more sense of solidarity among the Naga people this "contribution" was overshadowed by the dangerous legacy it left behind: the creation of artificial boundaries,[152] the swift transfer of power to India, and the bloody struggles that followed in the history of the Naga people in their quest for independence. In fact, the Nagas are not fighting for their independence; rather they are defending their independence from an invading/occupying force namely India.

The Indian government and the critics of Naga's independent movement blame the British administration for allowing the Nagas to follow their own traditions, customs and practices. Even when the British administration decided to extend their administrative control and grouped the Nagas under the umbrella category of "Excluded Areas" with the rest of the Northeast tribes, the Nagas were pretty much left on their own. Critics argue that such policies accounted for the Naga peoples' reticence to identify themselves as Indians.[153] There was hardly any effort on the part of the British administration to bring them together with the rest of Indians whether culturally, socially, politically or even emotionally. The practical effect was that there couldn't be any bonding between the Naga people and the Indian people socially or emotionally as national identity implies.

This accusation could not be further from the truth. The fact is that the British administration chose to employ a separate administrative policy for the Nagas when it was realized that they were a distinct group of people who had nothing in common with India or Indians. The British realized that the Nagas had their own distinct cultures and tradition, history and religion, life styles and foods

---

[151] West, *The most Dangerous Legacy*, 19.

[152] The Treaty of Yandabo, signed on 24 February 1826 between the English East India Company and the Kingdom of Myanmar laid the ground work for the disintegration of Naga ancestral homeland.

[153] Udayan Misra, *The Periphery Strikes Back: Challenges to the Nation-State in Assam and Nagaland* (Shimla: Indian Institute of Advanced Study, 2000), 25f.

and eating habits.[154] There are also obvious physiognomy differences between the dominant Indians and the Nagas. The inclusion of the Nagas within India is not only a matter of great consternation, it is quite illogical! It was an historical accident as was acknowledged by one of the British administrators when he stated that the Nagas "are not Indian in any sense of the word neither in origin, nor in language, nor in look, and it is only historical accident that they have been tacked on to an Indian province."[155]

Nagas' Struggle, Resistance Movement and Freedom

Pre-Independence of August 1947

Historically, the struggle of the Nagas in defending their independence began in the early 19th century when they fought gallantly but ultimately unsuccessfully against the invading British forces. In 1918 the first ever national Naga organization called the Naga Club was formed in Kohima for the purpose of expanding their national consciousness and supporting the Naga solidarity movement.[156] Perhaps, it was the Naga Club that officially represented the Nagas before the Simon Commission in 1929 when the commissioners visited Kohima to ascertain the views of the Nagas. The Naga leaders categorically stated that the Nagas did not want to be part of either a British Colony or India and that they should be left to govern themselves should the British decide to leave Nagaland and India.

Interestingly, during 1929 to 1933 a Naga resistance movement emerged under the leadership of Jadunang Rongmei. As Asoso Yonou describes, "From 1929 to 1933, a politically worthy, but religiously more significant movement that we may call the Naga renaissance or religious nationalism, took place in Naga inhabited frontiers... where Zemai, Liangmai and Rongmei Nagas live.[157] Jadunang claimed to be the Messiah King of the Nagas and "declared an independent Nagaland in an aggressive, warlike form"[158] against British rule. He had a large following from his own tribe and his movement for freedom steadily gained momentum. By 1931 the British viewed this movement as a direct threat to their power and they wasted no time arresting and hanging Jadunang on 29th

---

[154] In fact, the Indians looked down upon the Nagas for eating beef, pork and dog's meat which were a delicacy to the Nagas, which was a matter of social alienation. Alemchiba, *A Brief Historical Accounts of Nagaland*, 164; Cf. Horam, Naga Insurgency, 64.

[155] Robert Reid, Governor of Assam from 1937-1942. Quoted in Maxwell Neville, *India, the Nagas and the North-east,* New Edition (London: Minority Rights Groups, 1980), 3.

[156] It has been widely commented that the exposure of the Nagas who went to Europe as part of the Labor Corps of the Allied forces contributed to feeling of Naga nationalism and ultimately in the formation of the Naga Club.

[157] Asoso Yonou, *The Rising Nagas: A Historical and Political Study* (Delhi: Vivek Publishing House, 1972), 126.

[158] Asoso Yonou, *The Rising Nagas: A Historical and Political Study* (Delhi: Vivek Publishing House, 1972), 127.

August of that year. Leadership of the movement was assumed by Jadunang's female cousin, Gaidiliu. Under Gaidiliu's able leadership the freedom movement continued its work. The veteran nationalist Jawaharlal Nehru recognized her gallant leadership and called her Rani Gaidiliu. To this day, she is known by everyone as Rani Gaidiliu.[159]

The majority of the Naga people, under the banner of Naga Club, were pressing for independent Nagaland once the British decided to live Nagaland. Their desires and aspirations were further reiterated in the succeeding meetings with both the British administration and the soon to be independent India government. In February 1947 under the leadership of A. Z. Phizo, the Nagas had formed a full fledged political organ called the Naga National Council (NNC) by utilizing and building the existing Naga Club. The NNC was to play the role of pressure group to gain political advantage from the British rulers. The Nine-Point Hydari Agreement,[160] a product of the negotiations between the NNC and the Indian Constituent Assembly in June 1947, appeared very promising until India unilaterally withdrew their endorsement of the agreement. The Indian Constituent Assembly even threatened of invasion of Nagaland and this threat was seen legitimate and serious by the Naga leaders. Fortunately the Nagas were able to bring this matter to the attention of Mahatma Gandhi in New Delhi on 19 July, 1947. Gandhiji assured them, "If you do not wish to join the Union of India, nobody will force you to do that....Nagas have every right to be independent."

Independent India Scenario: Conflicts and Negotiations

The Historic Naga Plebiscite of 1951 and its Aftermath

On 15 August, 1947, the very next day after the Nagas declared their independence, India proclaimed more than its own independence, she also claimed authority over Nagaland. Despite the obvious insult, the Nagas were still willing to negotiate with India for an amicable resolution. Nagas were committed to non-violence and dialogue as the means to peace. It is not surprising then that they were profoundly dismayed when their positive gestures were simply ignored and instead they were confronted with the threat of military invasion if they didn't accept outright the offer to join the Indian Union. With no satisfactory resolution forthcoming the NNC decided in April, 1950, to affirm their refusal to accept the Indian

---

[159] The movement started by Jadunang exists yet to this day but is confined to a small and exclusive group which is named the "Haraka Cult." The movement is overtly against British rule and Christianity.

[160] The Agreement contains nine points and was fully to the advantage of the Nagas. The agreement recognized the right of the Nagas to shape and develop themselves in accordance with their own free wishes. However, disagreement arose concerning the last point of the agreement. Article 9 states, "Upon completion of ten years of the observance of the agreement the NNC would be free either to extend the agreement or decide to be on their own." India claimed this meant that a new agreement has to be adopted and Nagas believed it meant that the Nagas could decide to be free.

Constitution and to assert the sovereignty of Nagaland state. By this time "the movement of the Naga people for self determination became more consolidated, defined and stringent"[161] thanks to the leadership of A. Z. Phizo. Things began to move quickly and in May 1951 the NNC launched the historic Naga Plebiscite which lasted nearly two months with an overwhelming majority of Nagas, 99.9 % to be precise, voting in favor of sovereign Nagaland state. The government of India was informed of the result but Prime Minister Jawaharlal Nehru refused to honor the declaration of the Naga people. Tajenyuba Ao puts quite succinctly the mood and emotion of the people and the significance of the plebiscite:

> Filled up forms with thumb impressions were dispatched to the President of India, the President of All India Congress Party and the General Secretary of the United Nations. For the Nagas the spirit of unilateral plebiscite held in the Naga country was accepted without any objections from any quarters and it became binding on all Naga tribes in India and Burma with their tacit support to the Naga national struggle. The solidarity and oneness of Naga people which was an impossible task due to traditional feelings of enmity, language difficulty and different tribal social set up was achieved through the spirit of plebiscite. All credits for unity of the Nagas go to the stewardship of Phizo.[162]

This was immediately followed by the launching of a movement of civil disobedience calling for the boycott of business with government offices, non-payment of taxes, and the boycott of the upcoming first general election of independent India in January 1952. The Indian government responded by sending in the military and conducting arbitrary and indiscriminate arrests. The situation further worsened when in 1953, Nehru and his Myanmarese counterpart Thakin U .Nu's visited Kohima. Miffed by the refusal to allow representation to Nehru, the Nagas en masse walked out from Nehru's public address.

This public humiliation was not taken lightly by Nehru and the relations between the Nagas and Indian government became even more tense. Upon his return to New Delhi, Nehru ordered more Armed forces to be sent to Nagaland and many more arrests followed. The Assam Maintenance of Public Order Act was enacted in 1953 followed by the introduction of Assam Disturbed Act in 1955 "to enable the Assam Armed Police and Assam Rifles to execute their tasks unabated and openly, without legal constraints."[163] The first Indian aerial bombardment

---

161 Vashum, *Nagas' Right to Self Determination,* 79.

162 Tajenyuba Ao, *British Occupation of Naga Country* (Mokokchung: Naga Literature Society, 1993), 285.

163 *Naga Resistance and the Peace Process* (New Delhi: Other Media Communications, 2001), 10.

of Nagaland took place on 27 November, 1954, the same year the Assam Rifles began their mission of genocide in Nagaland. By this time, two divisions of the Indian Army and thirty-five battalions of the Assam Rifles and Armed Police had been deployed in Nagaland.

> This invasion, by the late 1950s reduced 645 Naga villages to ashes resulting in the deaths of over a hundred thousand lives who died from bullets, torture, starvation and diseases. By 1960, the Naga landscape was a wasteland of razed houses and broken lives.[164]

Given the situation, the Nagas were left with no other option but to take up arms of resistance in 1955. On 22 March, 1955, the NNC established its Federal Government of Nagaland (FGN) and created their own army called the Federal Army.

Meanwhile, differences among the rank and file of the NNC had arisen which resulted in the killing of T. Sakharie, one of the prominent leaders of the NNC. The moderate Nagas who had been so far silent began to find their voice. They organized to form a Naga Peoples' Convention (NPC) with the goal to be the mediator between the more radical NNC and the Indian government. The NNC was not pleased with the plan but gave the NPC a cautious welcome to the struggle. The NPC appealed to Phizo and NNC to lay down their arms in exchange for withdrawal of the Indian military from Nagaland, but the NNC flatly rejected their appeal.[165] In 1957 India agreed to the merger of the Naga Hills Districts with the Tuensang Frontier Division which made an autonomous district to be administered by a single Commissioner.[166] In a significant development:

> The Manipur Naga Council, which was formed in 1956, merged with the NNC . . . in 1957. Upon this a number of Manipur Naga Council office bearers, among them Angal Anal, the President, and Z. Ramyo, the Secretary, went underground and joined hands with the NNC.[167]

---

[164] Kaka Iralu. "16 Point Agreement - The Greatest Betrayal in Naga History," available from http://www.nscnonline.org/nscn/index-2.html

[165] In fact, from the very beginning NNC was suspicious of the hands of Indian Intelligence Bureau and Assam Government behind NPC and had dubbed it as "stooges of Indian government" out to destabilize the solidarity of the Nagas. A. Z. Phizo, the NNC supremo simply dismissed the NPC saying it "was nothing more than a 'bribe' given by the Government to the members of the Naga People's Convention." Ashiko Daili-Mao, *Nagas: Problems and Politics* (New Delhi: Ashish Publishing House, 1992), 75.

[166] Until that time Naga Hills Districts and Tuensang Frontier Division were administered separately under Assam state.

[167] M. Horam, *Naga Insurgency – The Last Thirty Years* (New Delhi: Cosmo Publishers, 1988), 84.

Creation of the autonomous district did nothing to improve the situation; rather, it sparked more intensified fighting between the national freedom fighters and the Indian armed forces. Further, the Armed Forces (Assam and Manipur) Special Forces Ordinances was passed on 11 September, 1958 and in 1972 the Act was amended to become the Armed Forces (Special Powers) Act (AFSPA) which brought more states and territories under its rubric. The Act was rightly described by many as draconian because it allowed soldiers of the Army to shoot to kill, to search, to arrest, to detain, or to remove anybody or anything without a warrant. Simply put, soldiers were now immune to prosecution by any court of law without first receiving the government's permission. In its review the South Asia Human Rights Documentation Center (SAHRDC) was highly critical of the AFSPA and accused it of contravening "both Indian and International law standards." The review also stated:

> The greatest outrage of the AFSPA under both Indian and International law is the violation of the right to life. This comes under the Article 6 of the ICCPR, and it is a non-derogable right. This means no situation, or state of emergency, or internal disturbance, can justify the suspension of this right.[168]

Sixteen Point Agreement, Nagaland State Formation and Its Impact on Freedom Struggle

The divide and conquer policy of India proved to be quite effective. The Indian government successfully engineered division among the Nagas; the NPC which was supposed to be playing the mediator role took upon itself the role of negotiator. NPC entered into negotiations with the government of India leading to the signing in 26 July, 1960 of the now infamous Sixteen Point Agreement. This agreement paved the way for the formation of Nagaland state as the sixteenth state of Indian Republic on 10 December, 1963 under the Ministry of External Affairs. The placement of Nagaland state under the Ministry of External Affairs (Foreign Affairs) rather than under the Ministry of Home Affairs produced a political and practical contradiction. Consider this: Why would India, while claiming Nagaland to be a natural part of India, place Nagaland state under the authority of External Affairs. The only logical conclusion we can draw from this is that it proves that the Nagas were never actually considered part of India and therefore were forcibly brought under Indian constitution.

The signing of the Sixteen Point Agreement and the subsequent establishment of Nagaland state raised the threshold of the Naga people's history of struggle. Indeed, it proved beyond doubt to be the most disastrous mistake ever endured

---

[168] South Asia Human Rights Documentation Center, "Armed Forces Special Powers Act: A study in National Security Tyranny," accessed 16 May, 2006, available from http://www.nscnonline.org/nscn/index-2.html

by the Nagas. Kaka Iralu termed it as "the greatest betrayal of Naga history." He went on to say:

> If there had been no NPC and no 16-Point Agreement in 1960, there never would have been a Revolutionary Government surrender in 1973 or a Shillong Accord in 1975, or an NSCN in 1980 and 1988, or a second NNC in 1990. In summary, the seeds of confusions, suspicions and fratricidal killings were all sown into Naga hearts and soil when the NPC singed the infamous 16-Point Agreement with the Government of India in 1960.[169]

The inevitable problem generated by the state formation was that it did not include the entirety of the Naga homeland. In keeping with the divide and conquer policy, the Indian government with the aid of NPC leaders, curved out a section of the Naga ancestral homeland in order to create an artificial state. Predictably, everyone who had been fighting for Naga sovereignty adamantly opposed the formation of this new state. A.Z. Phizo, the leader of the NNC denounced the state formation and reaffirmed that, "The Naga people will accept neither the Indian 'bribe' of statehood nor India's offer of 'internal autonomy' as something to be eulogized. It is only a means to conceal her [India's] crime against humanity."[170] The freedom fighters accused the Indian government and the NPC leaders who were part of the new deal of trying to undermine the Naga peoples' struggle for independence.[171]

Visier Sanyu rightly argues that the creation of this Nagaland state effectively drove a wedge between the already estranged Naga leadership factions. Those who favored statehood within Indian union focused their attention to Indian electoral politics, power and money; whereas "a large section of Nagas kept alive their quest for sovereign nation state."[172] The creation of Nagaland state not only divided the Nagas geographically and politically but also emotionally.

---

[169] Iralu, "16-Point Agreement."

[170] Daili-Mao, *Nagas: Problems and Politics,* 75.

[171] The debate still continues among Naga people. In 2000, the Nagaland State Congress Party published a political pamphlet entitled Bedrock of Naga Society in which the authors defended the sixteen point agreement and the subsequent formation of Nagaland state arguing that Nagaland state "gave the Nagas worth and significance in the eyes of the world". The document was denounced by Naga National organizations and civil societies alike including NSCN-IM, Naga Hoho, Naga people's movements for Human Rights, Naga Students' Federation and others. They consider the document as a distortion of Naga history.

[172] Visier Sanyu, "What Nagaland State did to the Nagas: A Historical Perspective," in S. M. Channa, ed., *Nagaland: A Contemporary Ethnography* (New Delhi: Cosmo Publication, 1992), 269; cf. J. Johari, "Creation of Nagaland: Triumph of Ebullient Infranationalism," in *Indian Journal of Political Science* 36, no. 1 (Jan-Mar. 1975), 13-38.

The state creation further aggravated the Naga's ongoing existing boundary disputes with Assam and other neighboring states none of which were of the Naga's making. As Asoso Yonuo states it clearly:

> At present as well as in the past, we know the boundary disputes assume a substantial subject of importance in relations between Nagaland, Assam, Manipur, NEFA and Burma. But following the creation of Nagaland state, this wuestgion became now and again, irritant. Many of the disputes were directly or indirectly inherited from the British rule when the traditional boundaries between them had been altered to administrative, strategic, economic and intrinsic gains or insufficiently explored.[173]

Of all the destructive effects which resulted from the arbitrary creation of this Nagaland state, it was the Balkanization of the population and traditional homeland that was most devastating. This had long been a practice perpetrated by the British administration and it was adopted quickly by the Indian government in order to incorporate certain Nagas communities into Manipur state and still more into Assam state.[174] This severely undermined the unity of the Naga people and made it much more difficult for the people to mount any concerted effort against the government. Not surprisingly, the unrest among the people intensified and attacks on the security forces escalated. The establishment of the new state also proved to be costly for the NPC when its President Imkongliba Ao was assassinated. To add to the woes and insults of the already suffering Nagas, in 1962 the Indian government promulgated the Nagaland Security Regulation, this is in addition to Armed Forces Special Powers Act established in 1958 with the purpose of making special provisions for the maintenance of public order by the suppression of subversive activities endangering the safety or security of Nagaland.

A cease-fire was negotiated between the NNC and the Government of India in 1964 through the initiative of the Nagaland Baptist Churches Peace Mission.[175] The first peace talks were held on 23 September, 1964 followed by several rounds of discussions. But the talks were destined to fail from the start because India had always viewed "Naga problem" as an issue of law and order within Indian constitution; soon the cease-fire broke down. Military operations re-commenced

---

[173] Yonuo, *The Rising Nagas*, 363-364.

[174] The British administration arbitrarily divided up the Naga people and their territory into Manipur state and Assam state. While Mao, Tangkhul and Tamenglong Naga areas were incorporated into Manipur state in 1842 the Angami areas were included in Assam, after which Naga Hills was created as a district in1886. Ibid., 369.

[175] And the Peace Mission consisted of three members of the following well known persons of the time: Rev. Michael Scott, (a British clergy), B. P. Chaliha (then Chief Minister of Assam), and Sri Jaya Prakash Narayan (a Member of Parliament and a Gandhian peace activist).

and heavy fighting between the two became the norm. Jaya Prakash Narayan, a member of the Baptist Peace Mission, went on record saying, "It is far more important to have friendly Nagas on our frontier closely associated with us than unfriendly and discontented Nagas kept forcibly within the Indian Union."[176] The situation deteriorated further in 1972 when the Indian government declared the NNC, the FGN, and the Naga Army as "unlawful associations" under the 1967 Unlawful Activities (Prevention) Act No. 37. In 1972 Nagaland state was arbitrarily transferred from the Ministry of External Affairs to the Ministry of Home Affairs.[177] The intention of the Government of India seemed very clear: India wished to capitalize as much as possible on the division it had brought about among the Naga people. It did succeed in destabilizing the solidarity of the Nagas and further weakening the struggle for Naga sovereignty.

The Impact and Ramifications of 1975 Shilling Accord

If the signing of the Sixteen Point Agreement opened up the whole Pandora's Box of problems for Nagas, the signing of the infamous Shillong Accord on 11 November, 1975 nailed the last blow to the unity and the ongoing Naga freedom struggle. The Accord was signed between certain members of NNC-FGN[178] and the Government of India. The Accord constituted a complete surrender of Naga aspiration; besides agreeing to lay down their arms the signatories "of their own volition, to accept without condition, the Constitution of India." Most Nagas were appalled at the outcome and immediately rejected the agreement. The strongest condemnation in fact, came from the rank and file of the NNC party itself. Thuingaleng Muivah and Isak C. Swu denounced it as an outright sell-out of Naga interests.

It has been said time and again that the NNC leaders signed the Accord under extreme duress. Some evidence corroborates this claim; however, the signatories' actions that followed seemed to also suggest otherwise. I do not in any way doubt the patriotism of those leaders nor do I question their sincerity. But the troubling reality is this: the Accord was a mistake and they did not admit their mistake; nor did they make effort to retract their decision. Rather, they devoted themselves to its implementation. The government of India, backed by its powerful military, embarked on its campaign to implement the Accord with a vengeance. They relied on the usual tactics of intimidation, arrests and

---

[176] Jaya Prakash Narayan was strongly criticized for speaking out; several Members of Parliament even demanded his arrest. He was one of few Indian leaders who appeared to genuinely understand the feelings and aspiration of the Naga people.

[177] The Sixteen-Point Agreement of 1960 placed Nagaland state under the Ministry of External Affairs of the government of India.

[178] The NNC team was led by Kevi Yally, the brother of A. Z. Phizo, and included, I. Temjenba, Veenyiyi Rhakhu, Z. Ramyo and M. Assa. The Accord reportedly had the blessing of Phizo who was by then in London, but he died in 1990 having neither endorsed nor condemned it.

imprisonment of all who opposed the agreement, especially politicians from the opposition parties and student activists.

Men were sent from Kohima to the Headquarters of the NCC to kill Isak and Muivah but providence provided their escape from their assassins. Isak and Muivah were arrested, not only ones but three times.[179]

Factionalism Follows the Shillong Accord

The Shillong Accord unfortunately brought about deeply destructive divisions among the Naga people. Isak, Muivah, and others pleaded to Phizo for his guidance but Phizo chose to remain silent. "Had Phizo uttered words of directions and guidelines, Naga unity and political movement would have taken a positive turn."[180] It was not until 1996, in other words, twenty years after the signing of the Shillong Accord, that the President of the Federal Government of Nagaland (NNC -A) Zashei Hurie, for the first time condemned the Shillong Accord as null and void.[181]

The inevitable consequence of the Shillong Accord was the splitting up of the NNC party. Under the leadership of T. Muivah and Isak Swu, a new party was founded in 1980 and christened as National Socialists Council of Nagaland (NSCN). As the NSCN became better organized and it also gained strength politically and militarily so that under its banner, the Naga's struggle for independence began to regain momentum. The party suffered a severe set back in 1988 when a coup was launched against Muivah and Isak Swu by the then vice President, Khaplang and his supporters assisted by Burmese which resulted in the death of over 140 freedom fighters. The plan for this coup was unfortunately engineered by the over ground Naga leaders who collaborated with the Indian intelligence network. They alleged that Muivah and Isak were planning to surrender themselves to India in return for leadership positions in the Indian administration. Further that they were planning to attack Konyak and Pangmi members of the NSCN before their surrender. However:

> The allegations against Chairman Isak and General Secretary Muivah were entirely concocted by Khaplang and Indian puppets who instigated Konyak Army Officers. Khaplang in his lust for power committed the most heinous crimes by butchering the most precious national workers.[182]

---

[179] Tajenyuba Ao, *British Occupation of Naga Country,* 301.

[180] Ibid., 299.

[181] Vashum, *Nagas' Right to Self Determination,* 103f.

[182] Ibid., 305.

Again Muivah and Isak made a providential escape from their enemies. The ultimate result was the emergence of two NSCN factions – NSCN-IM (Isak-Muivah) and NSCN-K (Khaplang).

In 1990 the NNC followed suit by experiencing its own split, one headed by Adino, the daughter of Phizo and the other headed by its Vice President, Khodao Yantan. Later on Yantan with some of his followers decided to join the Isak-Muivah faction of the NSCN. The leadership of the faction group was taken over by one I. Panger Walling. In 2007, NSCN (U) – Unification was formed by the breakaway groups from both NSCN (IM) & (K) under the leadership of Kitovi Zhimomi. With this split, the Naga struggle for independence came full circle and factional clashes and violence further continued as though the Naga people's suffering at the hands of Indian government is not enough. Furthermore, the internecine squabbles have taken on tribal overtones thereby complicating an already complex situation. It must be also noted that as late as 2015 another faction NSCN (R) led by Wangtin Konyak was formed. Wangtin and his followers broke away from NSCN (K).

However, there is much that is positive to be noted. Among the factions, the NSCN-IM has without question emerged as the influential organization politically and militarily and it has the greatest support. It has accomplished the most in the Naga cause for self-determination and is responsible for gaining recognition internationally for the cause of Naga peoples' struggle. Muivah and Isak, for the first time in the history of Naga politics, were able to earn international sympathy when they attended the Hague Unrepresented Nations and Peoples Organizations' (UNPO) Third General Assembly on January 23, 1993, and the United Nations World Conference on Human Rights in June 1993. As Chairman of the NSCN-IM, Isak honored members of the Third General Assembly of the UNPO with these words:

> On January 23, 1993, the National Flag of Free Nagaland was hoisted among the flags of their Nations for the first time in our history. At 10:11 midnight of January 23, 1993 Naga Standard Time (Suplee Time) the Chairman of the Unrepresented Nations and Peoples Organizations, Mr. Erkin Alptekin, announced the acceptance of Nagaland's membership in the UNPO at the Hague UNPO Third General Assembly Hall.[183]

Henceforth, Nagaland is a member nation of the UNPO. Since the very beginning of their struggle, the Nagas' have been trying to gain International support so this is no small achievement. Additionally, IM has been able to

[183] The Introductory preface to the address Isak gave to the honored members of the Third General Assembly of the UNPO in Hague, on behalf of the people of Nagaland when Nagaland was declared as a member of the Organization.

successfully represent the cause of the Nagas to the UN forum on several occasions.

The Indo-Naga Peace Process: A Critical Analysis

A meeting of the NSCN-IM leadership, Muivah and Isak, and India's Prime Minister P.V. Narasimha Rao, in Paris in February, 1995 opened the way for the eventual signing of a ceasefire agreement on 25 July, 1997 between NSCN-IM and Government of India (GOI) led by the Prime Minister I. K. Gujral.[184] The parties agreed to three months' ceasefire effective 1 August, 1997. The ceasefire has in fact continued to this day as have the peace talk. The following four points form the framework of the cease-fire agreement: 1) That there be a total suspension of armed conflict between the two sides (initially) for three months, beginning August 1, 1997; 2) That peace talks begin with no preconditions; 3) That peace talks shall be conducted at the highest level, i.e. at the Prime Minister's level; 4) That peace talks shall be held in a neutral country.[185]

The ceasefire agreement was greeted with a mixture of reactions although the majority of Nagas were certainly happy with it. There were however, persons and organizations who were apprehensive of the agreement. Their reactions ranged from cautious optimism to outright skepticism based on past historical experience. This history shows two patterns of behavior by India in its negotiations with the Nagas: unilaterally pulling out of the peace agreements, and its bullying tactics against the Nagas in forcing upon them to accept its (GOI) terms and conditions.[186] Many Nagas were therefore apprehensive despite the fact that they were also very willing to give peace a chance.

A joint Ceasefire Monitoring Committee (CMC) was formed; ground rules were established and adherence was expected of both sides. However, from the very beginning, the process was plagued with violations charges and counter charges by both sides. While the NSCN-IM accused the GOI of abusing the ceasefire by conducting operations against NSCN cadres, making arrests and detentions; the

---

[184] By this time the Congress led government was succeeded by United Front government under the leadership of Deve Gowda and later I. K. Gujral. In fact, it was Deve Gowda who on 4 March, 1997 announced in the Parliament that the dialogue between GOI and NSCN-IM had been initiated. Unfortunately, Deve Gowda was ousted from the Prime Ministership and was succeeded by I. K. Gujral who eventually signed the Ceasefire.

[185] Isak C. Swu, "Announcement of Cease-Fire Agreement between the Government of India and the National Socialist Council of Nagaland," in Naga Peoples Movement for Human Rights, *The Nagas: Truth and Hope for the Living* (Kohima: NPMHR, n.d.), 33.

[186] The peace agreement of the 1960s and the signing of the Shillong Accord in 1975 were such examples. Even prior to that there were instances such as the Hydari Agreement of 1946 which was never actually implemented since the GOI unilaterally pulled out of the agreement. On the other hand, Naga people's steadfastness and perseverance in the face of such challenges (India's betrayals) is well documented in the work of Kanwar Randip Singh, *The Nagas of Nagaland: Desperadoes and Heroes of Peace* (New Delhi: Deep and Deep Publications, 1987).

GOI, on the other hand, accused the NSCN of taking the law into their hands by enforcing NSCN's laws upon the civilians.

The most persistent disagreement concerned the geographical scope of the ceasefire agreement. While the GOI argued it's limited to present Nagaland state only, the NSCN-IM insisted that the ceasefire was not limited to Nagaland state only but covers all Naga inhabited areas.[187] The Indian Prime Minister's own emissary, Swaraj Kausal, who was a participant in the ceasefire agreement stated in an interview with *North East Sun* that, "Wherever they are, we observe ceasefire, even abroad…it covers Delhi and even Paris."[188] Regardless, India continues to refuse to officially extend the ceasefire beyond Nagaland state. Rajinder Sachar, former Chief Justice of the Delhi High Court, echoed the views of many when he said, "The biggest impediment in the peace process…is the refusal of the Government of India to officially extend the ceasefire to all Naga inhabited areas."[189] The NSCN began to seriously question the sincerity of the GOI on the ongoing peace negotiations.

The GOI refused to hold negotiations at the Prime Ministerial level as agreed upon in the ceasefire framework, while negotiations were taking place at the secretarial or emissarial level. No substantive issues could be addressed until that was changed. Consequently, the NSCN accused India not only of playing delaying tactics but that they also continued to pursue a campaign of suppression and oppression of Nagas in direct violations of the agreement under the garb of cessation of fire. Moreover, to add insult to the suffering already afflicted on the Naga people, in February 1988 India decided to go ahead with the election to fill the seats of the Assembly of Nagaland State which the Nagas strongly opposed while the peace negotiation was in progress. Nearly all the NGOs[190] and political parties, except the ruling Congress party led by Chief Minister, S.C. Jamir opposed the election. The Naga Hoho, in its summit held in Kohima in 18 December, 1997 resolved not to have assembly elections in Nagaland state.[191] "The Nagas want solutions not elections" was the slogan splashed all across Nagaland. Meanwhile, NSCN threatened to walk away from the peace process

[187] The Naga inhabited areas include besides the present Nagaland state, parts of Manipur, Assam, and Arunachal Pradesh states.

[188] Swaraj Kausal, "An Interview with Swaraj Kausal," in *North East Sun* (October 15-31, 1998); cf. Sanjoy Hazarika, 'Bordering on Peace: Naga Talks: Just a few Words More," available from http://www.nscnonline.org/nscn/index-2.html

[189] Rajinder Sachar. "Peace Process in Nagaland," in Mainstream. 2 August, 2000.

[190] The NGOs include, the all powerful Naga Hoho (the apex body of the non political organizations of the Nagas), Naga Student Federation (NSF), Naga Peoples' Movements for Human Rights (NPMHR), the Nagaland Baptist Churches Council (NBCC) and others while the political parties include, Nagaland People's Convention (NPC), National Democratic Movement (NDM) and the Bharatija Janata Party, Nagaland Unit (BJP).

[191] *North East Sun* (January 15-31), 1998.

unless India agreed to call off the election.[192] At one point in the talk Muivah the General Secretary of NSCN-IM felt impelled to declare, "We are not toys to be played around with."[193]

Muivah's arrest and subsequent imprisonment in Bangkok in January 2000 for traveling on illegal documents was a huge setback to the peace process.[194] The NSCN refused to nominate a replacement and pressed for Muivah's immediate release.[195] Meanwhile, India entered into ceasefire with the rival NSCN-K on 10 April, 2000. This move was seen by many as an attempt to divide the Nagas and to discredit the NSCN-IM. A number of people and organizations from around the world appealed to both the Thai and Indian governments for the release of Muivah. Muivah was eventually released in 2001 and the two sides agreed to continue with the peace negotiations.

A major breakthrough in the peace negotiations occurred in 14 June, 2001 when the BJP-led government of India officially announced that the ceasefire was "without territorial limits."[196] However, this was retracted in 9 July, 2001 when the neighboring states, particularly Manipur opposed this expansion of the ceasefire.[197] This act of retraction did not set well with the NSCN-IM and the Naga people who felt betrayed. The NSCN-IM was seriously contemplating pulling out of the peace negotiations. The comments of Ajoy Bose, a BBC News reporter articulated the sentiment of the Naga people.

> While the Manipuris are in no mood to be reasonable, the Nagas are far too upset with Delhi's betrayal to give any concessions. Interestingly, this is the second time within a year that the government has botched the ceasefire agreement with insurgent groups.[198]

---

[192] Muivah warned in a communication addressed to the Prime Minister of India, I. K. Gujral, that "the NSCN will not seek solutions against the will of the Naga people because it is a total negation of all democratic principles... if elections in the Naga areas are not stopped/deferred there will be no solution." Free Press (Imphal), 2 February, 1998.

[193] Muivah, "We are not Toys to be Played Around." *Hindustan Times* (New Delhi), 7 September 1997.

[194] Muivah was arrested twice in January 2000. The first arrest was made on January 19 but was released on bail. The second arrest occurred on January 30 on his way to Netherlands for talks with India. During this time GOI tried its Best to malign Muivah and NSCN by leveling charges against, even accusing the organization of having nexus with Pakistan's intelligence wing, Inter Services Intelligence (ISI). "Muivah has links with ISI: Center," The Assam Tribune (Guwahati), 5 February, 2000.

[195] "NSCN won't Replace Muivah for Talks," The Statesman (New Delhi), 22 March, 2000.

[196] United Naga Council and NPMHR, "Naga Peace Process and the Response of the Neighboring Communities," in Naga Peoples Movement for Human Rights, *The Nagas*, 98-99.

[197] The Manipuris resorted to mass protest and rallies which resulted in mob violence, vandalizing of government properties, and the killing of at least 10 protestors by the armies. The Manipuris were able to successfully upstage the peace process. Ibid., 108.

[198] "India's Naga Truce Confusion," BBC (London), 12 July, 2001.

In a positive gesture in 11 July, 2002, India agreed to officially recognize "the unique history of the Naga people"[199] which was seen even by the critics as a positive development in the peace process. In the same year the collective leadership of the NSCN-IM, Isak and Muivah who work from Bangkok, were able to visit India on the invitation of Atal Behari Vajpayee, the Prime Minister, and to engage in extensive consultations with both the ruling government and the leaders of the opposition parties. By this time, the two sides were beginning to address the substantive issues. While political sovereignty continues to be the bargaining goal of the NSCN-IM, unification of the entire area inhabited by Nagas has taken center stage in the negotiations.[200]

Despite the glitches that continue to afflict the ongoing peace negotiations, there seems to have developed better understanding and trust between the two sides. For the second time the collective leadership was able to visit India on the invitation of the Prime Minister, Dr. Manmohan Singh, in early December, 2004. Unlike the first visit, this time the leaders were able to visit Nagaland and enjoy Christmas and New Year with their own people. The collective leadership made maximum use of their time in Nagaland consulting and collecting views of the Naga people from all walks of life and seeing for themselves how the people were faring.[201] They have time and again made it clear that any solutions negotiated with India will not be at the expense of the Naga peoples' aspirations and desires. It must be an honorable solution for the Nagas.

The Naga peoples' expectations soared with the return of the collective leadership to their homeland[202] but it was to be short-lived since India again

---

[199] "Recognition of the Naga Unique history and situation of by the GOI through the Joint Communiqué, Amsterdam 11 July 2002," in Naga Hoho, White Paper on Naga Integration (Senapati: Naga Hoho, 2002), 43.

[200] At times the NSCN favor the multi-issue based negotiations over preconditioned one-issue based approach. As recently as February 2006, the Naga people reiterate their yearnings for unification of all Naga inhabited areas. "The responsibility of achieving our desire to live together lies not only with our leaders, but also each and everyone of us" says Mani Charenamei in Ukhrul during LUI-NGAI-NI, seed sawing festival, February 15-16, 2006. "Nagas see goal closer," available from http://www.telegraphinida.com/archives/archive.html; Nagaland Chief minister, Rio said, "Unification of the Naga inhabited areas is the route to the solution," available from http://www.kuknalim.com/modules.php/name=News&file=article&sid=2586

[201] Nagas representing both political and civil societies from all Naga inhabited areas were able to meet and air their views to the leaders during this visit. "The meetings are going on very well.... The people are very hopeful. Today (December 22) also the ladies met us to share their views.... We are here to take the people's opinion...", Muivah told to ANI at the NSCN-IM Headquarters, available from www.nagarealm.com, 23 December, 2004.

[202] Here are some of the sample comments from the people: "We are hopeful that as the collective leaders are here... this time Christmas will be more better. We also want that peace should be brought." "It's good that they (NSCN-IM collective leadership) are here during Christmas time. They would definitely come up with some solutions for us," available from www.nagarealm.com, 19 December, 2004.

refused to engage in substantive issues in the talks. Muivah left for Bangkok soon miffed by the non-committal attitude of India. The testiest moment was witnessed when NSCN-IM literally kept Indian government on tender hook on whether to extend the ceasefire which was supposed to expire at the end of January 2006. The ceasefire was finally extended but for only six months and on the condition that the peace talks must be pursued rigorously.

The Roles of Civil Society in Resistance Movement and Peace Process

The civil society has always been an integral part of the resistance movement, and for years they have played significant roles in the struggle of the Naga people. Very often however their role is overlooked and the credit due them is not acknowledged. But if not for the resilience, persistence, and support of the civil societies, the Nagas' struggle could not have existed, let alone come this far. From the beginning, they have played mediating roles either between different factional groups or facilitating the peace process between GOI and the Naga national movement groups. One important example of this work is the ceasefire between the GOI and the NNC in the 1960s which was the result of the initiative of the Nagaland Baptist Churches Council. The Naga Mothers' Association (NMA) which came to its existence in the '60s has been championing for peace among the Nagas and they are today a powerful voice in the peace process.

The roles of the Naga social organizations have been much more visible and significant since the late 1970s when the students' organizations, women's associations, tribal hohos[203] and human rights movements became better organized. The rejuvenated Naga Students' Federation (NSF),[204] which is the apex body of the Naga students, became much more involved and vocal in the ongoing Naga struggle. Through the initiative of a few Naga students, the Naga People's Movement for Human Rights (NPMHR) came to its existence in the late 1970s in response to the atrocities and numerous human rights violations committed against the Naga people by the Indian armed forces. The Naga civil society was further strengthened when for the first time in the mid 1990s the various tribal hohos came together and formed the Naga Hoho which became the apex body of the Naga socio-political organization. The formation of the Naga Hoho was a significant development in the history of the Naga people, a sure testament to the desire of the Nagas for unity. In Manipur, the United Naga Council (UNC) which is the apex body of the various Naga hohos spearheads in supporting the peace process between the GOI and the Nagas as well as the demand for Alternative Arrangements for the Nagas in Manipur.

---

[203] Hoho is a Naga term for association/organization.

[204] The NSF was first formed in the late 1940s but after just a few years the Federation became defunct due to differences among the students. In 1960s few Naga students tried to revive the Federation but did not succeed. Only in 1970s that NSF was restructured.

The Naga civil society has been actively involved in a wide range of issues. They have worked tirelessly for the cause of peace and reconciliation, human rights, and have voiced their outrage at the Indian military forces for their crimes against people. They have spoken critically of the Indian government and its military forces for the former's non-committal approach to the Naga's problem, and most of all, for the latter's continuous reign of terror in Nagaland. They have even successfully challenged the Indian government and its military forces in the court of law to account for human rights violations and atrocities committed against fellow humans in Nagaland.

For the first time in the history of the Naga resistance movement, the civil society has taken the initiative to carry the Naga cause to her neighbors and larger Indian populations. In January 2000, representatives from various social organizations, with the initiative of the NPMHR undertook a "Journey of Conscience" to Delhi with the view to generate dialogue and discussion with Indian civil groups concerning the ongoing peace process between GOI and NSCN-IM. The NPMHR's press release of 31 January, 2000, reads as follows.

> Mass-based Naga Civil Society organizations (including Naga Hoho, the traditional apex body of the Nagas), intellectuals and concerned citizens have undertaken a "Journey of Conscience" to Delhi to express their goodwill for a 'people-to people dialogue' with the initiative coming from the Naga Peoples Movement for Human Rights (NPMHR). This journey is being undertaken to different parts of the sub-continent to foster political and cultural understanding through interaction and mutual respect. It is a process whereby we recognize the distinction between the government and the civil society; and the need for intellectuals, human rights groups, and civil and democratic rights groups to come and contribute to the struggle towards larger values including democratic values.[205]

Many Indians were impressed to the extent that in March 2001a group representing various civil organizations and intellectuals reciprocated the good will demonstrated by the Nagas and toured Nagaland. The initiative has certainly generated better understanding and appreciation between Nagas and Indians. It is of particular significance that these Indians were able to escape their ignorance so that they now feel they have come to understand and appreciate better the struggles of the Nagas and even expressed their solidarity with them.

The Naga civil organizations have also initiated dialogues with the civil organizations of the neighboring states of Assam and Manipur to hammer out the long-standing issues and problems that exist between them based on mutual trust and understanding.

---

[205] Press Release (New Delhi), 31 January, 2000.

Naga civil society has also expanded its initiative beyond India by visiting neighboring countries with the view to promote the Naga cause and to spread the larger message of peace through cultural exchange programs. In 2002, the NPMHR and the NSF led a Naga cultural troupe to Thailand under the theme "Nagas Call for Peace: Creating a Vision of Hope for Our Nation and the World."[206] In addition to visiting neighboring countries, Naga representatives have made a number of appearances at the Indigenous Peoples' Convention and Human Rights Forum of the United Nations in order to carry the Naga cause to the world community.

While this international effort has been exciting the most important role of the Naga civil society is its tireless effort to bring the Nagas together as one people through dialogue and reconciliation. In recent years, the initiatives taken by the Forum for Naga Reconciliation (FNR) under the leadership of Rev. Dr. Wati Aier and many other committed church leaders have made a substantial contribution in its efforts to bring together the various Naga political groups in particular and peace and unity in Naga society in general. The FNR under the banner "Naga Reconciliation: A Journey of Common Hope" has been proactively pursuing for peace and unity since its formation in 2008. Some of the major breakthroughs in the peace process include signing of the Covenant for Reconciliation by the various Naga political groups as well as leading the Naga leaders and their respective groups to apologize and forgive each other in the spirit of reconciliation.

In 2013, Against Corruption and Unabated Taxation (ACAUT) came into being with the objective to fight against corruption and unabated taxation in Naga society. Its slogan "One Government One Tax" became the rallying point for the people's movement against corruption and illegal taxation. Whereas, the Naga political groups have been highly critical of the ACAUT and its activities, to the extent of accusing the movement to be anti Naga national movement.

Mediating between and among the various Naga political groups and serving as basically unbiased peace brokers is seldom easy or pleasant. A number of times, they have been accused of favoring one group over another and some critics have gone so far as to accuse them of working for a particular group. They are made scapegoat when things do not go well as when reconciliation is consistently elusive. However, the Naga civil society remains undeterred and is determined to continue with its work until there is no more need.

Obstacles to the Solution

The Naga struggle has lasted 58 years and counting, and has claimed over a hundred thousand Naga lives in addition to the physical and psychological suffering inflicted on the people and still resolution is no more than a dream. There is no Naga family which has not been affected and likewise, there is no family which

[206] "Nagas Call for Peace: Creating a Vision of Hope for Our Nation and the World," available from http://www.nscnonline.org/nscn/index-2.html

does not long for a solution to what at times seems an interminable problem. The questions before us then are these: What is ailing the Nagas? What are the obstacles to solutions? Why is it that the Nagas are still without the solutions? Are the Nagas doing something wrong? Is there truly any chance for total success?

There are no easy answers to these questions and there is no single reason that can adequately explain the difficulties. There are as we shall see many relevant factors both from within Naga population and outside that we must identify and examine.[207] In some cases, certain factors may actually be the product of a clandestine nexus formed between the external and internal players. One possible example is that NSCN-IM has often accused the Indian government, especially the intelligence gathering section known as the Research Agency Wing (RAW), of clandestinely assisting NSCN-IM's rivals providing them arms, ammunitions, and even protection when necessary.

External Factors

India and Myanmar are the foremost external factors in that they have forcibly governed Nagaland for nearly seventy years and that in itself is the source of the entire problem; consequently, the resistance movement must not only engage with two powerful nations, they also must be bale to fight on two distinct fronts so to speak. The preceding historical discussions have amply shown just that – exposing the sins of Indo-Burmese aggression against the 4 million Nagas and their continued policies to keep the Nagas under subjugation.

The other significant external factors also involve artificial boundaries and non-Naga political administrations which further divide the Naga people. In 2002 the Naga Hoho issued a, *White Paper on Naga Integration* which categorically stated that:

> Integration of all Naga inhabited areas (compact and contiguous) including the present Nagaland state by the removal of all imposed boundaries, imposed government and imposed system is the desired meaning of Naga integration.[208]

The Nagas want to live together as one people and determine their own future as a nation. Regrettably, these neighboring states[209] have strongly objected to this move and they have worked tirelessly for the status quo, i.e. to not disturb the existing state boundaries as these were drawn up by the British and Indian governments. They have been busy mobilizing their own people and demanding

[207] Cf. R. Vashum, *Indo-Naga Conflict: Problem and Resolution* (New Delhi: Indian Social Institute, 2001), 92-107.

[208] *White Paper on Naga Integration*, viii.

[209] The neighboring states include Arunachal Pradesh, Assam, and Manipur. For the reaction of these states to Naga Peace process see, "Naga Peace process and the Response of the Neighboring Communities," in *The Nagas: Truth and Hope for the Living*, 96-116.

India "protect the territorial integrity of the states." Regrettably, the Government of India has agreed to the demands of these states as demonstrated by their retraction of "without territorial limits" in the ceasefire agreement in 2001.

The issue of territorial integrity has unfortunately become particularly a difficult issue in the ongoing peace negotiations between India and Nagaland. NSCN-IM has accused India of elevating the interests of other people above the interests of the Nagas in arguing against the Naga case.[210] It has questioned the sincerity of the Indian Government and accused of lacking political will to resolve the long standing Indo-Naga problem.

The demands for the integration of the contiguous Naga areas have been further misconstrued as demands for "greater Nagaland." For the Nagas there is neither greater nor smaller Nagaland, there is only Nagaland. The Nagas rightly argue that they are not demanding anything that does not belong to them and that they will not touch an inch of land or territory that belongs to someone else. What they want is to right the wrongs done to them by the British and Indian governments and to reclaim their homeland.

Internal Factors

It is no less important to this discussion that we identify and examine the mistakes of the Nagas themselves. The Nagas have come a long way in their search for lasting solutions to these decades-old problems. What impediments prevented the Nagas from finding a lasting solution? What might have gone wrong with the Naga people during this process? Should the Nagas be held, at least, in part, accountable for their situation? In other words, shouldn't the blame be placed squarely at the feet of the Nagas themselves?

The divisions and disunity among Nagas continues to pose most harmful impediment quest for lasting solutions. The Naga nation is comprised of over 40 tribes and sub-tribes. Each tribe speaks its own dialect and it is not intelligible to others in most cases.[211] This diversity of dialects has severely handicapped all unification efforts to resist the colonial powers and has in fact exacerbated the already problematic adherence to narrow tribal interests. This is visible in every aspect of Naga society, the political, the social and the religious. The Naga political groups are equally if not more beset by division and disunity on the basis of the narrow tribal interests.

Such divisions have further aggravated the situation among the Nagas themselves. For over twenty years, the factional rivalries and clashes have taken center stage in the history of the Naga peoples' struggle and still the pleas for

[210] This has prompted T. Muivah to come with a scathing remark against Indian Government, "If you wish to talk with the Nagas then talk about the issues that concern the Nagas and not the interests of the other people. Otherwise, go and talk to them."

[211] Some neighboring tribes like the Angamis and Chakhesangs can understand and even speak each others' dialects.

reconciliation and unity have gone unheeded. Clearly, while the NSCN-IM remains the most powerful of all the groups and commands the greatest support there has been no lessening of the casualties of factional rivalries. There have even been occasion when factional rivalries have escalated and triggered ethnic violence directed at a particular tribe(s).[212]

Now becomes a question which should come first, a satisfactory agreement with India or the ideological and political unification of the Naga people. While one group, led by NSCN -IM favors a solution with India first, others have argued for unity of all the Nagas as a precondition for working on the solution. The view maintained by IM is that while they are committed to the unification of all factions and Nagas and will continue to work towards that end, it should not be allowed to stall the peace process in which they have already invested so much. Unity for the sake of unity is not desirable unless it is accompanied by accountability; so it must be principled and grounded historically. Given these convictions, IM has chosen solution as the priority and accordingly has engaged in peace negotiations with India when the opportunity was presented.

The civil organizations such as the Naga Hoho, NPMHR, NSF, ANSAM, Naga Mothers Association (NMA) and the Church continue to appeal for unity and act as neutral mediating parties and they have also put their weight behind the NSCN-IM led peace process with India. Hence, although not all the Nagas are united in their support for IM, at least most Nagas want to give the benefit of the doubt to IM in this ongoing peace process. The IM's claim that they have the Naga people's mandate may not be too far fetched. IM continues to advance its argument that since solution is the goal and when it is within reach and the time seems to be right it must be sought first and foremost.

One could sympathize with IM's position whether one supports them or not; there is some truth to their views. IM is critical of unprincipled unity because many people have abused "unity" by manipulating it for political and vested purposes. The irony is that the Government of India has raised the hype of the appeal for unity as a precondition for solutions, while at the same time working to engineer divisions among the Naga people. There can be no integrity in their call for Naga unity when at the same time they work to destabilize that very unity. It is nothing more than a political ploy.

In general, the Naga people support the ongoing NSCN-IM led peace negotiation with India just as they also push for the unity of all the Naga people. They all recognize that there must be at least the essence of unity among all sections of Naga people if a lasting and satisfactory solution to the decades-old Naga struggle is to be reached.

Peace Accord 2015: On August 3, 2015 a Peace Accord was signed between the Government of India and the National Socialist Council of Nagalim (NSCN

[212] In many such factional violence the Tangkhul people have often been the target and many lives have been lost and much properties destroyed in the process.

–IM) after a long protracted negotiations since they entered into peace negotiation in 1997. The Accord was actually a framework agreement agreed upon by the two entities for resolving the long standing Naga national issue. The accord envisaged the need for time bound solution. The peace accord was signed by Th. Muivah, the General Secretary of the NSCN-IM and Mr. R.N. Ravi the Indian Interlocutaor, in the presence of Mr. Narendra Modi, the Prime Minister and hosts of other dignitaries from both sides.

The framework agreement was based on the recognition of the unique history of the Nagas, shared sovereignty of the two entities, and the uniqueness of the Naga situation.

The agreement was signed after over 80 rounds of talks between the GOI and the IM spanning 18 years since they entered into peace negotiation in 1997.

Meanwhile the demise of Isak Chishi Swu, the Yaruiwo of the IM in June 28, 2016 has cast a spell of uncertainty on the overall situation. However, both the GOI and the IM continue to reassure the people that the death of Swu will not in any way affect the ongoing peace negotiation.

Socio-Economic Situation of the Nagas: An Overview

Naga social structure is predicated on a closely-knit community and emphasizes the well-being of the community over the individual, such that the individual's loyalty belongs to the community. Economically, they followed subsistence economy based on reciprocity and sharing unlike the western economic system that focuses on surplus and profit. Not too long ago, they were a self-sufficient people and agriculture was and is still their main occupation. Most people continue to live in the villages although many have moved to towns and cities; many more because of their jobs, others for other reasons including the lure of 'modern' urban life. The per capita income of Nagaland at current prices in 1998-99 stood at Rs. 12,08.[213]

Traditional social and economic systems have come under severe pressure from the influences of the modern economic system and globalization.

The forces of modernization and globalization swept over the region at the time when the people were least prepared. They have been forced to make the transition from the traditional to modern and it has severely disrupted both the social fabric and rhythm of Naga society. The market-driven economy of globalization with its need for "efficiency, productivity, individual ability to exploit and extract, profit margins, and the ability to stockpile accumulated wealth as financial capital"[214] has overwhelmed the traditional subsistence economy practices. We live today in a world where the ideals of capitalism –

[213] Directorate of Economics & Statistics, Government of Nagaland 2001, 314. The exchange rate stands as $1 = Rs. 43 (approximately).

[214] Luingam Luithui, "Brief Background on Nagalim (India and Burma)," in http://www.nscnonline.org/webpage/Articles/brief_background_on_nagalim.htm

or in the words of Fredric Jameson, "the cultural logic of capitalism" – and its triumph over communism/socialism are being cited as justifying the validity of capitalism.[215] The "free" market economy of globalization spearheaded by powerful multinational corporations, World Bank and International Monetary Fund (IMF) and supported by legal apparatuses such as the World Trade Organizations, GATT and other trade agreements has become the dominant economy across the world. The globalizing effects of capitalism especially on the Third World nations is undeniably alarming and Nagaland is no exception; in fact, the impact could be described as having the effects of an earthquake which caused multiple fractures in Naga society and no one knows whether the people will ever recover. Today the majority of Naga people are reeling in the grip of poverty condition with most of the wealth and resources concentrated in the hands of a very small number of persons who, not surprisingly also control the political and state machinery. These are the national elites of Naga society. Franzt Fanon, writing in the context of newly liberated Algerian state, described the few rich elites as the "national bourgeoisie" of Algerian society.[216] According to Fanon, the national bourgeoisie was comprised primarily of influential politicians, doctors, lawyers, traders, and commercial travelers and he argued that this local bourgeoisie of the Third World not only controlled the national resources and wealth but they also represented the interests of bourgeoisie of the "developed" world through their connections with the former European colonizer states.[217]

In this context of free market capitalism we may simply describe the poor people in society as simply left out of the economic process. In the words of Ankie Hoogvelt, they are simply rendered unbankable in the traditional sense of the term.[218] According to Hoogvelt, the capitalist economy is now experiencing a process of shrinking or intensifying what he calls involution rather than continuing in a mode of unchecked expansion. Globalization:

> In its manifestations of international trade, production and finance, in fact amounts to an accelerated withdrawing, a shrinking of the global map, rather than an expanding phenomenon, and one which expels ever more people from the interactive circle of global capitalism.[219]

---

[215] Frederic Jameson, *Postmodernism or the Cultural Logic of Late Capitalism* (Duke: Duke University Press, 1991), xviiif.

[216] Franz Fanon, *The Wretched of the Earth*, Preface by Jean-Paul Sartre (New York: Grove Press, 1963), 152.

[217] Ibid., 152-153.

[218] Ankie Hoogvelt, *Globalization and Postcolonial World: The New Political Economy of Development* (Baltimore: John Hopkins University Press, 2001), 89.

[219] Ankie Hoogvelt, *Globalization and Postcolonial World: The New Political Economy of Development* (Baltimore: John Hopkins University Press, 2001), 71.

In a similar vein, Haider A. Khan argues that:

> Global poverty can be viewed as a state that is brought about by the operation of the same forces that create wealth. However, by denying the poor the opportunities to acquire skills to participate in the market (and the society at large) in any meaningful sense the autonomy of an individual is constrained severely.[220]

What we see today is the intensifying of international exchanges and investments among the richest countries which concentrates the flows of capital among these same rich countries. Ngũgĩ wa Thiong'o calls such consolidation of finance capital the reality of imperialism. "Imperialism is the rule of consolidated finance capital .... Imperialism is total: it has economic, political, military, cultural and psychological consequences for the people of the world today. It could even lead to holocaust."[221] Further, the elites of the Third World are participants as economic players along with the wealthiest nations' elites thereby leaving out the majority of the world population. According to the UNCTAD report of 1996, there were already three hundred banking entities from ten leading developing countries operating in OECD countries.[222]

Even though the Naga elites are not yet players in the world economy, they are certainly well connected to the wealthy of India. They have succumbed to the lures of accumulation and profits so they invest their wealth and resources in Indian financial institutions rather than in Nagaland which means the majority of the Naga people are excluded from realizing any improvement in their standard of living.

The Most Alienated, Exploited and Neglected Region

Nagaland and the neighboring Northeast Indian states constitute the most neglected and alienated region in India.[223] There is total neglect of the people on all fronts: economic, social, political and development projects. Northeast India is comprised of seven states, often known as seven-sister states which are home to

---

220 Haider A. Khan, *Technology, Development and Democracy: Limits of National Innovation Systems in the Age of Postmodernism* (Cheltenham: Edward Elgar, 1998).

221 Ngũgĩ wa Thiong'o, *Decolonizing the Mind: The Politics of Language in African Literature* (Oxford: James Currey Ltd., 1986), 2.

222 Quoted in Hoogvelt, *Globalization and the Postcolonial World,* 89.

223 For a detailed discussion on the problems and challenges faced by the people of Northeast India refer to: Sanjoy Hazarika, Strangers of the Mist: Tales of War and Peace from India's Northeast (New Delhi: Viking, 1994); Udayan Misra, *The Periphery Strikes Back: Challenges to the Nation State in Assam and Nagaland* (Shimla: Indian Institute for Advanced Study, 2000); B. Pakem, ed., *Nationality, Ethnicity, and Cultural Identity in North-East India* (New Delhi: Omsons Publications, 1990); Prafulla Royhowdhury, *The North East: Roots of Insurgency* (Calcutta: Firma KLM Pvt. Ltd., 1995); V. I. K. Sarin, *India's North-East in Flames* (Ghaziabad: Vikas Publishing House Pvt. Ltd., 1982).

many large indigenous/tribal communities. Geographically, in relation to India, the Northeast states are connected with the rest of the country by a narrow strip of land that is often called the "chicken neck" - because it is long, narrow, and void of meat. However, this narrow strip of land has come to symbolize much more than being a meatless part of a chicken's anatomy; the real significance of this "neck" is that it symbolizes the conditions of profound isolation, neglect and exploitation the people of this region suffer which are the result of decades of underdevelopment and the extraction of resources by India. The lack of substantial development projects on one hand combined with the processes of globalization on the other have created a precarious and even fatal situation for the majority of these people.

The economic exploitation of the region's natural resources has deeply impacted the economic life of the people. The region is endowed with valuable natural resources and minerals such as oil, natural gas, coal, gold, silver, and titanium and others. According to an editorial in the well known daily *Nagaland Post*, "Nagaland has around 600 million metric tones of oil reserves in its basin mainly at Changpang and Naginimora areas…."[224] It goes on to cite the rich deposits of natural resources including a huge reserve of coal, high grade limestone, semi-precious stones, granite, marble, etc. But these natural resources are being tapped and removed to other parts of India where big factories and industries are located, so the people gain nothing.

The region has never been treated on a par with the rest of India; it is treated as second-class. In the context of the Indian electoral system in which majority representations rule, the Northeast states, with their small contingent of representatives in the parliaments, are often overlooked and sometimes ignored. In most cases, the problems and concerns of the region might not find a place on the national agenda. Very very few genuine efforts are made to address the problems of the region other than the usual token acknowledgements of sympathy.

Additionally, all the important developmental policies and decisions are made in India's capital, New Delhi and in most cases, the so-called "experts" and politicians in New Delhi actually know very little about the people in the Northeast. New Delhi adds to the alienation by regarding the people as the object of development rather than the subject of development. The total lack of transparency and accountability has alienated the people from the government.

Historically, with the introduction of India's new phase of development and monetary economy, corruption became rampant and a new economic class emerged in a supposedly classless Naga society. Sanyu makes this succinct observation:

---

[224] "Editorial" Nagaland Post (Dimapur), 1 February, 2006, In http://www.nagalandpost.com/editorialdesc.asp?sectionid=4547

> All these changes accentuated the formation of a nouveau rich class and an uneven social structure. The nature of political activities were mainly responsible for the emergence of the bourgeoisie and this provided them the initial capital to multiply further their resources through business, transport or construction works. All this led to social stratification based on material strength. The exploitation of the Naga by the fellow tribesman commenced speedily, for the first time Naga millionaires came to existence.[225]

Most scholars[226] argue that the Sixteen Point Agreement of 1960 and the subsequent creation of Nagaland state in 1963 paved the way for economic prosperity for the few and the culture of corruption in the Naga society. Subsequent to state formation, the Indian government with the view to lure away the Nagas from independent struggle, began to pour in funds for the development of the newly created state. The large infusion of money was of no help because there were no proper plans for development work, or how exactly the funds were to be used, nor was there even an agency to keep accounts on the money. As a result, the money found its way to the hands of a few politicians and bureaucrats who only exploited the situation for their personal benefit. The funds meant to improve the lives of the people thus ended up in the pockets of a corrupt few people. In the words of Kumar S. Singh:

> In order to create a subservient political elite the government accepted the responsibility to give financial incentive to the politicians euphemistically termed as grant in aid in the accord meant ostensibly to supplement the revenue of Nagaland. Yet a perusal of the text of the accord brings out the peculiarity of the aid. If the aid were actually meant for aiding development projects in Nagaland it should have been ear marked for specific heads of expenditure, instead the Government of India resorted to a lump-sum payment (cf. Clause II. I). History reveals us that the loophole left by making grant, without any identified head of expenditure was utilized to create a thoroughly corrupt political elite.[227]

---

[225] Visier Sanyu, "What Nagaland State did to the Nagas," 270.

[226] Visier Sanyu, "What Nagaland State did to the Nagas," Kumar S. Singh, "Naga Accords," 35.

[227] Kumar S. Singh, "Naga Accords," 35.

Today Nagaland state is known as one of the most corrupt states in India. The germs of corruption are wide spread and infest every nook and cranny of the state machinery, from top to bottom.[228] Ordinary Naga people are simply trampled on and rendered nearly helpless in every facet of their life. Sustainable development and social justice will remain elusive to the people until and unless the culture of corruption is eradicated. We need a development that is centered on the people and the people should be the subject of development, not be the object of development.

Finally, the Naga people are facing an acute ecological/environmental crisis as a result of deforestation by timber and log businesses in the region.[229] In the name of development large portions of forested lands are being destroyed so that once thickly forested Nagaland is now becoming more barren everyday; the beautiful and rare flora and fauna are disappearing. The eco-system is in a perilous state and there is great concern that unless steps are taken, it will soon be simply too late.

We need development that will seriously address the issue of deforestation and environmental well-being not merely for the sake of the people but for all creation. As I have noted in a previous paper:

> Any development projects that do not take the ecological/environmental concerns into serious consideration will always be deficient and lopsided. There is today a growing concern for recognizing our human relatedness with creation and the need for developing an ethics that is centered on creation. A globally responsible ethics will therefore include caring for all creation and working toward eco-justice.[230]

Situating Naga-Indigenous Christology

It is said that a living and empowering theology emerges only when it is produced in the context of the people's experiences and reality. In other words, a living theology is always contextual and situation-based as such that an analytical consideration of Naga people's socio-economic and political history is therefore a critical component in the construction of a Naga-Indigenous Christology as part of a relevant, empowering, and liberating Indigenous theology. So far I have demonstrated that Naga-Indigenous Christology does not occur in a vacuum but,

---

228 "Stop illegal Taxes; Wide Corruption Alleged", in *The Morung Express* (News Online, February 21, 2006), available from http://www.morungexpress.com/

229 Deforestation also results from slash and burn form of agriculture known popularly as jhum cultivation which is practiced by the villagers for their subsistence.

230 Ahao Vashum, "The Pertinence of Ethics in Development Debates", in *Naga Journal of Indigenous Affairs* 2, no. 1 (December-May 2003), 61; cf. K. Thanzauva, "A Theology of Development in the Context of Hill Tribes in North East India," in A. Wati Longchar and Larry E. Davis, ed., *Doing Theology with Tribal Resources: Contexts and Perspective*, Tribal Study Series no. 3 (Jorhat: Tribal Study Center, 1999), 43-59.

rather, it engages in a critical interaction with the socio-economic, political, and historical realities of the people. It takes into serious consideration the people's experiences of suffering, and their needs, desires and aspirations. It also interacts critically with people's cultural milieu as part of the process of liberating them from the oppressive and dehumanizing forces under which they live. A Naga-Indigenous Christology must emerge out of the socio-economic, political, and cultural realities of the Naga people if it is to be a living and empowering theology for the people.

Chapter 3

Christology
Christological Traditions and Approaches through the Centuries

Jesus Christ through the Centuries

In the preceding chapter, I have tried to situate Naga-Indigenous Christology in the socio-economic, political, and historical context of the Naga people. In this chapter I intent to situate Naga-Indigenous Christology in the existing bodies of Christological traditions and towards that end I present an overview of Christological understanding and traditions in different cultures in history. In other words, I will identify some of the ways in which Jesus has been interpreted and portrayed in different cultures and contexts. There is no single interpretation or image that could be said to represent the authentic or correct conception of Jesus; in fact, no one knows what he looked like or really anything of his "biography," and St. Augustine of Hippo attested to this fact in *The Trinity*.[231] In the history of Christianity several images of Jesus have been used.

> At the very beginning Jesus was represented symbolically or allegorically, two of the most popular representations in this connection being the fish and the lamb. The alpha and omega (the A and the Ω) were used as the Christ-monogram.[232]

---

[231] Quoted in Anton Wessels, *Images of Jesus: How Jesus is Perceived and Portrayed in Non-European Cultures*, trans. John Vriend (Grand Rapids: William B. Eerdmans Publishing Company, 1990), 3.

[232] Ibid.; Cf. John F. O' Grady, *Models of Jesus Revisited* (Mahwah: Paulist Press, 1994), 17.

According to Anton Wessel the earliest representation of Jesus in human form was as a youthful-looking "good shepherd" carrying a male sheep on his shoulders in the painting that is found in the catacombs of Rome and in the Church of Dura Europos which date to the third and fourth centuries.[233] The image was soon modified to depict a more mature Jesus with beard and long hair appropriate to the "Exalted Lord." At the end of Christian persecution and emperor Constantine's declaration that Christianity was the only religion of the empire, the image of Jesus was modified to "*Christus Victor*, crowned by the hand of God, the world-ruler, Pantokrator."[234] The emphasis is clearly on the world and the church became the imperial church.

A different image of Jesus was created in the Middle Ages; he was God in human form and a wrathful Judge of the living and the dead. The image of the long suffering Christ began to find favor with the people under the influence of St. Bernard of Clairvaux and St. Francis of Assisi, so the "Christ triumphant" became a "long-suffering Christ." Suffering and death dominated in the late Middle Ages. In the words of R. Koning:

> Thick tangles of clotted blood adhere to his wounds, while his arms and legs hang limp. The head, with eyes closed and mouth slightly open, the last breath just having escaped, falls over backward.... Mary in her grief blends in with this. Thus originated a statue of concentrated sorrow and deep gloom. The effect is one of ghastly realism which in its starkness has become a totally shattering cry.[235]

The images of Jesus portrayed through the centuries are indicative of how the church authorities want him to be seen. These Images and other art forms were the only way "the people" could know Jesus on their own since they were not allowed to read scripture. They are therefore not ends in themselves but means to an end; they point to the ultimate goal, in this case to Jesus Christ. Images are human constructs and therefore have certain limitations. John O' Grady rightly cautions:

> When examining the many images of Jesus they suggest attitudes, feelings, courses of action and devotion. They help to unite people in a common bond of affection and commitment. But always, as images, they are incomplete and should not be seen as perfect in themselves. The images express the reality toward which they lead but for which they cannot substitute.[236]

---

233 Wessels, *Images of Jesus*, 3-5.

234 Ibid., 7.

235 Quoted in Wessels, *Images of Jesus*, 9.

236 John O' Grady, *Models of Jesus,* 17.

Additionally, even the best of the image will always have limited value since "believers always faces mystery, inexhaustible intelligibility." But, to the extent that images can sometimes lead a person to profound experience of faith in Jesus Christ, the importance of the images should not be rashly minimized.

Jaroslav Pelikan, in *Jesus through the Centuries,*[237] offers an extensive study of the place of Jesus in cultures historically. Following the work of Albert Schweitzer Pelikan argues that the way people perceive and interpret Jesus varies according to place and time. Jesus is depicted in "each successive epoch" in accordance with the character of its history and context.[238] From the first century depiction of Jesus as a Rabbi to the nineteenth and twentieth century's image of Jesus as liberator, Pelikan enumerates the impact of Jesus on cultural, political, social and economic history through the centuries. Some of the images discussed include the Light of the Gentiles, the King of Kings, the Cosmic Christ, the Son of Man, Christ Crucified, the Monk who Rules the World, the Universal Man, the Prince of Peace, the Teacher of Common Sense and the Man Who Belongs to the World.

Christ and Culture

One of the important aspects of this study is to examine the relations between Christ and culture in history. A classic work in this area is that of H. Richard Niebuhr's *Christ and Culture.*[239] Niebuhr identified five different approaches in regards to how people conceived the relation between Christ and culture in history, some of these are: 1) Christ against culture, 2) Christ of culture, 3) Christ above culture, 4) Christ and culture in paradox, and 5) Christ the transformer of culture. It was Niebuhr's position that the first two should be characterized as negative while the last three positions imply a more positive attitude towards culture.

In "Christ against culture," the two are seen to be opposing forces where no common denominator between the two can be found. Christ is presented as having totally rejected all human culture and culture is seen as the domain of darkness and evil. The great North African theologian Tertullian fits this model according to Niebuhr. The second approach, "Christ of culture," has Christ portrayed as the fulfiller of human culture. Christ fulfills all human yearnings and the highest expectations of a given culture. These two approaches could be very well identified with the western missionaries who worked with and among people in non-Western-world. Missionaries to the Nagas were known for their hostile attitude toward traditional culture.

---

[237] Jaroslav Pelikan, *Jesus through the Centuries: His Place in the History of Culture* (New Haven: Yale University Press, 1999).

[238] Ibid., 2.

[239] H. Richard Niebuhr, *Christ and Culture* (New York: Harpers & Brothers Publishers, 1956).

"Niebuhr's preference obviously lies in the last three positions because, while on the one hand they bring culture under judgment, they nevertheless find a way to confirm it." [240] Advocates of "Christ above culture" recognize some goodness in human culture but it is only through Christ that the fullness of humanity can be realized. Niebuhr cites Thomas Aquinas as representative of this position for his method of synthesis, in which he attempted to find the appropriate meeting ground between Christ and culture. Aquinas taught that humans have the potential to attain happiness, but he maintained that "what a man can gain in his culture . . . is only an imperfect happiness."[241] Ultimate happiness could only be found in Jesus Christ. Niebuhr has criticized of this approach because there was no room for critical interaction between Christ and culture. The adherents of this view are generally conservatives.

The fourth view, "Christ and culture in paradoxical relation," maintains belief in human sinfulness on one hand and the reality of God's forgiveness and atonement on the other. The relation between Christ and culture is paradoxical in nature yet they maintain a certain unity. "In this the duality and inescapable authority of both Christ and culture are recognized, but the opposition between them is also accepted."[242] Niebuhr identifies Martin Luther as representative of this position in light of Luther's two Kingdoms theory in which he contends that the Kingdom of God and the Kingdom of the world are two distinct worlds. "God's kingdom is a kingdom of grace and mercy . . . but the kingdom of the world is a kingdom of wrath and severity."[243] However, Luther does recognize there are close relations between the life in Christ and the life in culture; Niebuhr describes it, "The Christian must affirm both in a single act of obedience to the one God of mercy and wrath, not as a divided soul with a double allegiance and duty."[244]

The fifth and final perspective is "Christ the transformer of culture" which is also known as the "conversionist solution" to the enduring problem of Christ and culture. "Christ is seen as the converter of man in his culture and society, not apart from these, for there is no nature without culture and no turning of men from self and idols to God save in society."[245] Niebuhr chose Augustine to represent this conversionist approach. Augustine was convinced of the total depravity of humans as a result of the fall, in other words, humans are by nature sinful and therefore incapable of transforming themselves. It is only in Christ that

---

[240] Wessels, *Images of Jesus*, 161.

[241] Niebuhr, *Christ and Culture*, 132.

[242] Ibid., 42.

[243] Quoted in Niebuhr, *Christ and Culture*, 171.

[244] Ibid., 172.

[245] Ibid., 43.

humans can experience a life of transformation and regeneration,[246] which means that Christ is the transformer of culture.

Niebuhr has offered specific ideas which facilitate a clearer understanding of the relationship between Christ and culture. Many theologians have engaged this relationship by relying on one or more of the perspectives enumerated by Niebuhr; however, they acknowledge that they did not go far enough to address the important question of the interplay between Christ and culture. In the words of Anton Wessels:

> However illuminating and useful Niebuhr's scheme may be, it still contains a tendency to assume that the identity of Christ is already known. The question which can be put to those who favor the fifth position is this: Who transform whom? Is it not necessary to say that one must speak of interplay between Christ and the cultures? Not only does Christ change and transform (the other) cultures, but it is also true that other cultures and religions bring out features in the face of Christ which had not been revealed before.... It is not only Christ who transforms the *nganga* (medicine man), but it is also the *nganga* who transforms Christ.[247]

Christological Trajectories

Colin Greene chose a different epistemological framework in which to identify three broad types of Christology: cosmological, political, and anthropological.[248] I shall discuss each one briefly below.

Cosmological Christology

Cosmological Christology refers to the Logos and wisdom traditions of the early church fathers, especially those of the third and fourth centuries, when they perceived Jesus Christ as the eternal Logos who also preexisted, and believed, "There was never a time when God was without the Logos."[249] Logos is often identified as the "Word of God;" however, it can be understood as more than that. Pelikan observes that Logos is also the "Mind" of the cosmos. He Writes:

> But 'Logos of God' when applied to Jesus Christ meant far more than 'Word of God,' more even than divine revelation . . . . Employing the

[246] Ibid., 208-209.

[247] Wessels. *Images of Jesus,* 163-164.

[248] Colin J. D. Greene, *Christology in Cultural Perspective: Marking Out the Horizons* (Grand Rapids: William B. Eerdmans Publishing Company, 2003).

[249] The prologue to John's Gospel tells of the pre-existent, creative and revelatory Logos. Similarly, the writer of I Corinth describes the cosmic Christ and his role as mediator in Creation (I Cor. 8: 6). Also, the writer of Christological hymn of Colossians 1:15-20 expresses of the cosmic dimensions of Christology (cf. Heb. 1:1-3).

> specific name Logos implied in addition to this that what had come in Jesus Christ was also the *Reason and the Mind of the Cosmos* [emphasis original].[250]

It was the Logos which acted as the cosmological link, the link between "the transcendent world of the eternal and the finite world of humanity" and Creation giving "shape, reason, structure and purpose to the universe."[251] The cosmic Christ was later identified with the personified Wisdom of the Old Testament who was also there with God before all things.[252] Joseph Sittler was one of the firsts to recognize the significance of the cosmic Christology in modern time. In "Called to Unity" a speech given at the World Council of Churches at New Delhi in 1961, Sittler following the writer of Colossians affirmed that:

> He [Christ] is not only the matrix and *prius* of all things; he is the intention, the fullness, and the integrity of all things; for all things were created through him and for him. Nor are all things a tumbled multitude of facts in an unrelated mass, for in him all things hold together.[253]

One of the effects of Logos Christology was the development of the Trinitarian conception of God - God the Father, the Son and the Holy Spirit, three persons in one Godhead, in which Jesus is the second person. The church fathers engaged in a series of theological debates to determine the nature of Jesus' personhood and, in the process, several theological positions emerged. Ultimately, there were two views: the Eastern position represented by the school of Antioch, upheld the full humanity of Jesus, and the Western position represented by the school of Alexandria, which affirmed the full divinity of Jesus. This debate on the nature of Jesus - was Jesus divine or human or both - was not resolved until the Council of Chalcedon, 451 CE[254] when representatives from the East and West (Rome) came up with a definition of Chalcedon in which the full humanity and divinity of Jesus was affirmed.

---

[250] Pelikan, *Through the Centuries,* 62.

[251] Greene, *Cultural Perspective,* 31.

[252] Prov. 8. This understanding led Jürgen Moltmann to remark that, "Logos Christology is originally Wisdom Christology, and is as such cosmic Christology." *The Way of Jesus Christ: Chrsitology in Messianic Dimensions,* trans. Margret Kohl (Minneapolis: Fortress Press, 1993), 282.

[253] Joseph Sittler, *Evocations of Grace: Writings on Ecology, Theology, and Ethics,* with a foreword by Martin E. Marty, ed. Steven Bouma-Prediger and Peter Bakken (Grand Rapids: William B. Eerdmans Publishing Company, 2000), 39.

[254] The issue was first taken up in the Council of Ephesus (431CE) which remained inconclusive. Emperor Marcian then convened the council of Chalcedon which brought together representatives from the East and the West which resulted in the formulation of the Chalcedonean orthodoxy.

> Following, therefore, the holy fathers, we confess one and the same Son, who is our Lord Jesus Christ, and we all agree in teaching that this very same Son is complete in his deity and complete – the very same – in his humanity, truly God and truly a human being, this very same one being composed of a rational soul and a body, coessential with the Father as to his deity and coessential with us – the very same one – as to his humanity, being like us in every respect apart from sin.[255]

The council affirmed two natures in one person. This Chalcedonian orthodoxy was further reaffirmed in the face of the challenges from the Nestorians and the Monophysites in the sixth and seventh centuries. However, "The search for Christological and soteriological consistency led to a level of theological abstraction that was far removed from the suffering servant of God described in the Gospels."[256]

Political Christology

A political Christology is derived from the examination of the political elements and contexts which contributed to the formulation of certain Christologies through the centuries and include the implications of titles accorded to Jesus in Christological confessions, such as Lord of Lords and King of Kings, which in certain contexts, would also carry political connotations.

Greene has also examined the relationships between state and Christianity and specifically the role of emperors in shaping political Christology in the history of the church. The importance of focusing on the political should require no explanation because from the advent of Jesus and his teachings Christianity has always been political since it involves authority and power, divine and human. For example, "Christian allegiance to Jesus as *kyrios* inevitably relativized the absolute authority of the Roman emperor and resulted in a recurring cycle of indiscriminate persecution and social ostracism."[257] Christians endured torture and persecution even to the extent of risking their lives on account of their loyalty to Jesus, the King of Kings. To the believers and their persecutors alike, to accord the title "King of Kings" to Jesus was an opposition to Caesar's claim to be the supreme King. The image of Jesus as the King of Kings was taken to mean that Jesus was about to establish an earthly kingdom – a political kingdom here on earth. This sentiment was reflected in Mark's Gospel when the people shouted during Jesus' triumphal entry into Jerusalem: ". . . . Blessed is the coming kingdom of our ancestor David! Hosanna in the highest heaven!"[258]

---

[255] The Chalcedon Definition. Quoted in Colin Greene, *Cultural Perspective,* 42.

[256] Ibid., 43.

[257] Ibid., 46.

[258] Mark 11: 9b-10.

However, as Pelikan and others have pointed out Christians were not totally opposed to their earthly rulers – the Caesars. They expressed their loyalty to kings and even prayed for them and their empire. What they were not prepared to accept was to treat the emperor as divine, to say, "Kyrios Kaisar" – Lord Caesar – and to worship him.[259] On the other hand, with Constantine's declaration of Christianity as state religion in 313 CE, there was a reversal of roles such that the emperor effectively absolutized the emperor's position by invoking divine authority. Constantine wrote to all churches in the provinces explaining, "Whatever is determined in the holy assemblies of the bishops is to be regarded as indicative of the divine will."[260] He further issued an edict against "heretics" banning them from gatherings and meetings and even to the extent of confiscating their church buildings. Greene describes the emergence of imperial Christology as follows:

> Not surprisingly, such a political use of Christology led to the emergence of imperial Christology. A transference took place where titles originally given to the emperor were attributed to Christ, who became *Christus Imperator*, ruler or Lord of the world. Correspondingly, the emperor was given titles that originally had a Christological meaning, such as servant of God, shepherd, and peace maker. The title Lord of Glory, which originally held an apocalyptic meaning was also politicized. With the continuation of the Holy Roman Empire, Christ was viewed as the *Rex Gloriae*, the triumphant Lord who continues to subdue the Kingdoms of this world by the power of the emperor.[261]

Anthropological Christology

Anthropological Christology refers to the modern or post-Enlightenment Christology that concentrates on the humanity of Jesus. Sometimes it is also known as Christology from below. According to Jürgen Moltmann, "Anthropological Christology is . . . used for the modern Christology, which is also called Christology from below.' The center of Christology is the human being Jesus of Nazareth, not the exalted or pre-existent Christ."[262]

According to Church history it was Nestorius, who popularized the idea of "the two persons, a divine and a human, existing in juxtaposition in the incarnate Christ."[263] While Cyril of Alexandria stressed on the unity of the person of Christ Nestorius denied any organic union between the man Jesus and the divine Christ;

---

[259] Tertullian, Apology 30-32. Quoted in Jaraslov Pelikan, *Through the Centuries,* 49.

[260] Eusebius, *Life of Constantine,* trans. and commentary by A. Cameron and S. G. Hall. (Oxford: Clarendon Press, 1999), 64-65.

[261] Colin Greene, *Cultural Perspective*, 48.

[262] Moltmann, *The Way of Jesus Christ,* 55.

[263] H. D. McDonald, "Nestorius," in Sinclair B. Ferguson and David F. Wright, ed., *New Dictionary of Theology* (Leicester: Inter-Varsity Press, 1988), 457.

that is, he maintained the separate presence of full humanity and full divinity in the incarnate Christ. Nestorius was condemned at the Council of Ephesus in 431 CE and upheld in Chalcedon. Interest in the humanity of Jesus was also found in the Byzantine theology which was connected to the emergence of Christ mysticism in the sixth century – a theology of negation or an apophatic theology of the East.[264] "In Christianity, Christ-mysticism is what emerged when the figure of Jesus of Nazareth became the object of mystical experience, mystical thought, and mystical language."[265] Religious experience played a vital role in this aspect of Christology; not the general experience involving feeling or sense of the divine presence (undifferentiated religious states or feelings), "but the way in which the believer actually encounters, is united with, or related to, the person of Christ."[266]

In accord with Pelikan, Greene notes that the development of this form of Christology owes a great deal to the influence of the writings of *Pseudo-Dionysius* in the sixth century.[267] Closely related to this mystical experience of Jesus was the ascetic and contemplative tradition developed in the monasteries in which the monks lived an exemplary life of simplicity, poverty and chastity in conformity to the life and teachings of Jesus Christ. Anthropological Christology also has roots in the New Testament, especially the ideas of Jesus is the new Adam and the prototype of a new humanity.[268]

Contemporary Christology

While the cosmic, political and anthropological approaches to Christology continue to have certain significance, there are today a number of more comprehensive and diversified criteria through which to understand contemporary Christologies. New dimensions and interpretations from various perspectives and contexts have clearly changed the ethos of present Christologies from that of the past. Christologies these days are not constructed according to nor restricted by Western traditional Christianity.[269] Since the beginning of twentieth century, there has been a dramatic shift geographically in the growth and development of Christianity. The majority of Christians are now concentrated in the non-Western world, the so-called Two Thirds World; that is generally, Latin America, Africa, the Pacific and parts of Asia. In his book *Whose Religion is Christianity?* Lamin Sanneh describes the decline of Christianity in the West, the ascension of Christianity in

---

[264] Greene, *Cultural Perspective,* 52.

[265] Pelikan, *Through the Centuries,* 123.

[266] Greene, *Cultural Perspective,* 54-55.

[267] Greene also mentions the influences of the allegorical interpretation of Song of Songs in medieval monasticism and the monastic tradition of Hesychat spirituality which was based on the contemplative tradition of prayer and silence. Ibid., 56-59.

[268] I Corinth. 15: 45f and Romans 5:21f.

[269] By West or Christian West, I am referring to Europe and North America.

the rest of the world and thereby makes the case that Christianity is truly a "World religion." By "world religion," Sanneh means the Christian faith taking root in the non-Western world and is distinct from "global Christianity" which is the "faithful replications of Christian form and patterns developed in Europe."[270]

This shift in the demographic landscape of Christianity means that the ways Christianity is viewed and expressed have also changed, as have the ways theology is constructed and practiced. Specifically, with the emergence of liberation theology in Latin America in the 1970s the gate to new, more relevant ideas was thrown open. Liberation theology sought to concern itself with a "critical reflection on praxis," and according to the "father" of liberation theology Gustavo Gutiérrez, the first priority of praxis is "real charity, action and commitment to the service of men [sic]. Theology is reflection, a critical attitude. Theology follows; it is the second step."[271] Similarly, Robert H. King has acknowledged these developments:

> The theologies of liberation have generated a strong response from women, blacks, Third World peoples, and others not previously a part of theological establishment. They have brought a sociological perspective to the study of theology heretofore unknown and in the process have challenged many traditional assumptions, such as the appropriateness of patriarchal and monarchical imagery for God.[272]

Contemporary theology and Christology will thus encompass theologies and Christologies of the West and the Two-Thirds World including theologies of the minorities in the first world nations. There are in fact multiple and different trends of Christologies in existence today. The words of Roger Haight capture well the contemporary state of Christology when he says:

> Few areas in theology have been as volatile over the past two decades as Christology. Many of the leading theologians of our time have proposed their Christologies; a plethora of Christologies respond to particular issues; the discipline itself is divided into a number of

---

[270] Lamin Sanneh, *Whose Religion is Christianity? The Gospel Beyond the West* (Grand Rapids: William B. Eerdmans Publishing Company, 2003), 22; cf. See also Andrew F. Walls, *The Cross-Cultural Process in Christian History: Studies in the Transmission and Appropriation of Faith* (Maryknoll: Orbis Books, 2002), 85, 31-32. In the light of this shift taking place, Walls acknowledges that, "Today, the signs suggest that what the Christianity of the Twenty-first century will be like, in its theology, its worship, its effects on society, its penetration of new areas, whether geographically or culturally, will depend on what happens in Africa, in Latin America, and in some part of Asia." 32.

[271] Gutiérrez, *A Theology of Liberation,* 16.

[272] Robert H. King, "Introduction: The Task of Theology," in Peter C. Hodgson and Robert H. King. ed. *Christian Theology: An Introduction to its Traditions and Tasks.* Newly Updated Edition (Minneapolis: Fortress Press, 1994), 24.

> subdisciplines that require specific expertise and have generated their own body of literature. More and more, what is subsumed within the area of Christology appears to be a confusing mass of accumulating data.[273]

Christology in Postmodern Context

Increasingly people are identifying contemporary reality as being postmodern; indeed the common refrain is we are living in the postmodern age. The terms "postmodern" and, "postmodernity" mean different things to different people; however, for our purposes, these words will be used in the very broadest sense as relates to material and intellectual culture. The material definition of postmodernity refers to the actual way of life that has developed in Western societies. In this material or economic sense, postmodernism is nothing but a "cultural logic of late capitalism" according to Fredric Jameson.[274] The intellectually postmodern refers to academic ideas and theories which act to guide and inform interpretive principles in the various disciplines and claim no allegiance to any meta-narrative or the grand universalizing narratives. It is used to convey the recognition that an "epistemic or ephocal" transition has taken place. While one school of thought which includes Lyotard argues that today we live in a postmodern age, the Habermas "school," for lack of better term, maintains that there is no historical rupture large enough to merit the designation "post." For Jameson, postmodernism:

> Is neither a narrowly cultural category designating specific features which distinguish postmodernism from modernism proper, nor a global category designating a new epoch and radical break from the past; rather the term serves to "correlate the emergence of new formal features in culture with the emergence of a new type of social life and a new economic order."[275]

This new social and economic order has been called "late" or multinational capitalism. The value given to the legitimacy of postmodernism can be seen as a function of difference of opinions regarding, 1) radical newness 2) the continuation of modernity with no dramatic shift happening, and 3) nostalgic and premodern.[276]

In light of these very brief observations, our question is, what does this mean to the work of identifying and understanding Christology today? What is

[273] Roger Haight, *Jesus Symbol of God* (Maryknoll: Orbis Books, 2002), 17.

[274] Fredric Jameson, *Postmodernism or, the Cultural Logic of Late Capitalism* (Durham: Duke University Press, 1999).

[275] Ibid., 331.

[276] Paul Lakeland, *Postmodernity: Christian Identity in a Fragmented Age* (Minneapolis: Fortress Press, 1997), 16-18.

the shape, color, and sound of postmodern Christology? Susan B. Thistlethwaite believes there are many Christs in today's Christianity.[277] Put another way, she perceives many types of Christologies according to different contexts and situations around the world. There is the white Christ as much as there is the Black Christ or, for that matter, Asian or African or Latin American Christs. There is also the male Christ as well as the female/woman Christ. Drawing insights from the postsructuralism's claim that reality is a product of history derived through language, and a Foucauldian analysis of power as series of intricate relations, Thistlethwaite argues that Christological formulation and understanding are shaped and affected by the power relations. [278]

Jürgen Moltmann proposes a postmodern Christology that will move beyond the classical dogma characterized by the metaphysics of substance and modern Christology as a category of history. In *The Way of Jesus Christ,* Moltmann proposes a postmodern Christology. He argues that the context of Christology should assume a much wider horizon that moves beyond human history to encompassing the whole of God's creation "which places human history ecologically in the framework of nature."[279]

Haight provides four useful themes which he believes characterize the postmodern consciousness which are also the critical factors in forming the direction postmodern Christology moves.[280] First, the postmodern consciousness includes a radical historical consciousness which affirms that all knowledge is local and truth and meaning are contingent on context. Christologically, a return to the historical Jesus is an indicator of historical consciousness. "Radical historical consciousness begins when one recognizes how deeply the meaning of Jesus Christ has changed when he is reinterpreted in different epochs and cultures, and why such change is necessary."[281] Second, postmodern consciousness means a critical social consciousness. Aided by the social sciences, the contemporary awareness of the social reality and social structures, from linguistic structures to institutional oppressions, has played critical roles in constructing socially mediated

[277] Susan B. Thistlethwaite, "Christology and Postmodernism: Not Everyone Who Says to me, 'Lord, Lord,'" in Interpretation 49, no. 3 (July 1995), 267-280.

[278] Ibid., 273. By way of illustration, Thistlethwaite notes that the significance of the Lordship of Jesus Christ shifted from the early centuries' usage as a site of resistance and protest against the Roman Empire by the persecuted Christians to the imperial identity of the church and its dominance over others during and after Constantine. "As power became organized through the stratification of society through gender, race, and class, the term 'Lordship' increasingly functioned to divinize these stratifications and to organize power relations in a hierarchical fashion. This stratification in the church became so complete that the first definition of hierarchy in English-language dictionaries is ecclesiastical." 274.

[279] Jürgen Moltmann, *The Way of Jesus Christ: Christology in Messianic Dimensions,* trans. Margaret Kohl (Minneapolis: Fortress Press, 1993), xvi.

[280] Haight, *Jesus Symbol of God,* 331-334.

[281] Ibid., 332.

Christologies, such as liberation theologies. It recognizes the fundamental sociality of human existence and the necessity of bringing change where there exists oppression, unjust, and unfreedom. "Socially conscious christologies unfold within a postmodern context and interpret Jesus Christ as standing for a human imperative to exercise corporate responsibility in the creation of just social structures."[282]

Third, the postmodern consciousness is a pluralist consciousness. It recognizes more than ever, the reality of the existence of a plurality of ethnicities, cultures, and religions which are manifested in the inevitable necessity of co-existing with people of different backgrounds and cultures. This is especially so religiously; no single religion, faith tradition, or belief system can be claimed as the best or most true. It appears that at least some claims to exclusivity are giving way to mutual respect and understanding. In this pluralist context, we look for a Christology that affirms and respects difference and others.

The fourth theme Haight identified is cosmic consciousness. With a shift in worldview from anthropocentrism to cosmos gaining momentum, cosmic Christology has assumed new meaning and dimension in contemporary Christological thinking. God's relation to humanity and the rest of Creation, and the soteriological implication this entails, take on new dimensions.

Theology of Liberation and Culture

The emergence of liberation theology precipitated an entirely new way of doing theology which sought to validate and alleviate the experience of the poor and the oppressed.[283] In other words, the economic exploitation and political oppression experienced by the poor are the basis of liberation theology. In the case of black theology it is the blacks' historical experience of slavery and their continued experience of discrimination and exploitation at the hands of the white oppressors which serve as the context of their theological reflection. Likewise, feminist and womanist theologies as well as theologies of other oppressed populations emerged out of their respective experience of oppression. Liberation theology follows praxis, the method of action-reflection, as its methodology. Theology is accordingly defined as the critical reflection on praxis:

---

[282] Haight, *Jesus Symbol of God,* 333.

[283] Gustavo Gutiérrez and James H. Cone are the pioneers of liberation theology. While Gutiérrez was theologizing from the perspectives of the socio-economic realties of the poor in Latin America, Cone did so in the context of black peoples' experience of slavery and racism. They were followed by a host of liberation theologians from the Third World as well as liberationists writing for women, women of color, and other oppressed populations. For an introduction to liberation theology refer to Alfred T. Hennelly, ed. *Liberation Theology: A Documentary History* (Maryknoll: Orbis Books, 1990). For black theology refer to James H. Cone and G. S. Wilmore, eds., *Black Theology: A Documentary History*, 2 Vols. (Maryknoll: Orbis Books, 1993).

> Based on the gospel and the experiences of men and women committed to the process of liberation in the oppressed and exploited land.... It is a theological reflection born of the experience of shared efforts to abolish the current unjust situation and to build a different society, freer, and more human."[284]

Liberation theology begins with the claim that all theology is contextual. No theology is universally valid for all people and for all time. James Cone states categorically thus:

> Theology is not universal language about God. Rather, it is human speech informed by historical and theological traditions, and written for particular times and places. Theology is contextual language – that is, defined by the human situation that gives birth to it. No one can write theology for all times, places, and persons.[285]

Feminist theology as liberation theology emerged soon after the books by Gutierrez and Cone were published. The main context of feminist theology is the experience of women suffering within the patriarchal systems of a male-dominated society. Feminist theology strives to extricate freedom for women from the androcentric social and cultural conditions in which they are subordinated and treated as less than equals with men. Its primary goal is to work for attaining equality among men and women in the society.[286]

There are feminist theologians writing from the vantage points of particular minorities and the Third World who claim that feminist theology ignores concerns and experiences of their own women. Feminist theology has come to be regarded as a product of women of and a theology for privileged women, and particularly white women. Non-Euroamerican female theologians and scholars primarily from the traditionally marginalized populations of the so-called Two-Thirds World have developed theologies which address the concerns and issues effecting

---

[284] Gustavo Gutiérrez, *A Theology of Liberation.* 15th Anniversary Edition with a new Introduction (Maryknoll: Orbis Books, 2000), xiii.

[285] James H. Cone, *A Black Theology of Liberation.* Twentieth Anniversary Edition (Maryknoll: Orbis Books, 1990), 1.

[286] Following are five of the most prominent feminist theologians and examples of their work: Elisabeth Schüssler Fiorenza, *In Memory of Her: A Feminist Theological Reconstruction of Christian Origins* (New York: Crossroad Publishing Company, 1983), and *Jesus: Miriam's Child, Sophia's Prophet: Critical Issues in Feminist Christology* (New York: Continuum, 1994); Rosemary Radford Ruether, *Sexism and God Talk: Toward a Feminist Theology* (Boston: Beacon Press, 1983), and *To Change the World: Christology and Cultural Criticism* (New York: Crossroad Publishing Company, 1981); Anne Carr, *Transforming Grace: Christian Tradition and Women's Experience* (San Francisco: Harper, 1988); Rita Nakashima Brock, *Journeys by Heart: A Christology of Erotic Power* (New York: Crossroad Publishing Company, 1988); Maryanne Stevens, ed., *Reconstructing the Christ Symbol: Essays in Feminist Christology* (New York: Paulist Press, 1993).

women in society in which they live. These relativized theologies are identified as womanist theology, Mujerista, Asian feminist theology, and African feminist theology to name only a few.[287] With each of these particular populations, and understanding of and relationship with God and Christ have been articulated to reflect the distinctive situations and experiences of these women.

Asian and African liberation theologies on the other hand, unlike the Latin American liberation theology, have moved beyond by bringing in the cultural and religious dimensions in their theological reflections. The theological phenomena taking place in Asia and Africa and in certain Indigenous peoples' nations around the world might be referred to as theologies of contextualization.[288] For Asian and African theologians, the political, socio-economic, and religious realities of the people go hand in hand in their theological reflections. In other words, their theologizing efforts and theological interpretations reflect the experience (socio-economic), language, traditions, and customs of their own culture.

Indigenous peoples around the world have for ages out of memory recognized their relationship within the whole of creation and have understood their reality according to this relationship.[289] Contrary to the traditional western worldview which is characterized by considerable, even disproportionate, tendency to anthropomorphizing, an Indigenous worldview affirms the inter-relatedness of all that is created. Accordingly, the datum relevant to the work of Indigenous theologians is Creation, not human beings. Indigenous people believe that human existence and their identity are inseparably linked with Creation, hence theological

---

[287] Some of the prominent figures and their representative works are as follows: Delores S. Williams, *Sisters in the Wilderness: The Challenge of Womanist God-Talk* (Maryknoll: Orbis Books, 1993); Jacquelyn Grant, *White Women's Christ, Black Women's Jesus* (Atlanta: Scholars Press, 1989); Virginia Fabella and Mercia A. Oduyoye, eds., *With Passion and Compassion: Third World Doing Theology* (Maryknoll: Orbis Books, 1988); Kwok Pui-lan, *Postcolonial Imagination & Feminist Theology* (Louisville: Westminster John Knox Press, 2005); Chung Hyun Kyung, *Struggle to be the Sun Again: Introducing Asian Women's Theology* (Maryknoll: Orbis Books, 1990); Elsa Tamez, ed., *Through Her Eyes: Women's Theology from Latin America* (Maryknoll: Orbis Books, 1989); Maria Pilar Aquino, *Our Cry for Life: Feminist Theology from Latin America* (Maryknoll: Orbis Books, 1993); Mercia A. Oduyoye, *Daughters of Anowa: African Women and Patriarchy* (Maryknoll: Orbis Books, 1997); Ada Maria Isasi-Diaz, Mujerista Theology: *A Theology for the Twenty-first Century* (Maryknoll: Orbis Books, 1996).

[288] While inculturation is an integral part of theologizing, I prefer to use the term contextualization. Contextualization is a much more broader term that encompasses the cultural and social realities of the people. In other words, it encompasses the total reality of people's experience socially, culturally, economically, spiritually and politically.

[289] Vine Deloria Jr, *The World We Used to Live In: Remembering the Powers of Medicine Men* (Golden: Fulcrum Publishing, 2006); *God is Red: A Native View of Religion*, 2nd ed. (Golden: North American Press, 1992); Graham Harvey, *Indigenous Religions: A Companion* (London and New York: Cassel, 2000); John A. Grim, ed., *Indigenous Traditions and Ecology: The Interbeing of Cosmology and Community* (Cambridge: Harvard University Press, 2001); George E. Tinker, *Spirit and Resistance: Political Theology and American Indian Liberation* (Minneapolis: Fortress Press, 2004).

reflection must begin with Creation. Additionally, their theoretical framework is based on spatiality and relationship rather than temporality and history. One way we can relate this concept is the method of gathering information; Indigenous people value all information. Vine Deloria Jr. explains:

> In most tribal traditions, no data are discarded as unimportant or irrelevant. Indians consider their own individual experiences, the accumulated wisdom of the community that has been gathered by previous generations, their dreams, visions, and prophecies, and any information received from birds, animals, and plants as data that must be arranged, evaluated, and understood as a unified body of knowledge. This mixture of data from sources that the Western scientific world regards as highly unreliable and suspect produces a consistent perspective on the natural world . . . . Knowledge about plants and birds can form the basis of ethics, government, and economics, as well as provide a means of mapping a large area of land . . . . In tribal systems there is never a sense of disorientation within the tribal understanding of the word.[290]

Liberation and Cultural Christology

Having discussed in brief the various liberation and cultural theologies, I will now turn my focus to the various Christological reflections and positions espoused by liberation and cultural theologies. My task is to identify and critically examine the most distinctive features of various Christologies.

Latin American Liberation Christology

Jesus Christ is portrayed first and foremost as liberator; however, Jesus the liberator is not concerned with the law as much as he is concerned with human beings and their liberation from all systems of death. In "The Political Dimension of Christ the Liberator" J. Severino Croatto states that:

> Jesus initiates his program of liberation by redeeming human beings, rescuing them from the structural power of the law, from the 'traditions,' and from the marginalizing prejudices of institution, sect, race, and religion. He denounces the legalistic 'justice' of the Pharisees...and the perverted and alienating 'authority' of the Sadducees.[291]

---

290 Vine Deloria Jr, *Spirit and Reason: The Vine Deloria, Jr., Reader* (Golden: Fulcrum Publishing, 1999), 66-67. Deloria also talks about the spiritual/intellectual journey of the American Inidan elders in his latest work, *The World We Used to Live In*, xxiv-xxxii.

291 J. Severino Croatto, "The Political Dimension of Christ the Liberator," in José Míguez Bonino, ed. *Faces of Jesus: Latin American Christologies,* trans. from the Spanish by Robert R. Barr (Eugene: Wipf and Stock Publishers, 1998), 120.

The image of Jesus as a political messiah who would liberate the poor and oppressed was very prominent in Latin American interpretation of Jesus Christ. This concept of Jesus as a political liberator is based on Jesus' use of the word "kingdom" which has a concrete political connotation.[292] Segundo defends the validity of this description of Jesus. He argues:

> People talk about how absurd it was for him to be killed for political reasons. They fail, or choose not, to notice the first visible effect of his preaching in Galilee and of his arguments in defense of the poor. What was it, according to the Synoptic Gospels? It was a conspiracy between the ideologico-religious authorities (the Pharisees) and the political authorities (the Herodians) to get rid of him: "The Pharisees went out, and immediately held counsel with the Herodians against him, how to destroy him" (Mark 3:6).[293]

Segundo goes on to assert:

> Jesus appears on the scene proclaiming the arrival of the kingdom, and disappears from that scene after having been accused of introducing a kingdom and of being its king. All four Gospels agree that the reason given for Jesus' death, the charge inscribed on his cross, was "Jesus of Nazareth, the King of the Jews" (John 19: 19-22; Mark 15:26; cf. Matt. 27: 37; Luke 23: 38). Three years (according to the majority of exegetes) were not enough for Jesus to dispel the ambiguity of the term and prove that he was using it in a purely religious sense![294]

In a similar vein, Leonardo Boff cites three reasons stated in the Gospels which explain the execution of Jesus:[295] the popularity of Jesus with the people was perceived by the authorities as a threat; Jesus disconcerted his opponents by not appealing to any accepted traditions and authorities; and Jesus not only taught and preached with authority, he also pronounced forgiveness of sin which was regarded as an act of blasphemy against God.

Second, following their insistence on orthopraxis over orthodoxy, they are critical of classical Christology which fails to take seriously the praxiological significance of Christology in Christian living. According to Boff:

---

[292] Both Jon Sobrino and Juan Luis Segundo maintained that Jesus was condemned to die as a political agitator.

[293] Juan Luis Segundo, *The Historical Jesus of the Synoptics,* trans. from Spanish by John Drury (Maryknoll: Orbis Books, 1985), 76-77.

[294] Ibid., 88.

[295] Leonardo Boff, *Jesus Christ as Liberator: A Critical Christological Essay for Our Time,* trans. by Patrick Hughes (Maryknoll: Orbis Books, 1978), 101-103.

> We know that for Christ and the primitive church, the essential did not consist in the reduction of the message of Christ to systematic categories of intellectual comprehension but in creating new habits of acting and living in the world.[296]

Third, for liberation theologians the starting point of Christology is the historical, living Jesus rather than the abstract Christ of faith and doctrine. The Christ of faith they argue, is susceptible to manipulation by the oppressive structures of society, while, the underlying reasoning for insisting on the efficacy of the historical Jesus is the power resides in what he said and did. According to Jon Sobrino the practice of Jesus is "his activity brought to bear upon the reality around him in order to transform it in a determinate, selected direction, the direction of the Kingdom of God."[297]

The effort to ground liberation Christology in the historical Jesus does not mean it is an attempt to construct a biography of Jesus; rather, it signals the invitation to "continue his practice – or, in Jesus' language, an invitation to his discipleship for a mission."[298] Liberation theologians claimed that the oppressive structures of Jesus' day and the contemporary situation in Latin America were similar. They also insisted that Jesus came to establish and work for the Kingdom of God here on earth. In his life on earth Jesus worked for justice, peace and liberation, which are certainly integral values of the Kingdom.

Sobrino has called to our attention the eschatological dimension of the Kingdom by analyzing Jesus' proclamation of the "kingdom at hand" as an eschatological statement. He suggests further that:

> The thought tension between the present and the future of the kingdom is experienced as undying hope. In the praxis of love and justice one knows that the kingdom is at hand, is becoming present; and in conflictive praxis in the midst of the world's sin one maintains hope in God's future.[299]

Latin American Christology sees Jesus Christ as the liberator - political and socio-economic – and his message of the immanence of the Kingdom is the basis for their belief. They have relied heavily on the concept of the historical Jesus, to give primacy to his ministry to the poor and oppressed. In other words, they highlighted the message that Jesus identified with and stood in solidarity with the poor and marginalized to the extent of giving up his life. The suffering and death

---

[296] Leonardo Boff, *Jesus Christ as Liberator: A Critical Christological Essay for Our Time,* trans. by Patrick Hughes (Maryknoll: Orbis Books, 1978), 47.

[297] Jon Sobrino, *Jesus in Latin America* (Maryknoll: Orbis Books, 1987), 66.

[298] Ibid., 66.

[299] Ibid., 95.

of Jesus was his act of love and unwavering commitment for all so that "they may have life in its fullness." This liberation theology calls out for the Justice of Jesus which demands a "preferential option for the poor."[300]

Black Christology

In *Introducing Black Theology of Liberation*, Dwight Hopkins has divided black theology into two strands: one, he calls it theology of liberation based in politics and the other a theology of liberation based in black cultures.[301] He identifies James Cone and J. Deotis Roberts as the main proponents of political theology, while Gayraud S. Wilmore and Charles H. Long are advocates for cultural theology. While all four theologians have the same theological goal, the liberation of the black Americans, they differ in their choice of methods and sources. Cultural theologians are critical of political theologians for not taking seriously black religious and cultural resources in their theological reflections and also for following the intellectual categories of white theology. Cultural theologians have instead pushed to distance black theology from "white" theology and to a focus on faith experience. They have proposed the use of four categories: 1) black religious thought or language, 2) sources, 3) Africanisms, and 4) liberation. [302]

Blacks have identified with Jesus because he had a dark complexion and not white as he had always been portrayed. Some forty years ago, Malcolm X proclaimed, "Christ wasn't white. Christ was a black man."[303] Likewise, Cain Hope Felder, a black biblical scholar, has asserted that "the sweet little Jesus boy of the Negro spiritual was, in fact, quite Black."[304] According to Kelly B. Douglas, the underlying assumption for the black Christ has long been there with Blacks in terms of skin color. However, it is only after the emergence of black theology in the 1960s that theologically black Christ was fully developed.[305]

Black theology emerged out of black people's historical experience of being torn from their homeland, sold into slavery, and treated as though they were less than human. Understandably, their Christological concepts and construction have been both informed and developed within this experience of suffering. Black's alienation and suffering has been and continues to be exacerbated by their skin color. Black theologians argue that discrimination against Black people is primarily a function of their skin color. James H. Cone, who can be rightly

---

[300] Gustavo Gutierrez, *The Power of the Poor in History*, trans. from Spanish by Robert R. Barr (Maryknoll: Orbis Books, 1988), 137-138.

[301] Dwight N. Hopkins, *Introducing Black Theology of Liberation* (Maryknoll: Orbis Books, 1999), 52-86.

[302] Ibid., 65-66.

[303] "The Playboy Interview: Malcolm X Speaks with Alex Haley" (May 1963). Quoted in Kelley Brown Douglas, *The Black Christ* (Maryknoll: Orbis Books, 1994), 1.

[304] Quoted in Douglas, *The Black Christ*. 1.

[305] Ibid., 6.

called the father of Black theology, argues that, "Since the black community is an oppressed community because and only because of its blackness, the Christological importance of Jesus Christ must be in his blackness."[306] Unlike some black theologians who emphasize the physiological characteristic of Jesus' blackness,[307] Cone contends that Jesus as a Black man is most valuable symbolically. Rather than emphasizing the ethnic characteristics of Jesus, Cone believes the Jesus' blackness symbolized the sufferings of oppressed peoples, and particularly Black Americans. This blackness gained even more power by virtue of Jesus' life and existential commitments. Cone understands "Black" or "blackness" as representative of all forms of oppression

Cone points to the scriptural record of the life and ministry of Jesus both of which indicate he identified and stood in solidarity with oppressed people in first century Palestine. In this sense for Cone, Christ's blackness is informed by Jesus' identification with the oppressed and by the fact that black people are the oppressed ones. Cone concludes thus, "Christ is black therefore, not because of some cultural or psychological need of black people, but because and only because God really enters into the world where the poor, the despised and the oppressed are."[308] Additionally, Cone believes in the humanity and divinity of Jesus Christ and on this basis he affirms that "the pain of the cross was God suffering for and with us so that our humanity can be liberated for freedom in the divine struggle against."[309]

In Dwight Hopkins' view Jesus is the Spirit of total liberation with us.[310] Jesus as the Spirit has always been with the oppressed and downtrodden empowering and laboring with them in their struggle for freedom. The goal of the Spirit of liberation is to provide freedom, dignity and quality of life: "freedom for the captives, liberation for those blind and emancipation for the broken hearted," as declared by Jesus.[311] Hopkins asserts that it is through the oppressed that the Spirit reveals its fullness to the rest of the humanity. He claims that the Spirit is partial to the poor because "Jesus is with those enchained in poverty."[312] Hopkins

---

306 James H. Cone, *A Black Theology of Liberation,* 20th Century ed. (Maryknoll: Orbis Books, 1990), 213.

307 Albert Cleage concluded that based on the genealogical information provided in the Bible Jesus of Nazareth was ethnically black. He explained that the Israelites were a "mixture of Chaldeans, Egyptians, Midianites, Ethiopians, Kushites, Babylonians and other dark peoples, all of whom were already mixed with black people of Central Africa." On this basis, he claimed Jesus was black, born of a black mother. Albert Cleage, *The Black Messiah* (Kansas City: Sheed and Ward, 1969), 3.

308 James H. Cone. *God of the Oppressed,* rev. ed. (Maryknoll: Orbis Books, 1997), 136.

309 Ibid., 127.

310 Dwight N. Hopkins, *Down, Up, and Over: Slave Religion and Black Theology* (Minneapolis: Fortress Press, 2000), 193.

311 Ibid., 194.

312 Ibid., 200.

further points out the meaning and implications of Jesus as the Spirit of liberation with us; it means two things:[313] first, the Spirit of liberation with us means being in the world for the least in society, for the poor, and for those who have less privileges than we have. Second, journeying and following the Spirit of liberation with us means our own liberation is inextricably linked with the liberation of everyone else; in other words, our liberation is incomplete until everyone else is liberated as well.

American Indian Christology: Christ as Corn Mother

Among the Indigenous theologians in the world the name George E. "Tink" Tinker stands out. Tinker, an American Indian of the Osage nation, has for thirty years been at the forefront in developing Indigenous theologies by incorporating traditional cultural values and ceremony. He has also written extensively on the subjects of oppression of the Euro-American Christianity and the missionaries' collusion with the colonial powers.[314] He has criticized Euro-American Christians of imposing their concepts of Jesus on American Indians.[315] Tinker is particularly critical of the title of Jesus as Lord. He has argued that the term "Lord" or "Lordship" presume systems of patriarchal hierarchy and inequalities of power which serve to reiterate and reinforce in American Indians their status as members of conquered and colonized nations. Such hierarchical structures and their attendant nomenclatures are alien to American Indian cultures and social structures. He explains:

> To call upon Jesus as Lord suddenly began to strike me as a classic example of the colonized participating in our own oppression. To call upon Jesus as Lord is to concede the colonial reality of new hierarchical social structures; it is to concede the conquest as final and to become complicit in our death, that is, the ongoing genocidal death of our peoples. It is an act of the colonized mind blindly reciting words that the colonizer has taught us which violate our own cultures but bring great comfort to the colonizer and his missionaries.[316]

---

[313] Dwight N. Hopkins, *Down, Up, and Over: Slave Religion and Black Theology* (Minneapolis: Fortress Press, 2000), 209-210.

[314] Some of his notable writings are *Spirit and Resistance: Political Theology and American Indian Liberation* (Minneapolis: Fortress Press, 2004); *Missionary Conquest: The Gospel and Native American Cultural Genocide* (Minneapolis: Fortress Press, 1993); and Clara Sue Kidwell, Homer Noley, and George E. "Tink" Tinker, eds., *A Native American Theology* (Maryknoll: Orbis Books, 2001).

[315] Tinker, "American Indians and Jesus: Reflections Towards an EATWOT Christology," in *Voices from the Third World* 18, no.2, (December 1995), 121-127.

[316] Tinker, "Jesus, Corn Mother, and Conquest: Christology and Colonialism," in Jeace Weaver, ed., *Native American Religious Identity: Unforgotten Gods* (Maryknoll: Orbis Books, 1998),

Tinker goes on to argue that the use of "Lord" is also not helpful to white Christians because, "The metaphor seems to excuse White Amer-Europeans from any earthly humility or surrender, and often to facilitate a lack of consciousness with regard to the impropriety of relationships of exploitation."[317]

In light of this, he contends that any effort to construct an American Indian Christology must simultaneously be a project of decolonization.

In his project to forge an American Indian Christology, Tinker has drawn upon a traditional story of the Corn Mother.[318] He notes that it is necessary to first make a distinction between Jesus and Christ. He argues that Christ is the preexistent Logos as described in John 1, while, "Jesus is a human who has a birth, a beginning in time . . . ."[319] So, to identify Jesus as the Christ who preexisted, as is done by Christians, is to in fact to limit God by virtue of finite human interpretation. A more accurate interpretation would posit that, "The Logos is some aspect of God, perhaps the creative aspect of God's self as God communicates with human beings."[320] Tinker then explains that, "This, suddenly, is a notion of Christ that Indian people can begin to understand naturally within their own experiences and knowledge."[321] From this perspective then Tinker cites the practicability of perceiving Christ as the Corn Mother. Christ is described as the Corn Mother who is said to have given her life for the sake of her children. Tinker attaches a great deal of significance on the vicarious suffering of the Corn Mother on behalf of the whole of her children. According to this story the people met their daily requirements for sustenance through the vicarious suffering of the death of the Corn Mother. Food is therefore sacred and to be shared. Sharing and eating of food has sacramental values because it involves the eating of the body of the Corn Mother. Additionally eating and sharing of food reminds our relatedness with the rest of Creation – animals and plants – because they also share and depend on the provision provided by the Mother.

> Corn and all food stuffs are our relatives, just as much as those who live in adjacent lodges within our clan-cluster. Thus, eating is sacramental, to use a Euro-theological word, because we are eating our relatives. Not only we are related to corn, beans, and squash, since these things emerge immediately out of the death of Corn Mother, but even those other relatives like Buffalo, Deer, Squirrel, and Fish ultimately gain their strength and growth because they too eat of the plenty provided

139; Clara Sue Kidwell, Homer Noley, and George E. "Tink" Tinker, *A Native American Theology*, 68.

317 Ibid., 140.

318 Ibid., 149-152.

319 Ibid., 148.

320 Ibid., 149.

321 Ibid.

> by the Mother – eating grasses, leaves, nuts, and algae that also grow out of the Mother's bosom.[322]

Asian and African Christology

Asian and African theologies have taken seriously the view that liberation and culture are inseparably related and they go together. They have fully recognized the people's experience of suffering and the need thereof for liberation and the rich traditions and cultural resources which serve as such a fecund reservoir for contextual theologies. Also, unlike Western theological epistemology which tends to require that distinction be made between the historical Jesus and the Christ of faith, Asians and Africans in general prefer to view Jesus and the Christ as one and the same, making no distinction between the two. For them, in the words of Sri Lankan theologian R. S. Sugirtharajah,

> The artificial dichotomy imposed by Western academics between historical exegesis and theology – between historical facts and faith formulations – does not exist. The crucial hermeneutical question is not what the historical Jesus looked like but what he means for Asia today."[323]

Asia's demographics are the single most important element for any discussion of contextual theologizing. Asia is the birth place of all the largest religions of the world including Hinduism, Christianity, Islam, Buddhism, Confucianism, Jainism and Sikhism. It also contains the world's most densely populated and destitute countries. These are the harsh realities out of which Asian theologies and Christologies are being imagined and articulated. Put another way, Asian Christologies are formulated and lived surrounded by long established non-Christian religious beliefs and traditions,[324] and they must be relevant and empowering for people suffering under crushing poverty, exploitation, and neglect. Asian proponents of liberation theology understand the logic and power in employing cultural metaphors and images in formulating a relevant Christology.

Asian theologians, such as Stanley J. Smartha, Aloyius Pieris, Michael Amaladoss and many others are known for their theologies of religious pluralism and their articulation of Christologies in the context of religious pluralism. In *One Christ Many Religions*, Smartha argues for a theocentric Christology as a

---

[322] Tinker, "Jesus, Corn Mother, and Conquest: Christology and Colonialism," in Jeace Weaver, ed., *Native American Religious Identity: Unforgotten Gods* (Maryknoll: Orbis Books, 1998), 139; Clara Sue Kidwell, Homer Noley, and George E. "Tink" Tinker, *A Native American Theology,* 68.

[323] R. S. Sugirtharajah, ed., *Asian Faces of Jesus* (Maryknoll: Orbis Books, 2001), x.

[324] Stanley J. Smartha, *One Christ - Many Religions* (Maryknoll: Orbis Books, 1991), x. Smartha wrote about how traditional Christologies, developed in the West and imported to other countries, fail to take into account the presence of other "lords" and "saviors" in a multirelgious context.

viable and relevant Christology in a religiously pluralistic society such as India. Pieris has engaged at length the aspects of conflicting truth claims among religious traditions. In one such case he examined the conflicting claims made for Buddha and Christ which convinced him that the efficacious methodology is to go beyond the philosophical debates to concentrate on the dimensions of human liberation and well-being. "What mediates liberation is the medium to which one culture as much as another can decide what name to give: Christ, Son of God, and so forth, or *Dharma, Tathagata,* and so forth – according to its own religious idiom."[325] Pieris concludes by observing:

> The real parting of ways, therefore, begins when either Guatama or Jesus is identified with that medium by means of these titles. It is at this point that dialogue must once more change directions if it is to avoid a blind alley, for we are dealing with kerygmatic affirmations.[326]

Buddha and Christ are seen as mediators of liberation. In the same manner, M. Thomas Thangaraj has developed a Christology of the Crucified Guru as an experiment in cross-cultural Christology based on the Hindu concept of Guru.[327]

Choan S. Song and Kosuke Koyoma are known for their pioneering works on developing theologies rooted on Asian cultural soils.[328] They both have formulated Asian Christologies using the image of rice, the staple food of Asian people, and Jesus is portrayed as the rice of life. Minjung theologians of Korea identify Jesus as a Minjung[329] who understands and shares their pain and suffering. Jesus is perceived as a liberator who liberates the people from the bondage of the feelings of *han*[330] which has crippled them for decades and decades.

---

[325] Aloysius Pieris, "The Buddha and the Christ: Mediators of Liberation," in R. S. Sugirtharajah, ed., *Asian Faces of Jesus,* 57.

[326] Ibid., 58.

[327] M. Thomas Thangaraj, *The Crucified Guru: An Experiment in Cross-Cultural Christology* (Nashville: Abingdon Press, 1994), 91-105. Of course, a number of Indian scholars in the past, Christian and non-Christian, including M. Gandhi, Raja Ram Mohan Roy, Robert De Nobili (a Jesuit missionary), have regarded Jesus as Guru/Teacher. However, it is Thangaraj who seems to have made full use of the concept in his formulation of Christology in Indian context.

[328] For their works refer to the following books. C. S. Song, *Theology from the Womb of Asia* (Maryknoll: Orbis Books, 1986); *Third – Eye Theology: Theology in Formation in Asian Settings,* Revised Edition (Maryknoll: Orbis Books, 1979); Kosuke Koyama, *Water Buffalo Theology,* Twenty-Fifth Anniversary Edition, Revised and Expanded (Maryknoll: Orbis Books, 1999).

[329] Minjung is a Korean term which means "masses of people." They are the oppressed, exploited, and discriminated people of the society. Cf. Chung Hyun Kyung, *Struggle to be the sun Again: Introducing Asian Women's Theology* (Maryknoll: Orbis Books, 1990), 120.

[330] Han in Korean means a deep feeling of "unexpressed anger and resentment" accumulated over the years. Ibid., 42.

In India the most exploited and oppressed people are Dalits and Tribals. Constructing Christology from the perspective of people underside history, A. P. Nirmal argues that the starting point of theology for the Dalits is the experience of suffering, not praxis. And he goes on to assert that in Jesus Christ the suffering dalits have found their identity as people. Sathiananthan Clarke, another dalit theologian constructs a Christology by drawing upon the "theological explications of the symbol of drum from the Dalit religious traditions.[331]

Africans are also known for their rich religious and cultural traditions which they believe have sustained them throughout their history. The influence of these traditions is quite obvious in their theologies. According to Charles Nyamiti, there are two general types of African theology today, inculturation and liberation.[332] While inculturation theologies focus on the process of making the Gospel incarnate in the cultural soil of Africa, liberation theologies emphasize on the socio-economic and political struggles of the people. Nyamiti observes further identify that African cultural Christologies could also be understood as fitting within two broad description; some in scripture and applied to the African reality and the others work from African reality to a Christology. While, John S. Mbiti, Douglas W. Waruta, Zablon Nthamburi and others follow the former approach, other theologians like Charles Nyamiti, Anselme T. Sanon, François Kabasélé, and Cécé Kolié follow the latter.

Some of the important cultural images employed metaphorically in the construction of African Christologies include Christ as Chief,[333] Christ as Ancestor and Elder brother,[334] Jesus as the Master of Initiation[335] and Jesus as Healer.[336] These images make it easier for African Christians to relate to and identify with Jesus Christ. Some African scholars call this the synthesis approach. François Kabasélé chooses the Bantu people as his example in order to elaborate on the synthesis approach. He writes:

> "As new cultures encounter Christ...certain Bantu values such as that of ancestor worship, will become Christian, by the fact that they will be experienced by Bantu Christians, in a synthesis that breaks neither

---

[331] Sathianathan Clarke, *Dalits and Christianity: Subaltern Religion and Liberation Theology in India* (Oxford and Delhi: Oxford University Press 1998), 5.

[332] Charles Nyamiti, "African Christologies Today," in Robert J. Schreiter, ed. *Faces of Jesus in Africa* (Maryknoll: Orbis Books, 2000), 3ff.

[333] François Kabasélé, "Christ as Chief," in Robert j. Schreiter, ed., *Faces of Jesus in Africa,* 103- 105.

[334] Charles Nyamiti, *Christ as Our Ancestor: Christology from an African Perspective* (Gweru: Mambo Press, 1984); Kabasélé, "Christ as Ancestor and Elder Brother," in Robert J. Schreiter, ed., *Faces of Jesus in Africa,* 116-127.

[335] Anselme T. Sanon, "Jesus, Master of Initiation," in Robert J. Schreiter, ed. *Faces of Jesus in Africa*, 85-102.

[336] Cécé Kolié, "Jesus as Healer," in Robert J. Schreiter, ed., *Faces of Jesus in Africa,* 128-150.

> with the Bantu nor with Christ, a synthesis over which the criterion of an unconditional, absolute love for God and our siblings ought to preside."[337]

Liberation Christology is the other type of Christology that has become quite prominent in African contexts and these can be roughly divided into two types of liberation theologies. The first is generally identified with South African Black theology and the second is simply called African liberation theology. While the first is informed by the exigencies of race, the second can be identified with a broader effort to "integrate the theme of liberation into the rest of the African cultural background…;"[338] nonetheless, the two have some common features. For example, both are Christologies done from below and both stress the life and ministry of Jesus.[339]

The words of Kofi Appiah-Kubi summarize well the prevailing Christological trends in Africa.

> "[African] concepts of Christology revolve around the genealogy, the *Rites de passage* – birth, baptism, eucharist and death; kinship and community aspects; such titles as Mediator, Redeemer, Savior, Liberator and Healer are pregnant with meaning for these Indigenous African Christians."[340]

Feminist Christology

Feminist theologies reflect women's faith in light of their experiences as females. They are critical of the male biased theologies which reify and perpetuate the subordination of females; they question the premise of traditional theology which privileges male over women; and they also challenge the church's teaching about God and Jesus Christ. To many the church is seen as a bastion for the advancement of the interests of men over women which is justified through selective biblical interpretation and biased theological positions.

As a part of the methodology feminist theologians insist on rereading the scripture through the lens of women's experiences and using the tools of critical biblical studies, these theologians have been able to expose the androcentric character of scripture as it reflects the patriarchal cultural milieu of the time.[341] Accordingly, they insist that the application of a social-historical critique gives a

---

[337] Kabasélé, "Christ as Ancestor and Elder Brother," 125.

[338] Nyamiti, "African Christologies Today," 13.

[339] Laurenti Magessa, "Christ the liberator and Africa Today," in Robert J. Schreiter, ed., *Faces of Jesus in Africa,* 151-163.

[340] Kofi Appiah-Kubi, "Jesus Christ – Some Christological Aspects from African Perspectives," in *Voices from the Third World* 16, no. 2 (December 1993), 24.

[341] Elizabeth Cathy Stanton, *The Woman's Bible* (New York: Arno Press, 1972).

much more accurate picture. In, *In Memory of Her,* Elisabeth Schüssler Fiorenza explains the importance of reclaiming the past for women and notes that, "Feminist theology as a critical theology of liberation therefore seeks to develop not only a textual-biblical hermeneutics but also a historical-biblical hermeneutics of liberation."[342] Fiorenza maintains that this approach is necessary if feminist biblical hermeneutics is to move beyond the "objective" textual interpretations and value-neutral historical reconstruction.

The point of departure for feminist theology is women's experience. There are naturally many sorts of experience such as an experience of the divine, of oneself, of community and of the world; most females affirm a marked difference in their experience as compared to a males' experience in the same set of circumstances, and reading the Bible is no different. They are acutely aware that they are neglected and even ignored in theological reflection.[343] Feminists feel that, "There is a sense in which women have not shaped or even known their own experience. What they have known is the false consciousness created by male ideology.[344] Ruether identifies the full humanity of women as the critical principle of feminist theology.

> Whatever denies, diminishes, or distorts the full humanity of women is, therefore, appraised as not redemptive. Theologically speaking, whatever, diminishes or denies the full humanity of women must be presumed not to reflect the divine or an authentic relation to the divine....[345]

Another point of concern of the feminist theology is the language used to express thoughts and ideas about God, sometimes referred to as God talk. Feminists rightly point out that within Christianity and Jewish tradition God is portrayed as male. Feminists argue that this exclusive male image of God has often been used to advance the idea that men are closer to God than women therefore men are superior to women; indeed, it is only through men that women are in relation with God. In the words of Ruether, "A symbolic hierarchy is set up: God-male-female. Women no longer stand in direct relation to God; they are connected to God secondarily, through the male."[346] Similarly, Mary Daly questions the image of God the 'Father' because it legitimizes male domination by:

---

[342] Fiorenza, In Her Memory, 29-30. Similarly, Ruether argues for appropriating prophetic principles which rejects any forms of oppression and discriminations including women oppression, in Feminist theology. Ruether, Sexism and God-Talk, 22-33.

[343] Ruether, Sexism and God-Talk, 12-13.

[344] Carol P. Christ & Judith Plaskow, ed., *Womanspirit Rising: Feminist Reader in Religion* (San Francisco: HarperSanFrancisco, 1992), 6.

[345] Ibid., 18-19.

[346] Ruether, *Sexism and God-Talk,* 53.

> Making its mechanisms for the oppression of women appear right and fitting. If God in 'his' heaven as father is ruling "his" people, then it is in the 'nature' of things and according to divine plan and the order of the universe that society be male dominated."[347]

Feminists argue for the use of alternative, inclusive language about God. While some argue for looking to pre-Judaic-Christian sources claiming that God was known as both God/Goddess, others argue for positive and constructive alternatives to the sexist theology within the Judaic-Christian tradition. Today, feminists identify "God" by many different names, among them are Father-Mother God, Goddess, and God-Parent. Daly has proposed that God be referred to by the androgynous "God the verb" rather than as a noun because the noun fails to convey the notion that God is Being. "Women now who are experiencing the shock of nonbeing and the surge of self affirmation against this are inclined to perceive transcendence as the Verb in which we participate – live, move, and have our being."[348]

Ecofeminism is a strand of feminist theology which focuses on the issue of women's relationship with nature and Creation. They are critical of the accepted dichotomy which identifies women with the domain of nature only while men are identified with culture. The point is that this artificial distinction further polarizes the status or positions prescribed to women and men rather than bridging them. Ecofeminism's focus is creating new cultures:

> . . . that would embrace and honor the values of caretaking and nurturing – cultures that would not perpetuate the dichotomy by raising nature over culture or by raising women over men. Rather, they affirmed and celebrated the embeddedness of all the Earth's people in the multiple webs and cycles of life.[349]

Theologians such as Ruether and Christ have proposed viewing the earth and nature in relation to God and humanity as a relational and holistic organism. "This whole is the earth and sky, the ground on which we stand, and all the animals, plants, and other beings to which we are related."[350]

In regards to Christology there is no one position that can be identified to represent the Christological position of feminists; - there is a myriad of

---

[347] Mary Daly, "After the Death of God the Father: Women's Liberation and the Transformation of Christian Consciousness," in Christ and Plaskow, ed., *Womanspirit Rising,* 54.

[348] Mary Daly, *Beyond God the Father: Toward a Philosophy of Women's Liberation: With an Original Reintroduction by the Author* (Boston: Beacon Press, 1985), 34.

[349] Irene Diamond and Gloria Feman Orenstein, ed., *Reweaving the World: The Emergence of Ecofeminism* (San Francisco: Sierra Club Books, 1990), x-xi.

[350] Carol P. Christ, "Rethinking Theology and Nature," in Irene Diamond and Gloria F. Orenstein, ed., *Reweaving the World,* 65.

Christologies being developed and articulated. One thing they seem to all agree on is that traditional Christologies like traditional theologies are influenced and formulated by men and therefore they are "malestream" Christologies. Generally speaking, feminist Christologies can be categorized within two broad categories: liberationist Christology and relationalist Christology. Many feminist theologians have been influenced by liberation theologies in their Christological approaches. Prominent among liberationists are Ruether and Fiorenza who believe that the ultimate goal of feminist Christology is liberation. Ruether begins her Christological articulation with this question: "Can a male Savior save women?"[351] For the answer to this question she goes back to the historical roots of Christology in the Ancient Near East, Judaism and the ministry of Jesus which offer evidence that Christology was patriarchalized over the course of the first five centuries of the church. Additionally, she reviewed various contemporary alternative Christological articulations including the androgynous and spirit Christologies.[352] She concludes that Jesus is the representative of liberated humanity.

> In this sense Jesus as the Christ, the representative of liberated humanity and the liberating Word of God, manifests the *kenosis of patriarchy*, the announcement of the new humanity through a lifestyle that discards hierarchical caste privilege and speaks on behalf of the lowly.[353]

Fiorenza while agreeing with Ruether on the premise that feminist Christology should be grounded in socio-political reality, observed that Ruether, like many other feminist theologians, did not challenge the "Western cultural sex/gender and its androcentric language, according to which the male Man is the paradigm of being human whereas woman is either his inferior or complementary 'other.'"[354] She argues:

> Any feminist use of the concept of "humanity" that does not radically displace the Western kyriarchal frame of reference, which understands gender as a biological given and masculinity as the paradigm for being human, is bound to reinscribe the sex/gender system in feminist terms.[355]

---

351 Ruether, *Sexism and God-Talk,* 116.

352 While androgynous Christologies affirm the female side of Christ, spirit Christologies affirm that the risen Christ continues to be revealed through spirit-possessed person, male or female. Ibid., 135.

353 Ibid., 137.

354 Fiorenza, *Jesus: Miriam's Child,* 47.

355 Ibid.

To avoid such pitfalls, Fiorenza proposes a feminist liberationist Christological method that is concerned with justice and well-being of all, that is, an approach that "critically scrutinizes its own presuppositions, methods, interests, and social functions and their kyriarchal positions."[356]

There are some feminists who have taken relationality as the interpretative framework in their christological proposals.

> This feminist christological discourse uses key concepts such as redemptive connectedness, power-in-relation, dynamic mutuality, erotic creativity, the language of lovers, mutual interdependence, passionate creativity, inclusive wholeness, healing energy of existence, and ontological priority of relationality.[357]

Carter Hayward and Rita Nakashima Brock, each, draw their insights from "Christa"[358] in their argument for relational Christology. While Hayward's central theme is "right relation", Brock's is 'broken-heartedness." According to Hayward, "the Christological task of Christian feminism is to move the foundations of Christology from the ontology of dualistic opposition towards the ethics of justice-making."[359] Brock focuses on the communal nature of Christianity and is critical of any theology or Christology that focuses solely on Jesus the heroic individual and liberator. She envisions a Christa/Community as the "healing center of Christianity."

> Jesus participates centrally in this Christa/Community, but he neither brings erotic power into being nor controls it. He is brought into being through it and participates in the co-creation of it. Christ/Community is a lived reality expressed in relational images.... Hence, what is truly christological, that is revealing of divine incarnation and salvafic power in human life, must reside in connectedness and not in single individuals.[360]

In addition to liberationist and relational Christologies, theologians such as Elizabeth Johnson have enlisted the wisdom traditions to assist them in articulating their Christology. Johnson argues that wisdom Christology is not androcentric

---

[356] Fiorenza, *Jesus: Miriam's Child,* 61.

[357] Ibid., 50.

[358] "Christa" is the statue of the female Jesus, sculpted by Edwina Sandys.

[359] Isabel Carter Hayward, *Speaking of Christ: A Lesbian Feminist Voice* (New York: Pilgrim Press, 1989), 21.

[360] Rita Nakashima Brock, *Journeys by Heart,* 52.

and hence will contribute to the empowerment of women as well as men.[361] The human being Jesus is identified with divine Sophia.

Sallie McFague is a proponent of a cosmological and theocentric approach to theology but also she acknowledges that this approach is shaped by what she calls the Christic paradigm. McFague holds the view that God is incarnate not only in Jesus, but in the whole universe which she illustrates by employing the body as metaphor; the universe is the body of God. In this sense Jesus is paradigmatic of how God is present in the whole universe; however, she insists that Jesus is not unique.

> Jesus is not ontologically different from other paradigmatic figures either in our tradition or in other religious traditions who manifest in word and deed the love of God for the world. He is special to us as our foundational figure: he is our historical choice as the premier paradigm of God's love. But all creation and all human beings have the potential as the beloved of God to reflect or respond to their lover.[362]

Womanist Christology

Womanist and feminist theologians from Third World countries are quite critical of the universalizing feminist Christologies. They rightly argue that feminist Christologies like feminist theologies are shaped and informed by the experiences of the white privileged women of the West/North whose realities and priorities are far different from the great majority of the world's women. Second, although mainstream feminist theologians deal with the issue of racism and classism, the model from which they construct theology remains is a product of Euro-American patriarchy. Jacquelyn Grant, an African American theologian, has gone so far as to indict European-American feminist Christological discourses as implicitly racist in so far as they have essentialized female experience and ways of knowing. Grant explains:

> In a racist society, the oppressor assumes the power of definition and control while the oppressed is objectified and perceived as a thing. As such, White women have defined the movement and presumed to do so not only for themselves but also for non-White women. They have misnamed themselves by calling themselves feminists when in fact they

[361] Elizabeth Johnson, "Jesus the Wisdom of God: A Biblical Basis for Non-Androcentric Christology," in *Ephemerides Theologicae Lovanienses 61,* no. 4 (1985), 261-294.

[362] Sallie McFague, *Models of God: Theology for an Ecological, Nuclear Age* (Philadelphia: Fortress Press, 1987), 136.

are White feminists, and by appealing to women's experience when in fact they appeal almost exclusively to their own experience."[363]

The matrix of womanist theology is the suffering endured historically by Black women. It is the reality of Black women to experience discrimination on at least three levels: race, sex, and class. Of course, while black women's reality is unique in several significant ways, to a certain extent they share in the reality of a broader community. In this context they believe that Jesus identifies and suffers with them; he is their "co-sufferer."[364] Grant notes that Black women regard Jesus' suffering as undeserved as is their own. Concomitantly, the significance of Jesus Christ in womanist theology is described as freedom. Of equal significance in womanist theology is Jesus as political Messiah.

> Jesus Christ represents a threefold-significance: first, he identifies with the 'little people,' Black women, where they are; secondly, he affirms the basic humanity of these, 'the least'; and thirdly, he inspires active hope in the struggle for resurrected, liberated existence.[365]

As Grant understands it, the challenge for womanist Christology are threefold: 1) investigating the relationship between the oppression of women and theological symbolism, 2) exploring what Christ can mean for a society in which class distinctions grow ever sharper, and finally, being vigilant in doing constructive Christology.

Third World Feminist Christology

What is commonly referred to as the Third World is those countries considered by the Euro West to "developing" and/or "underdeveloped" countries particularly of Asia, Africa and Latin America. "The Third World is a cross-ridden universe of economic, political and religio-cultural oppressions within which women are doubly or triply burdened."[366] Third world feminist theologians share their Womanist sister's weariness of feminist theology and have come up with theologies informed by their own experiences and appropriate to their realities. While feminist theology in Latin America focuses on economic oppression, and

[363] Grant, White Women's Christ, *Black Women's Jesus,* 199-200.

[364] Ibid., 212.

[365] Ibid., 217.

[366] Virginia Fabella and Mercy Amba Oduyoye, ed., *With Passion and Compassion: Third World Women Doing Theology: Reflections from the Women's Commission of the Ecumenical Association of Third World Theologians* (Maryknoll: Orbis Books, 1988), xi. At the same time Kwok Pui-lan rightly cautions that since "Third World" "is a mental construct covering a vast territory with many cultures, languages, and peoples, we must not homogenize the diverse regions or generalize feminist theologies from a radically different backgrounds." Kwok Pui-lan, *Postcolonial Imagination & Feminist Theology* (Louisville: Westminster John Knox Press, 2005), 151.

institutional patriarchy, and violence against women, Asian and African feminist theologies tend to focus on the cultural and religious oppression "because of the impact of the entrenched cultural myths, rituals, and traditions on women's role in society."[367] Chung Hyun Kyung explains that, "Asian Women's theology was born out of Asian women's tears and sighs and from their burning desire for liberation and wholeness."[368] Their overarching vision is to seek liberation and wholeness of life and this search has focused primarily on the suffering, death and the liberation messages of Jesus Christ.

While critical of the colonialist portrayal of the suffering Jesus in which Jesus is portrayed as a resigned, passive sufferer, Third World women relate to and identify with the sufferings of Jesus.[369] They see the Christ brought by the missionaries as a conquering Christ imposed on them by the imperialist Western Christianity. Despite this, Third World women are also attracted to certain characteristics of the missionary Christ because they are able to see the empowering and liberating images of Jesus in scripture.

Kyung has identified both traditional and emerging images of Jesus Christ.[370] Traditional images include Jesus the suffering servant, Jesus as Lord, and Jesus with us. Asian Women have identified their sufferings with the sufferings of Jesus and they draw strength from their belief that God suffers with them. Jesus as liberator, Jesus as mother, woman, and Shaman, and Jesus as worker are some of the emerging images of Jesus Christ. Jesus Christ is perceived and identified in a much more engaging manner as a liberator, mother and worker; he is actively involved in their struggle as women, mothers and workers for liberation and wholeness.

Teresa M. Hinga offers four popular liberating images of Jesus from an African perspective.[371] First, Jesus Christ is perceived as an empowering friend and savior who values the lives of men and women equally. Second, the image of Christ is the embodiment of the spirit who is always there with them, speaking for the voiceless and the weak. Third, Jesus is envisioned as the prophet who subverts existing power relations and challenges the status quo. And the fourth understanding is Jesus as the healer. Anne Nasimiyu-Wesike explains the holistic view of African feminist Christology:

---

367 Pui-lan, *Postcolonial Imagination,* 152.

368 Chung Hyun Kyung, *Struggle to be the Sun Again: Introducing Asian Women's Theology* (Maryknoll: Orbis Books, 1990),

369 Teresa M. Hinga, "Jesus Christ and the liberation of Women," in Mercy Amba Oduyoye and Musimbi R. A. Kanyoro. ed., *The Will to Arise: Women, Tradition, and the Church in Africa* (Maryknoll: Orbis Books, 1992), 187.

370 Chung Hyun Kyung, *Struggle to be the Sun Again,* 53-73.

371 Hinga, "Jesus Christ and the Liberation of Women," 190-191.

> The African woman's experience calls for a Christology that is based on a holistic view of life. She needs the Christ who reflects the whole of her life, whose presence is felt in every corner of the village and who participates in everything and everybody's daily life. This God, the Christ, is the one who takes on the conditions of the African woman – the conditions of weakness, misery, injustice, and oppression.[372]

Latin American feminists, like their counterparts in Asia and Africa, take seriously their own experiences and context. Thus their christological reflections are informed and shaped by their experiences and realities. In "Women and Christology,"[373] Nelly Ritchie has reflected on images of Jesus in the Latin American context and identified the following images: Jesus as the Christ of life, Christ of grace, the Liberator Christ, and the Christ of the Kingdom. The words of Elsa Tamez, also a Latin American feminist theologian, sum up very well Latin American women's Christological views:

> We searched for ways to assist with the birth of the Christ child among us, among Latin Americans. This Son, whose father is the God of Life, is dedicated to saving the world, liberating men and women, and building a new way for human beings to live with each other in justice, love, peace, and freedom."[374]

Christology and Naga-Indigenous Theology

It should now be clear that an appreciation of Christological traditions and approaches as distinct and historical products of culture provides a broader perspective from which to formulate a Naga-Indigenous Christology. Although brief, the preceding discussion of particular Christologies demonstrates that understandings of Jesus Christ are of necessity contextual; that is, every tradition is influenced by its particular cultural milieu and conditioned by time and space. Indeed all Christological formulations intent to interpret the significance of Jesus Christ in a specific historical situation. It should also be clear that a community's reliance on certain culturally specific resources and philosophies means that each Christology is intrinsically limited, because, what is relevant and meaningful to one particular group of people in one particular historical setting is not likely to be relevant to people in another culture and/or context.

Regarding the classical Christologies we examined, again briefly, within the three broad trajectories – cosmic, anthropological, and political – I have

---

[372] Anne Nasimiyu-Wasike, "Christology and an African Woman's Experience," in Robert J. Schreiter, ed., *Faces of Jesus in Africa,* 77.

[373] Nelly Ritchie, "Women and Christology," in Elsa Tamez, ed., *Through Her Eyes: Women's Theology from Latin America* (Maryknoll: Orbis Books, 1989), 85-95.

[374] Tamez, "Introduction: The Power of the Naked," in *Through Her Eyes,* 2.

illuminated how Christologies of early Christians were developed and shaped. The Christological debates revolved around the nature, substance, and personhood of Jesus and his relation to the "Father" according primarily to Greek philosophical concepts as these were pertinent to the challenges Christians faced at the time. Our survey of contemporary Christologies, beginning with the postmodern, showed they were heavily biased by Western philosophical influences which espouse little if any relevance for Christians outside of the Euro-american World. The emergence of liberation theology over the past forty years has opened a very useful space for conceiving of and doing theology and Christology from the perspective of those whose history and culture have been denied. Nonetheless, as I noted above, a large percentage of the liberation theologies and Christologies are not themselves applicable to the experiences and cultures of the Indigenous peoples. My interest in formulating a Naga-Indigenous Christology stems from observing and experiencing the pain caused by the fragmentation and disintegration of the cultural fabric of the Naga people. I believe the identity crisis which spawned the calamitous situation that now exists for the Naga people can be improved considerably if they are offered an accessible and relevant Christology.

The Naga-Indigenous Christology I articulate must likewise be informed by the socio-economic and a political context of a people who have struggled and suffered under the oppressive colonial domination of India. A relevant Naga-Indigenous Christology will therefore require the retrieval and rehabilitation of certain enduring traditions and cultural values of the Naga people and this task will be the focus of the following chapters, the result being a vision of the future which liberates and empowers the Naga people.

Chapter 4

Methodological Issues of Indigenous Theology Sources of Indigenous Christology

I have, in the preceding chapter, provided a general overview of the various Christological traditions in the history of culture as a way of locating Naga-Indigenous Christology in the existing bodies of Christological discourse. I have also engaged in critiquing those various Christologies in the light of the experience of the Indigenous peoples. In this chapter I will address the most important methodological issues concerning Indigenous theology. I will begin by situating Indigenous theology within the wider context of postcolonial discourse and informed by its discourse I will theorize the whole category of Indigenous situation/theology. I will also discuss the various models of contextual theology in my efforts to establish an appropriate methodology for Naga-Indigenous theology. Then I will delineate and analyze its sources consisting of past cultural and religious traditions and values, myths and folktales, people's history, and contemporary experiences of the Naga society.

Postcolonial, Postcolonialism, and Postcolonial Theory

Defining Postcolonialism

The term "postcolonial" is widely used and recognized in contemporary academic discourse. Initially the term referred to the political and economic reconfigurations occurring worldwide as former colonies gained their independence in the years following the Second World War. With more use the definition gained prominence and scope to the extent that, "it has become increasingly a fundamental universal category along with race, and class, and caste, and age, and gender."[375] According to Sugirtharajah, when postcolonial is

---

[375] R. S. Sugirtharajah, *Postcolonial Reconfigurations: An Alternative Way of Reading the Bible and Doing Theology* (St. Louis: Chalice Press, 2003), 4.

considered in its broadest sense it conveys three meanings.[376] First, historically the term signifies the social, political and economic conditions of the contemporary world while at the same time distinguishing them from the colonial situations. Secondly, the term refers to the critical discursive enterprise geared toward critical analysis of texts and societies, engages in assessing the totalizing forms of dominant Eurocentric theories and knowledge, and offers viable alternatives to the dominant Western constructs and discourse. "It provides openings for oppositional readings, uncovers suppressed voices, and more prominently, has as its foremost concern victims and their plights."[377] Thirdly, postcolonial signifies in a way the political and ideological stance of the people engaged in anti-colonial and anti-globalizing theory and reflection. In sum it is a resistance discourse.

Postcolonial literatures began to appear as early as late1940s in the works of Franzt Fanon,[378] Albert Memmi,[379] Aime Cesaire[380] and others but, the writings were conveniently subsumed under the category of "Commonwealth Literature." "Commonwealth literature" was a term literary critics began to use from the 1950s to describe literature in English emerging from a selection of countries with a history of colonialism."[381] However, by the 1980s, the term 'commonwealth' was losing currency and was being replaced by "cultural studies"[382] and "postcolonial;"[383] and by the 1990s the use of "postcolonialism" became quite popular and it has been increasingly employed to signify both the categories and methods of such writings. Contemporary postcolonial thinking has moved to a different level from having been first conceived as a pedagogical tool to the status of advancing particular theoretical concepts. It was later in the 1980s and 1990s that cultural critics such as Edward Said, Gayatri Chakravorty Spivak and Homi Bhabha "gave postcolonialism its theorization and practice."[384] While each works

---

[376] R. S. Sugirtharajah, *Postcolonial Reconfigurations: An Alternative Way of Reading the Bible and Doing Theology* (St. Louis: Chalice Press, 2003), 4.

[377] Ibid.

[378] Franz Fanon, *The Wretched of the Earth* (New York: Grove Press, 1963); *Black Skin White Mask* (New York: Grove Press, 1967, first published in French in 1948).

[379] Albert Memmi, *The Colonizer and the Colonized* (Boston: Beacon Press Book, 1967, first published in French in 1956).

[380] Aime Cesaire, *Discourse on Colonialism,* trans. P. Joan (New York: Monthly Review Press, 1972, first published in French in around 1952).

[381] John Macleod, *Beginning Postcolonialism* (Manchester and New York: Manchester University Press, 2000), 10.

[382] Stuart Hall, a Jamaican scholar was one of the firsts to designate the writings of the formerly colonized in his notion of "cultural studies." For a detailed discussion on the origin of Cultural Studies refer to Stuart Hall, "The Emergence of Cultural Studies and the Crisis of Humanities," in October 53 (Summer, 1990), 11-23.

[383] Postcolonial was a designation first adopted by a cadre of scholars in India.

[384] Sugirtharajah, *Postcolonial Reconfiguration,* 14.

from distinct site, and each employs different philosophical categories, they have a common objective in their approach which is "to investigate and expose the link between knowledge and power" in the literary works of the West. According to Sugirtharajah in the works of Said, Spivak, and Bhabha two separate uses emerge regarding postcolonialism; Said and Spivak apply it as a reading strategy and Bhabha conceives postcoloniality a state of being.[385]

One of the changes which has emerged in the course of postcolonial thinking is that today postcolonialism is not so much about marking the contrast between the colonizer and the colonized, as it is focused on the interrelationship of the two. In other words, the traditional binary reading which holds things in strict essentialist and oppositional ways of thinking, such as: colonizer-colonized, East-West, and civilized-primitive has now given way to "a radical syncretizing of each opposition."[386] It is now understood that the colonizer and the colonized are intimately interconnected so that in the process of decolonization both parties experience moments of liberation and re-evaluation of the nature of their relationship.

Said calls this shift to postcolonial hermeneutical thinking "contrapuntal reading," by which he means "we . . . re-read it not univocally but contrapuntally, with a simultaneous awareness both of the metropolitan history that is narrated and of those other histories against which (and beyond which) the dominating discourse acts."[387] Reading contrapuntally means that we read by juxtaposing the histories of both the metropolitan and the subaltern, rather than considering them mutually exclusive contexts. The effect of such contrapuntal reading, or postcolonial hermeneutic, can be liberation. In the words of Samia Mehrez,

> For both parties it must be a process of liberation: from dependency, in the case of the colonized, and from imperialist, racist perceptions, representations, and institutions which, unfortunately, remain with us till this very day, in the case of the colonizer.[388]

Postcolonial Imagination and Naga Situation

There is debate on the appropriateness of describing the contemporary situation as "postcolonial" in which critics argue that the political independence of the former colonies did not in most cases mean a complete break with the colonizing country. Even though the physical aspects of colonial rule have disappeared, the values and ways of thinking of colonialism are apparent to this day. Stuart Hall in his essay, "When Was 'the Post-Colonial?': Thinking at the Limit," argues that the relationship between colonialism and postcolonialism is much more complex

---

[385] Sugirtharajah, *Postcolonial Reconfiguration,* 15.

[386] Of course, Fanon and Memmi were already employing this method in their work.

[387] Edward Said, *Culture and Imperialism* (New York: Vintage Book, 1993), 59.

[388] Quoted in Sugirtharajah, *Postcolonial Reconfigurations,* 16.

and intricate than it is assumed to be because the condition of post-independence in many ways "is characterized by the persistence of many of the effects of colonization."[389] Regrettably, the contemporary life situation continues to revolve around colonial ways of knowing and colonial agency continues to operate.[390] These arguments beg the question: Just how free are these so-called countries independent nations? A significant number of nations/countries/peoples are still living in a "colonial situation." Numerous peoples, especially Indigenous peoples around the world are continuously subjected to the impositions, machinations, and oppressions of colonial power, and for these peoples it would be unconscionable to even suggest that they are free.

Criticism has also come from scholars who claim postcolonial discourse to be just another invention of western academic discipline.[391] One point they note is that, the well known postcolonial theorists, Spivak, Bhabha and Said may have come from colonized nations, they all migrated to the West and their academic accomplishments are steeped in the dominant Western paradigms. Also of concern is the critics' indictment of the postcolonial theorists on grounds that they ignore the problems and concerns of neo-colonialism.[392] It is argued that postcolonial theory is not capable of dealing with the class issues exacerbated by neocolonialism.

John McLeod has attempted to strike a balance for this problematic relationship between colonialism and postcolonialism.

> "Postcolonialism" recognizes both historical continuity and change. On the one hand, it acknowledges that the material realities and modes of representation common to colonialism are still very much with us . . . . But on the other hand, it asserts the promise, the possibility, and the continuing necessity of change, while also recognizing that important challenges and changes have been achieved.[393]

---

[389] Stuart Hall, "When was 'the Post-Colonial?' Thinking at the Limit," in Iain Chambers and Lidia Curti, ed., *Postcolonial Question: Common Skies, Divided Horizons* (London: Routledge, 1996), 248.

[390] For contemporary situation of hegemony refer to Noam Chomsky, *Hegemony or Survival: America's Quest for Global Dominance Global Dominance* (New York: Henry Holt and Company, 2003); Ward Churchill, *Acts of Rebellion: The Ward Churchill Reader* (New York: Routledge, 2003); Arundhati Roy, *An Ordinary Person's Guide to Empire* (Cambridge: South end Press, 2004); Lise Noël, *Intolerance: A General Survey,* trans. Arnold Bennett (Montreal & Kingston: McGill-Queen's University Press, 1994).

[391] Meenakshi Mukherjee, "Interrogating Postcolonialism," in Harris Trivedi and Meenakshi Mukherjee, ed., *Interrogating Postcolonialism: Theory, Text and Context* (Delhi: Indian Institute of Advanced Studies, 1996), 3-11.

[392] Arif Dirlik, "The Postcolonial Aura: Third World Criticism in the Age of Global Capitalism," in *Critical Inquiry* 20, 1994, 328-356.

[393] McLeod, *Beginning Postcolonialism,* 33.

Speaking now to the Naga situation, the issue of postcolonialism is particularly complex and complicated given the fact that the Nagas have been subjected by multiple colonizations. When the Nagas declared their independence from British rule in 14 August, 1947, it was only to discover that they would have a new colonizer, India. To this day, Nagas are reeling under the control of Indian colonial rules. For the Nagas, from the historical and political points of view, a postcolonial situation has not happened. Where and how then do we apply the tools of postcolonial discourse to analyze the Naga situation? Put another way; do we even want to employ postcolonial hermeneutics to understand the Naga situation? Indeed it can be of use.

Although, the Naga situation cannot be properly described as a postcolonial moment, postcolonial theory can be very useful in unraveling and understanding the political situation of the Nagas. With the passage of time the colonial situation in Nagaland has evolved and taken a more complicated and nuanced character which in certain ways provides postcolonial moments. It is for this reason the methods of postcolonial studies offer significant tools to deal with the Naga problem. In addition this hermeneutic has discursive and heuristic values to facilitate constructing the identity of the Nagas as a people. This issue will be dealt in detail in the following discussion of postcolonial identity, hybridity, and the Nagas.

Postcolonialism: Identity, Hybridity, and the Nagas

The postcolonial situation is generally characterized by "in-between spaces" as opposed to binary oppositions and likewise postcolonial identity can be recognized by its hybridized identity. Historically, this hybridized identity is a natural by-product of colonialism. According to Bill Aschroft:

> Hybridity occurs in post-colonial societies both as a result of conscious moments of cultural suppression, as when the colonial power invades to consolidate political and economic control, or when settler-invaders dispossess indigenous peoples and force them to 'assimilate' to new social patterns.[394]

Generally speaking, hybridity is a process that normally occurs when two or more communities of differing cultures come into contact and live side by side for a period of generations.

In the *Location of Culture,* Bhabha defines postcolonial identity as situated on the border, "in-between" spaces, and in the landscapes of migration and diaspora. In Bhabha's thinking "beyond" and "border" serve as crucial discursive keys to understanding postcolonial identity. While "beyond" is an in-between

---

[394] Bill Aschroft, Gareth Griffiths, and Helen Tiffin, ed., *The Post-Colonial Studies Reader* (London: Routledge, 1995), 183.

site of transition, the border is the place of possibility and agency for new ideas. "The 'beyond' is neither a new horizon, nor a leaving behind of the past…we find ourselves in the moment of transit where space and time cross to produce complex figures of difference and identity past and present, inside and outside, inclusion and exclusion."[395] Bhabha sees identity as a discursive product. He is opposed to idea of sovereign or essentialized subjectivity and maintains that identity can be and is remade and remodeled; accordingly, postcolonial identity is constantly remodeled and reconfigured. People who live at the border or on the edge/margin therefore must constantly remake their group and communal identities. Bhabha notes that, "The imaginative crossings at the 'beyond' offer ways of thinking about communal identity that depart from older ideas, such as the 'deep horizontal comradeship' of the nation which can fall foul of the binary logic of same/different, inside/outside, citizen/stranger."[396]

As stated above, Bhabha's contribution to the concept of postcolonial identity has also come under criticism for its totalizing conceptions of postcolonial identity. While, Bhabha's understanding of identity as being situated in the border and in-between spaces is certainly helpful in understanding the postcolonial condition, not every people or nation who has experienced colonization should be thrown together under the totalizing representation of migration and diaspora. Bhabha has also been criticized for not giving sufficient consideration to the historical specifics in his works.[397]

Hybridization is simultaneously the result and cause of complex problems in the ethnic and racial composition of the once colonized natives in their contemporary existence as communities. These complex problems are further compounded by the perpetual never-ending exodus of the people from traditional homelands to ever growing towns and cities where they become just lost in the sea of poverty, desperately attempting to chart their way along. In a number of his writings, George E. "Tink" Tinker grapples with the issues and problems of hybridization among the American Indian communities.[398] He eloquently describes the experience with the identities faced by American Indians in this "postmodern moment of miscegenation, immigration, urbanization and diasporaization."

> A lasting result of five hundred years of colonialism and conquest, of intentional and persistent church and colonial government policy, is the continued dilution of Indian blood, a phenomenon referred to as

---

[395] Homi Bhabha, *The Location of Culture* (London and New York: Routledge, 1994), 1.

[396] McLeod, *Beginning Postcolonialism,* 218.

[397] Ibid., 221-222.

[398] George E. Tinker, *Spirit and Resistance: Political Theology and American Liberation* (Minneapolis: Fortress Press, 2004); "Lost Bloods: Biological Claims to Indianness in the Postcolonial Conquest," TMs.

> "mixed blood," which has infused Indian communities with colonial religion and colonial culture in general. The contemporary result is a confusing plethora of questions. Who is Indian today? How can we validate claims to "tribal" blood? Can one be "Indian" and "Christian"? . . . . Who is a member of any Indian national community ("tribe")? Does one have to be a "member" of a "tribe" in order to be Indian? How is membership determined and who determines it?[399]

Recognizing the enormity of the challenge and the complexities of the problems, Tinker proceeds to address the issues theoretically and practically by noting first that although blood is an essential category that alone is not sufficient to determine the identity of the Indian person. Instead, he proposes cultural competence to be a "much more important indicator" for determining the Indian Identity. Tinker states:

> By culturally competent here I mean where the traditional culture continues to be lived in some consistent trajectory of development from the ancient national community's aboriginal existence. Cultural competency is a term I created ... to help us come a little closer to understanding what 'Indian' means in this postmodern and so called postcolonial world of confusion and uncertainty.[400]

In making his case for cultural competence as a litmus test for determining the Indian identity Tinker acknowledges that the complex problems of cultural hybridity can never be completely and satisfactorily dealt with. He perceives more complications in cultural competency itself and concedes that, "It is a battle we are regularly losing as our children find their places in the gang infested landscape of America's end of the millennium cities - assimilated into the mainstream of America's urban communities of color and poverty."[401]

Although Tinker's focus is the identity crisis among American Indians, the problems he addresses are certainly not unique to American Indians but are in many ways true for many other formerly colonized people in communities around the world. The problems of identity– ethnic, cultural, religious, social and political – also confront Indigenous peoples in Africa, Asia and Latin America where they are simply overwhelmed by the enormously powerful forces of a dominant Western culture and its values. Most Indigenous peoples are driven to the cross-roads where identity and survival intersect. The reality is that their

---

[399] Tinker, *Spirit and Resistance,* 37.

[400] Tinker, "Lost Bloods," 3. In his *Sprit and Resistance,* Tinker identifies a number of specific tests that can be considered factors for determining Indian cultural competence. 43ff.

[401] Tinker, *Spirit and Resistance,* 47.

present and future existence are predicated on and conditioned by the problems of identity that besiege them.

It is not surprising then that there are certain striking similarities between the American Indian experiences of new and mutable identities and those of the Naga people. Both American Indians and Nagas still struggle under the heel of colonial powers and both are fighting for their political freedom. The Naga nation is composed of a number of tribes and sub-tribes with distinctive cultures, dialects, and languages as are American Indians, but irrespective of their tribal differences they all understand and acknowledge common history as a people.

Now, having identified some similarities, there are problems that can be considered unique to the Nagas. The Nagas too suffer from multiple identity crises but with a distinct difference. The Nagas, unlike most other Indigenous peoples, continue to live on and remain the sole custodians of their ancestral homelands.[402] The situation with which they must deal is the result of the tangle of two influences, the Indian state and the Indian nation. On the national level Nagas are identified as Indians because they are politically under Indian control, which is not a little ironic because many Indians do not even know where Nagaland is and who the Nagas are; indeed, very often Nagas are regarded as "foreigners" by most Indians. At the state level, Nagas have been divided up and grouped together with other states where they are reduced to minority status as a consequence of the infamous divide and conquer policy of British and Indian governments. Consequently, Nagas are identified by and with the name of a state to which they are a part. For example, apart from Nagaland state, Naga populations are found in adjoining states such as Manipur, Assam, and Arunachal Pradesh and a third of Nagas live across the border in Myanmar. The Nagas of Manipur are thus known as Manipuries by state imposition and it is the same case with the Nagas in the other states and those in Myanmar.

Also, while American Indian tribal identity has often been based on certain blood quantum, the Nagas' tribal identity is seldom questioned or challenged. This is true even for those whose blood is mixed due to inter-marriage. As it is with all Indigenous people around the world, Nagas are increasingly becoming integrated with non-Nagas and particularly with Indians. There are Indian businesses in Naga towns, there are laborers from all over India, there are immigrants and refugees from Bangladesh, and there is also a large Nepali population.[403]

Liberation Theology and its Limit

The emergence of liberation theology in the aftermath of colonialism, that is, in the postcolonial context provided a new opportunity for doing theology outside of

[402] Except for the migration of Indian people and refugees from Bangladesh and settling in Naga territory, especially in towns and cities.

[403] Intermarriages are happening at all levels of the Naga social stratum. In many cases, the men who are married to Naga women are co-opted into the family clan or tribe of the bride.

the decadent monolith traditional theology had become. The theme of liberation came alive in theological discourse and it reverberated across all the continents including the Euroamerican world. The focus of the theological task shifted from orthodoxy to orthopraxis, where practice and reflection, action and faith were conceived as dialogical movement rather than a movement *from* faith to action, and *from* theory to practice.

Indeed, liberation theology began to unravel and expose the multiple forms of oppression coinciding the issues of economic, social, and racial injustice in the world, especially in the so-called Third World countries. A number of diverse theologies emerged and developed within the particularities of identity and context resulting in liberation theologies in Latin America, Asia, and Africa. Also Black theology, Feminist theologies, and Womanist theology; each of these was rooted in the lived particularities of context and identity.

However, by mid 80s, despite its ostensible diversities liberation theology had become just another monolithic movement predicated and dependent on ideologies of binary opposition and a Marxist class analysis. Within a few short years, the limits of this simplistic essentializing methodology became apparent. Catherine Keller spells out the problems of liberation theology thus:

> … early liberation movements did not face: the oppressive dynamics internal to oppressed communities; the ambiguous and shifting complexities of national, cultural, even sexual identities; and the difficulties of creating sustainable coalitions – including coalitions with progressives who do not embody a specifically oppressed identity."[404]

Particularly problematic was the reliance on a Marxist critique, focused on the lone category of the oppressed revolting against the oppressive, which is after all a Euro-western construction, because its analysis is far too narrow for addressing the "complexities of postmodern power structures."

The postcolonial situation is a complex one and its complexities are manifested in myriad forms and locations. An enduring problem which continues to confront liberation theology is how to address the forces of oppression. In her book *Indecent Theology*, Latin American feminist theologian Marcella Althaus-Reid explains the very complex nature of oppression:

> Oppression is perhaps what we cannot have in common, because oppression is built in overlapping levels of multiple and contradictory elements which, according to context, produce variably dense, saturated effects…. Any theology concerned with issues of wealth and

[404] Catherine Keller, Michael Nausner, and Mayra Rivera, "Introduction" in Catherine Keller, Michael Nausner, and Mayra Rivera, eds, *Post Colonial Theologies: Divinity and Empire* (St. Louis: Chalice Press, 2004), 5; Cf. Elina Vuola, *Limits of Liberation: Feminist Theology and the Ethics of Poverty and Redemption* (London: Sheffield Academic Press, 2002), 3f.

> poverty needs to consider more the incoherence of oppression and its multiple dimensions rather than its commonalities."[405]

Liberation and Inculturation

One of the main criticisms of liberation theology centers around its failure to take the cultures and traditions of the people seriously. Liberation and inculturation have been treated as two separate concerns or realities and therefore have failed to see the important connections between the two. While liberation theology emphasizes on the socio-economic and political liberation of the people, theology of inculturation tend to focus on the religious and cultural dimensions. The relationship that has existed between liberation and inculturation has been ignored in most theologies whether it be liberation or traditional theologies of the West. Expressing his obvious frustration with this artificial distinction between liberation and inculturation, Aloysius Pieris laments that:

> At the EATWOT Asian consultation in 1979, I tried to forestall this futile debate by avoiding the liberation/inculturation schema and by defining theology as discovery rather than an invention - that is, as a Christian participation in and a Christic explicitation of all that happens at the deepest zone of a concrete ethos wherein religiosity, poverty, each in its liberative dimension, coalesce to forge a common front against mammon, the anti-God.[406]

Tinker holds liberation theology accountable for its failure to take into consideration Indigenous peoples' cultures and religious traditions despite the large and in some countries its the majority, Indigenous population in Latin America where, ironically liberation theology was born. "The problem with modern liberation theology, as with marxist political movements, is that class analysis gets in the way of recognizing cultural discreteness and even peopleness."[407] The problem with such a narrow theological enterprise is that it treats people's socio-economic problems as distinct from their cultural life as though the two are not related. The truth is that it is inconceivable to expect political liberation without cultural liberation. Any theology that maintains such a dichotomy is doomed to inadequacy and failure. Affirming the intrinsic connections between liberation and culture from African perspective, Emmanuel Martey asserts that:

---

[405] Marcella Althaus-Reid, *Indecent Theology: Theological Perversions in Sex, Gender and Politics* (New York: Routledge, 2000), 168f.

[406] Aloysius Pieris, "The Place of Non-Christian Religions and Cultures in the Evolution of Third World Theology" in Virginia Fabella and Sergio Torres, ed. *Irruption of the Third World: Challenges to Theology*: Papers from the Fifth International Conference of the Ecumenical Association of the Third World Theologians, August 17-29, 1981, New Delhi, India (Maryknoll: Orbis Books, 1983), 114.

[407] Tinker, *Spirit and Resistance,* 104.

> The foundation of a people's liberation...is in their inalienable rights to have their own history whose continuity lies in culture. That is why in Africa, liberation is necessarily an act of culture; and, the liberation movement in Africa is seen by theorists and analysts as "the organized political expression of the struggling people's culture."[408]

Indigenous theology comes as a corrective to the theologies which fail to account for culture and thereby ignore the natural and necessary interrelationship of liberation and culture. Indigenous theology makes no such distinction; rather, it takes seriously both political liberation and cultural liberation and the critical link between the two.

Indigenous Theology: Methodological Consideration

Models of Contextual Theology

For a theology to be authentic it must be grounded in certain methodological assumptions; additionally, every theology has characteristic features which constitute its very nature. While some theologies are naturally dogmatic and apologetic, those such as liberation theology place the emphasis on praxis. Indigenous theology is the latter and, as a contextual theology, is rooted in the historical and cultural reality of the people. In my project to determine the appropriate methodology for Indigenous theology it will be helpful to discuss the extent models of contextual theology.

Using the work of Stephen B. Bevans,[409] as his starting point, K. Thanzauva has identified and explicated six different models which are present in Indigenous theology in Northeast India. These models are transplantation, fulfillment, translation, dialogical, synthesis and praxis.[410] Transplantation and fulfillment models account for context by marking the literal transportation of the gospel message from one place to another, particularly as this was done by missionaries from the Christian West to the non- Christian world, without making any adjustment or change to acknowledge differences in language and culture. The gospel message is proclaimed using the West's epistemological categories and is draped in the cultural garb of the Western Christianity as the "Truth" for all people everywhere. The proponents of these two models hold the native cultures and traditions in the utmost disdain and contempt and believe they must be condemned as demonic and evil. The early Christian missionaries embodied these models and, unfortunately, their powerful influence on the susceptible

---

[408] Emmanuel Martey, "Theology and Liberation: The African Agenda," in *Voices from the Third World,* vol. 28, no. 1 (June 2005), 44.

[409] Stephen B. Bevans, *Models of Contextual Theology*, revised and expanded edition (Maryknoll: Orbis Books, 2002).

[410] K. Thanzauva, *Theology of Community: Tribal Theology in the Making* (Aizawl: Mizo Theological Conference, 1997), 54-88.

tribals means that to this day most Christians in Northeast India subscribe to these models. Naga Christians have been convinced that their own traditional culture and values are antithetical to authentic Christian faith. Even those who acknowledge that traditional culture is both valid and efficacious insist that Christ is above all cultures, therefore, only Christ has the means and ways to fulfill the people's needs and aspirations. The four remaining models described by Thanzauva are not as blatantly antagonistic of the traditional culture and values

Proponents of the translation model recognize the positive nature of Indigenous cultures and traditions; on the contrary, they are in fact disposed to using Indigenous cultural metaphors and images to facilitate translation of the gospel message to the native languages. This method could be manifest as a literalistic, word-for-word translation, or it could take a functional and dynamic form. The functional translation looks for the dynamic equivalence rather than the literal meaning of the original word. The underlying assumption of this model is that, "Christianity contains an essential element, a supra-cultural message which can be separated from a culturally bound mode of expression."[411] In other words, the essence of the gospel cannot be altered but must be translated in a way that is meaningful to the reader or listener. This model, in addition to transplantation and fulfillment models, is being widely applied in Northeast India. Although the translation model requires the gospel message be made linguistically meaningful to the listener/reader, it ignores the actual cultural context within which the translation will be learned thereby precluding all critical interaction between the gospel message and the people's experience. Two noted adherents of this model are Renthy Keitzar and Zairema.[412]

The dialogical model, which is primarily a contribution of the Asian theologians,[413] recognizes the importance of dialogue between or among more cultures in order to find common ground in matters of faith. Put another way, the relative validity of every culture is presumed as is the necessity for mutual enrichment through dialogue. Indeed, the dialogical model recognizes the compatibility of every culture with Christian faith including the cultures disdained and denigrated by proponents of transplantation models. This model makes it possible to find common ground among ostensibly disparate religious groups in order to promote harmonious and peaceful co-existence. Now, the dialogical model is good as far as it goes, however, it falls short in at least two ways: First is its failure to challenge the existing social and economic inequalities in the society, and second, it shies away from addressing the core issues of the respective beliefs.

---

411 K. Thanzauva, *Theology of Community: Tribal Theology in the Making* (Aizawl: Mizo Theological Conference, 1997), 67.

412 Both Renthy Keitzar and Zairema are known for their works on indigenizing the gospel message in Northeast Indian context.

413 Some of the well known proponents of dialogical methods are Stanley J. Smartha, M. M. Thomas, S. Wesley Ariarajah, Raimundo Pannikar, and Aloysius Pieris.

The synthetic model focuses on synthesizing two or more cultures, particularly Christian traditions and cultures and the traditions of the Indigenous peoples from which a new form of Christian expression or theology emerges.[414] In other words, there is a fusion of two or more traditions resulting in the formation of a new theology or faith expression. As with the dialogical model this model recognizes the inherent goodness of culture and it allows for critical interaction between Christian tradition and Indigenous people's cultures and traditions. It takes very seriously the cultural context of the people in the formulation of a relevant faith expression and also allows for the critical interaction with other contexts and differing theological expressions. "This model is synthetic in the Hegelian sense of not just attempting to put things together in a compromise but of developing, in a creative dialectic, something that is acceptable to all standpoints."[415] In Northeast India, this synthetic interaction is occurring in the fusion of Western and traditional music, it has yet to be a dominant factor in theological expression.

The last of the six models is the praxis model which refers to the contextual character of liberation theology and the emphasis on the action-reflection method of doing theology. The praxis model presumes the significance inherent in the socio-economic, political and spiritual contexts. Jon Sobrino rightly states that the praxis model "in its most profound sense is understood as the unity of knowledge as activity and knowledge as content."[416] This model is based on the conviction that, "Truth is at the level of history, not in the realm of ideas"[417] and is concerned with social transformation and liberation in the light of the Kingdom's values.

The six models of contextual theology we have examined outline a range of possible approaches to employ in our theological formulation. While some theologians opt to rely on one specific, others have found it most beneficial to combine models; in fact, there are instances in which models overlap one another. After his search for a relevant method or methods for the formulation of theology in Northeast India Thanzauva has proposed a combination of the synthetic and praxis models which he refers to simply as the synthetic-praxis model.[418] He argues that this method is appropriate in a context like northeast India where marginalization, discrimination and social injustice as well as cultural alienation of the people are rampant and endemic. While the synthetic model emphasizes the cultural identity of the people, the praxis model facilitates the social and economic transformation of the people. Thanzauva further states that

[414] K. Thanzauva, *Theology of Community*, 74-77; cf. K. P. Aleaz, "Gospel and Culture: Some Indian Reflection," in *Indian Journal of Theology* 36, no. 2 (1999), 64-79;

[415] Bevans, *Models of Contextual Theology*, 90.

[416] Quoted in Bevans, *Models of Contextual Theology*, 72.

[417] José Miguez Bonino, *Doing Theology in a Revolutionary Situation* (Philadelphia: Fortress Press, 1975), 72.

[418] Thanzauva, *Theology of Community*, 84-88.

employing the synthetic-praxis method allows for the much needed critique of the interaction between Christianity and tribal culture, a social analysis of and reflection about the people's struggle, and the reclamation of past culture and values.[419]

This synthetic-praxis method Thanzauva proposes is without question a viable model that can be applied in the construction of Naga-Indigenous theology for three reasons. First it takes seriously people's cultures and their distinct socio-economic and political contexts. Second it allows for critical interaction between Christian traditions and the Naga people's cultures and values that results in a new form of Christian expression of faith and theology. And third it requires reclaiming past cultural traditions and values. Now having noted the positive aspects, I would be remiss if I neglected to identify two of the model's shortcomings. One problem is that it assumes that Indigenous cultures are essentially identical, failing to recognize the diversity that exists among Indigenous communities. Second, it fails to recognize the "differentiated complexities" which are the consequence of the hybridity that is contemporary Indigenous peoples' reality. While the synthetic-praxis model is critically important for articulating an Indigenous theology, it will benefit considerably with the additional clarity provided by a postcolonial theory of difference for a result that is a fuller and more empowering treatment of Indigenous theology.

Indigenous Theology as Postcolonial Theology: A Further Discourse on Methodology

According to Mark L. Taylor, the ethos of postcolonial theology is defined by the combination of the discourse of difference and the discourse of liberating struggle, what he calls it "differentiated liberating struggle."[420] It is "differentiated" because of the fluid and hybrid nature of the postcolonial situation and a "liberating struggle" because of its commitment to liberation from colonizing powers and agents. "In this ethos" Taylor writes, "the discourses of difference are taken up as intrinsic to, facilitative of, liberating struggle."[421] In this sense, a postcolonial ethos exists simultaneously with the ongoing anticolonialist struggles and thereby showing cognizance of the differentiated complexities.

It should now be clear that Indigenous theology is a form of postcolonial theology in that it emerges out of a people's struggles against the forces of marginalization and oppression. A successful Indigenous theology will undertake three main functions as it seeks to expose and emasculate the body of global forces which undermine the very existence of its peoples and their cultures. I will discuss

[419] Thanzauva, *Theology of Community*, 84.

[420] Mark L. Taylor, "Spirit and Liberation: Achieving Postcolonial Theology in the United States" in Catherine Keller, Michael Nausner, and Mayra Rivera, ed., *Postcolonial Theologies: Divinity and Empire* (St. Louis: Chalice Press, 2004), 46.

[421] Ibid.

these elements in no particular order. One main concern of Naga Indigenous theology is certainly a "liberating struggle;" struggle for liberation in all its social, political, and economic contexts is a focal point of Naga Indigenous theology. Just as any other liberation theology, Naga Indigenous theology inevitably follows the method of praxis and must begin by addressing the existing conditions or situation of the people with the objective to ensure a better and healthier tomorrow. By first engaging the people's experiences of oppression, exploitation and alienations an Indigenous theology takes seriously the longings and aspirations of the people and it must also be the struggle's motivating force.

Another essential function of Naga Indigenous theology is to take seriously the history, memories, and experiences of the people. Remembering the past is critical, not merely for its own sake, but to serve as both affirmation and expectation for building and shaping the future the people want. Tinker articulates this understanding as it would apply in his own context when he states:

> An American Indian theology must be a liberation theology . . . . This American Indian theology will begin with a clear memory of how we got where we are today in order that we might begin to create a future that is healthier than our present.[422]

He goes on to explain that the process of dreaming for the future must be done following, as closely as possible, traditional Indian values and ways of thinking. "We remember the past in order to dream the future, in order to dream or imagine the future into existence, just as the Spider Woman thought the world into existence in the act of creation."[423] Naga Indigenous theology, in like manner, must reclaim their past for shaping and building a better future they want.

The third main concern of a Naga Indigenous theology is that it be equipped to recognize the "differentiated complexities" that go beyond the simplistic binary of colonizer/colonized. An Indigenous theology that is influenced by postcolonial thinking and discourse must be amenable to the fluidity and hybridity which characterize tribal existence. In other words, it must reject the West's worldview which is organized according to, "discreet and mutually exclusive categories,"[424] such as: same/other, spirit/matter, subject/object, civilized/primitive, pure/impure, and rational/chaotic. Modern history is replete with evidence of how such binary thought pattern were manifested in the ways that the colonizer work continuously to delineate and reinforce a clear differentiation between himself and the colonized. Fortunately for projects such as Indigenous theology postcolonial

---

422 Tinker is here referring to the creation story of the American Indians. American Indians believe Spider Woman was involved in creation of the world. *Spirit and Resistance,* 4.

423 Ibid.

424 Keller, Nausner, and Rivera, "Introduction," in Keller, Nausner, Rivera, ed., *Postcolonial Theologies*, 11.

theory recognizes that things are never organized in such exclusive, rigid, and hierarchical terms. Indeed, there are nuances, in-between spaces, intersections, and psychological manipulations at work in relationships. Spivak suggests that postcolonial theory turns its "critical glance not specifically at the putative identity of the two poles of a binary opposition, but at the hidden ethico political agenda that drives the differentiation between the two."[425]

Some of the most common metaphors of postcolonial identity are the borderlands, crossroads, and frontiers and which are clearly indicative of the "interstitial" nature of identity.[426] Identity as viewed through a postcolonial lens is not a "fixed set of traits, but rather evolves through a continuing process of interrelation, identification and differentiation. A person's identity is formed as she or he negotiates a sense of belonging to some groups and being distanced from others."[427] For over fifty seven years now Nagas have been struggling to negotiate their identity as a people over against that which is imposed on them by India. Their search for their own identity is conducted in the midst of their struggle for political sovereignty on the one hand, and religious and cultural selfhood on the other.

Still postcolonial theorists continue to employ terms that constitute collective identity for a group of people, a race or an ethnicity. There are numerous examples such as Latin American, Asian, African, Feminists, American, the poor which continue to be used in spite of the fact that there are clearly few if any "pure" ethnic/racial groups or cultures any where anymore. In reference to Asia, Kwok Pui-lan argues that the use of "Asian" does not necessarily mean an essentialized notion of Asia since Asia is constitutive of multiracial and multicultural groups.[428] There are some who would argue there is no such thing as "Asia." In this sense "Asian" serves heuristic and discursive role to group together all aspects of Asian people and their cultures. It signifies that there is some sort of collective consciousness of the Asian people. Further more, Asian culture is not monolithic, it is multifaceted and stratified and hence the use of "Asian" must be seen as a discursive and political construct.

Sugirtharajah makes the following observation regarding the task of theological reflection: "In the postcolonial context Christian theological reflection needs to take on board not an imagined homogeneity but a plurality of identities and coalescing of cultures."[429] In a similar manner and in order to be relevant, Naga Indigenous theology must take into serious consideration the plurality of

[425] Gayatri Chakravorty Spivak, *Critique of Postcolonial Reasons: Toward a History of the Vanishing Present* (Cambridge: Harvard University Press, 1999), 332.

[426] Homi Bhabha calls such perception of identity as an "interstitial perspective" which challenges the conventional understanding of identity.

[427] Catherine Keller, et al, "Introduction," 11-12.

[428] Pui-lan, *Postcolonial Imagination,* 40.

[429] Sugirtharajah, *Postcolonial Reconfigurations,* 7.

identities and coalescing of cultures within the broad spectrum of tribal peoples. Rather than resorting to painting all the Naga peoples with one broad stroke, Naga theology should be able to accommodate and affirm the diverse and variable identities that exist within the Nagas themselves.

Reclaiming the Past: Sources of Indigenous Christology

Western Science and Indigenous Knowledge

Christianity and Western scientific knowledge have always dominated the fields of theology and academic disciplines. Non-Christian religious traditions and wisdom are very often dismissed and even ignored for theologizing and academic pursuits. In other words, the Christian tradition is considered the only valid source of theology and faith. Writing in the context of the vast, poor, and non-Christian Third World, Aloysius Pieris forcefully argues that:

> The irruption of the Third World is also the irruption of the non-Christian world. The vast majority of God's poor perceive their ultimate concern and symbolize their struggle for liberation in the idiom of non-Christian religions and cultures. Therefore, a theology that does not speak to or speak through this non-Christian peoplehood is an esoteric luxury of a Christian minority. Hence, we need a theology of religions that will expand the existing boundaries of orthodoxy as we enter into the liberative streams of other religions and cultures.[430]

Indigenous knowledge and religious traditions have largely been dismissed as unscientific and therefore invalid as a way of knowing by the Western world. Unlike the Western science, they are not objective and cannot be scientifically verified therefore they are described as superstitious, primitive and unreliable. Western science has always been regarded as the superior way of knowing. In fact, Western forms of knowledge and knowledge acquisition are considered the only valid way of knowing. Linda Tuhiwai Smith, a Maori Indigenous scholar, rightly argues that Western scholars and researchers establish the superiority of Western knowledge over the knowledge of the Indigenous peoples by simply relegating it to the periphery.[431] By doing so, the wisdom of Indigenous peoples and people of

---

[430] Aloysius Pieris, "The Place of Non-Christian Religions and Cultures in the Evolution of Third World Theology" in Virginia Fabella and Sergio Torres, ed., *The Irruption of the Third World: Challenge to International Economic Order, Challenge to Theology: Papers from the Fifth International Conference of the Ecumenical Association of Third World Theologians, August 17-29, 1981, New Delhi, India* (Maryknoll: Orbis Books, 1983), 113-114.

[431] Linda Tuhiwai Smith, *Decolonizing Methodologies: Research and Indigenous Peoples* (London and New York: Zed Books Ltd., 1999), Similarly, Jacob K. Olupona argues that Western religious scholarship by privileging "World" religions has effectively marginalized Indigenous religious traditions for years. He calls this, "Arbitrary and capricious bifurcation of religious scholarship." Jacob K. Olupona, ed., *Beyond Primitivism: Indigenous Traditions and Modernity* (New York and

color is rendered inconsequential. Indeed, Western science offers very powerful means of knowing and has brought innumerable discoveries, inventions, and improvements to the world. Western science has taken humans to moon, and to the bottom of the seas; it has produced energy for unimaginable power and medicines and machines to heal the human body.

Today we live in an age of the incessant "free" flow of information and communication and people around the world are amazed at how fast and conveniently, information are received and exchanged. Communication across all manner of borders has become much easier and faster. For all its remarkable developments and technological advancements, the claim of Western science as the only valid way of knowing becomes even more powerful.

While some might argue that Western science is more dominant than ever, there is a growing resurgence of the value of Indigenous knowledge taking place all over the world. In fact, Indigenous peoples have been honing and preserving the validity of their knowledge and their ways of knowing for centuries. However, with the imposition and expansion of Western science and its methods through the projects of European colonization, Indigenous knowledge has been effectively undermined, ignored, and in many cases obliterated. But recent attempts by Indigenous peoples around the world to reassert the importance of Indigenous knowledge have resulted in growing interest in recovering Indigenous knowledge among both Indigenous and non-Indigenous researchers and scholars. Bradley R. Howard speaks to the ongoing activism of the Indigenous peoples as follows:

> Parading down a technoconsumer superhighway into the new millennium, we are unintentional witnesses to an extraordinary event: a resurgence of activism among indigenous peoples, energetically asserting their international rights not only as individual human beings but as self-determining peoples, unique and independent cultures."[432]

The rights of the Indigenous peoples must include their claim for recognition of the validity and value of their collected knowledge and ways of knowing.

Indigenous Theology and Indigenous Resources

Theological reflection based on tribal life experiences and traditional heritage is an essential task of Indigenous theology. The Indigenous peoples are endowed with rich cultural and religious resources and, rather than condemning them as evil and demonic, every effort should be made to reclaim these resources for the

---

London: Routledge, 2004), xiv. In "White Studies: The Intellectual Imperialism of U.S. Higher Education," Ward Churchill argues primarily that the whole American "field of knowledge" is structured around a predominantly White-Euro American studies. *Since, Predators Came: Notes from the Struggles for American Indian Liberation* (Littleton: Aigis Publications, 1995), 246-264.

[432] Bradley R. Howard, *Indigenous Peoples and the State: The Struggle for Native Rights* (DeKalb: Northern Illinois University Press, 2003), 3.

purpose of theological reflection. In this search for an articulation of meaningful theology we must retrieve the cultural values that are known to be life affirming and liberating. This search will involve processes of recollection, remembering and sharing with a view to formulating a theology that will ultimately be inclusive, dialogical, liberating, and above all empowering. What follows are pointers to how our rich traditional heritages might be rediscovered for developing a relevant Indigenous theology.[433]

Traditional heritages include past and present socio-cultural traditions, customs, religious beliefs, and practices. This includes, but is not limited to, myths and legends, folktales and stories, wisdom and proverbs, mores and songs which were mostly transmitted orally from generation to generation and serve as the text of what Renthy Keitzar calls the unwritten "Prime Bible."

> These may be called the unwritten "Prime Bible" of the tribal/indigenous people. One can find in these oral traditions their beliefs, norms, and practices; hence a great and rich treasure of theological value is hidden with this "Prime Bible" of the people.[434]

Indigenous Worldviews: Basis of Indigenous Knowledge

Understanding Indigenous worldview is key to understanding Indigenous knowledge and ways of knowing. Worldviews both inform and are informed by the thinking and understanding of a people about the world and how it operates. This is of particular importance for Indigenous peoples because theirs is fundamentally different from that of Western culture. What follows is a brief but essential discussion of Indigenous worldviews. According to Gregory Cajete, an American Indian scholar:

> A worldview is a set of assumptions and beliefs that form the basis of a people's comprehension of the world. The stories, symbols, analogies, and metaphors that express a worldview in coded form are called mythology. Worldviews are conveyed via mythology in informal, art, media, economic, spiritual, governmental, and educational institutions.[435]

---

[433] Yangkahao Vashum, "Sources for Studying Tribal Theology" in A. Wati Longchar, ed. *An Exploration of Tribal Theology,* Tribal Study Series no. 1 (Jorhat: Tribal Study Center, 1997), 63-77.

[434] Renthy Keitzar, *In Search of a Relevant Gospel Message* (Guwahati: Christian Literature Center, 1995), 21. According to Jan Vansina, oral traditions are documents of the present since they are told in the present. They are also of the past since the stories told belonged to the past. Therefore, oral traditions have both the past and present dimensions simultaneously. Jan Vansina, *Oral Tradition as History* (Madison: University of Wisconsin Press, 1985), xii.

[435] Gregory Cajete, *Native Science: Natural Laws of Interdependence* (Santa Fe: Clear Light Publishers, 2000), 62.

A worldview is thus an underlying foundational principle that holds together peoples visions, orientations and thinking in life as a community. It is a foundational principle that informs and directs all aspects of a peoples' existence: how people relate to one another as well as how they interact with nature, and creation, and God(s). The worldview thus shapes and is shaped by attitude and orientation toward life and the world. Ninian Smart thinks worldviews can be maps of how to live and explains, "From one perspective different worldviews are maps of how to live. From another they themselves depict those powers in human experience and the cosmos that stir people to action."[436] Smart explains further that worldviews are comprised of belief systems and ideologies to the extent that the study of religions and ideologies can be regarded as "worldview analysis."

Indigenous worldviews can be described as the recognition of the undifferentiated unity of all things, meaning, there is no distinction drawn between the spiritual and physical, material and immaterial, sacred and profane, and spiritual and earthly. Nor does an Indigenous worldview recognize any structure of hierarchy in creation. They see the world and all its surroundings in holistic perspective. While a Western worldview is essentially anthropocentric, an Indigenous worldview is creation-centered and is characterized by understanding the interdependence and the inter-relatedness of *all* creation, including human beings. Therefore, Indigenous peoples all across the world believe that the whole of creation are our relatives. The Lakota nation of American Indians has an expression which describes beautifully all that concerns the Indigenous worldview "We are all related." According to Standing Rock Sioux scholar Vine Deloria, Jr, the similar phrase, "All my relatives" is not merely a religious sentiment which many people have supposed, but it also "describes the epistemology of the Indian worldview, providing the methodological basis for the gathering of the information about the world."[437] Deloria goes on to explain the implication of this worldview when he states:

> "We are all relatives" when taken as a methodological tool for obtaining knowledge means that we observe the natural world by looking for relationships between various things in it. That is to say, everything in the natural world has relationship with every other thing and the total set of relationships makes up the natural world as we experience it. This concept is simply the relativity concept as applied to a universe that people experience as alive and not as dead or inert.[438]

---

[436] Ninian Smart, *Worldviews: Crosscultural Exploration of Human Beliefs.* Third Edition (Upper Saddle: Prentice Hall Inc., 2000), 54.

[437] Vine Deloria, Jr, *Spirit and Reason: The Vine Deloria*, Jr., Reader, Eds. Barbara Deloria, et al (Golden: Fulcrum Publishing, 1999), 52.

[438] Vine Deloria, Jr, *Spirit and Reason: The Vine Deloria*, Jr., Reader, Eds. Barbara Deloria, et al (Golden: Fulcrum Publishing, 1999), 34.

Here then is another key characteristic which distinguishes an Indigenous worldview and its knowledge from a Western worldview and its scientific methods. In a similar vein, Leroy Little Bear observes that the Indigenous "paradigm is comprised of and includes ideas of constant motion and flux, existence consisting of energy waves, interrelationships, all things being animate, space/place, renewal, and all things being imbued with spirits."[439]

As noted above, Indigenous "peoples do not differentiate their world of experience into two realms that oppose or complement each other. They seem to maintain a consistent understanding of the unity of all experience."[440] Referring to Naga religious view, J.H. Thumra asserts that "unlike many modern Christian belief in the dichotomy of the 'sacred' and the 'secular' or the 'spiritual' and the 'material', the traditional Naga religion does not have such a dichotomy. For them the 'sacred' and the 'secular' are one."[441] In "An Emerging Asian Theology: Tribal Theology," Wati Longchar makes a useful comparison between dominant Christian worldview and traditional tribal worldview in which he underscores their differences.[442] Indigenous peoples around the world view reality in its wholeness and perceive life as one single web and many smaller webs of relationships which is the antithesis of the dominant Christian dualistic and individualistic views. Further, their cultural and religious values are governed by respect for one another and reciprocity is the norm for their day-today interactions.

The well-being of all creation including that of human beings depends upon preserving and restoring the harmonious inter-relationships of all creation. All living creatures including humans are meant to work toward maintaining balance and harmony and these are to be seen as the ultimate concern of all beings. Indigenous peoples do not believe in the superiority of humans over against the rest of creation. In fact, most Indigenous people believe, as their stories and mythologies attest, humans are thought to be at the lowest strata of creation order.[443] Arguing against the Euro-western theories of evolutionary ascendancy, Tinker asserts that:

> Rather than elevate human beings to the apex of an evolutionary ascendancy (i.e., common descent), the lack of human privileging over against these other life forms means that Indians understand that

[439] Leroy Little Bear, "Foreward", in Gregory Cajete, *Native Science.* x.

[440] Deloria, *Spirit and Reason.* 354.

[441] Jonathan H. Thumra, "The Naga Primal (Traditional) Religion and Christianity: A Theological Reflection," in V. K. Nuh, ed. *In Search of Praxis Theology for the Nagas* (New Delhi: Regency Publications, 2003), 54.

[442] For a detailed comparison see A. Wati Longchar, *An Emerging Asian Theology: Tribal Theology: Issue, Method and Perspective* (Jorhat: Tribal Study Center, 2000), 64.

[443] Ibid., 131.

> all life shares equal status and that value, personhood, intelligence, and the like must be recognized in all life. If there is a hierarchy of beings in the Indian experience of the world, humans are found at the bottom rather than at the top, the youngest and least wise of all living things."[444]

Indeed, Indigenous peoples consider animals, other living creatures, and all created as "'people' in the same manner as the various tribes of human beings are people."[445] Indigenous peoples claim they have reciprocal relationships with all living things, which includes the so-called "inanimate" objects such as rocks, plants, and other natural forms.[446] Every thing is imbued with spirit so all is sacred for Indigenous peoples. Because, all Creation is sacred the very land we walk and till must be treated with respect and reverence. Therefore, they treat life and creation with respect and reverence. One reason land is sacred for Indigenous peoples is that it is the dwelling place of the spirits; the ancestors have lived and worked the same land and they take their final rest and their bones becomes the land.[447]

Indigenous worldview is further characterized by being spatially oriented rather than temporally focused as is of the Euro-american worldview. This worldview of spatiality essentially accentuates and locates the all important life qualities of relationships among and between human beings and the whole of creation. This understanding extends and embraces the way Indigenous peoples view the world and relate themselves to the spirits and God(s). In "Full Circle of Liberation: An American Theology of Place," Tinker argues that the traditional Christian Euro-centric notion of God's action in time, which incidently, is also embraced by Black theologians and Latin American theologians, is not how American Indians could understand a relation to God. God acts in space and in place. Tinker explains, "God reveals God's self in creation, in space or place, not in time."[448] For Tinker and other indigenous thinkers, the traditional linear

---

[444] George E. Tinker, "The Stones Shall Cry Out: Consciousness, Rocks and Indians", TMs, 3.

[445] Vine Deloria, Jr, *God is Red: A Native View of Religion.* 2nd ed.(Golden: North American Press, 1992), 89.

[446] Walking Buffalo articulates this truth: "Did you know that trees talk? Well they do. They talk to each other, and they'll talk to you if you listen. Trouble is, White people don't listen. They never learned to listen to the Indians, so I don't I suppose they'll listen to other voices in nature. But I have learned a lot from trees: some times about the weather, some times about animals, sometimes about the Great Spirit." Quoted in Deloria. Ibid., 90.

[447] M. Horam, *Nagas Old Ways, New Trends* (Delhi: Cosmos Publications, 1988), 15f.

[448] George E. Tinker, "The Full Circle of Liberation: An American Theology of Place," in David G. Hallman, ed., *Ecotheology: Voices from South and North* (Geneva: WCC Publications, 1994), 221; Spirit and Resistance, 91-92.

thinking of temporality that is fundamental to the Western intellectual tradition is quite alien to Indigenous peoples and is in fact destructive to their livelihood.

Indigenous Religious Tradition

Western scholarship, literature and film would have the world believe that Indigenous peoples don't have "real" religion. This has been the "truths" since European first made contact with native peoples. On the contrary Indigenous people are deeply religious. Their religious understanding does not make distinctions between sacred and secular, spiritual and physical, heavenly and earthly, because all these together constitute the wholeness of life. In this sense, for the Indigenous people, religion would simply mean living in the continual awareness of the reality of the presence of the Sacred Other whom they encounter and acknowledge in obedience everyday.

Indigenous people believe in the Sacred Other (for lack of a better term), who is the Creator and Sustainer of the Universe. The Tangkhul Nagas call it *Varivara* and the Aos refer to it as *Lijaba*. In Ao *Lijaba* means God who enters the earth or dwells in the earth; thus *Lijaba* is the creator God.[449] They also believe in a Creator that is loving and merciful, just and compassionate. Most tribes have a masculine name for their Supreme Creator although some use both masculine and feminine names; a feminine name for this Sacred Other thus indicate the feminine nature of God as the mother. Certain tribal conceptions of the Sacred Other as male and female could be helpful in formulating an inclusive theology of God. In like manner, the tribal belief in spirit, the spirit who pervades and controls the whole universe, might be applied to interpret an understanding of the Holy Spirit from a tribal perspective.

One reason the West has been so reluctant to recognize the validity of Indigenous religion is the obvious lack of an equivalent of the Christian bible. There never have been scriptures such as those of the "recognized' religions. Rather their religious ethos is embodied in myths, legends, and stories that everyone learns. Myths especially unravel and teach how the Sacred Other works and reveals his/her mysteries through creation and the purpose or role of the myriad actors within this Creation. Thus myths are our scripture and creed.

Mercea Eliade defines myth as, "A 'true story' and, beyond that, a story that is a most precious possession because it is sacred, exemplary, significant."[450] Myths can convey profound theological meanings and religious truths of a

---

[449] For a detailed discussion see O. Alem, Tsüngremology (Mokokchung: Clark Theological College, 1994), 34ff; A Wati Longchar, "Lijaba – the Earth Entering Supreme Being: The Ao-Naga concept of God and Ecology," in A. Wati Longchar and Yangkahao Vashum, ed., *Tribal Worldview and Ecology*, Tribal Study Series no. 2 (Jorhat: Tribal Study Center, 1998), 24-33.

[450] Mercea Eliade, *Myth and Reality* (London: George Allen & Unwin Ltd., 1963), 1. For a detailed discussion of myth refer to Eric Csapo, Theories of Mythology (Malden: Blackwell Publishing, 2005).

particular group of people. They could tell us about God, spirits and their relations with human beings and creation. They could tell us how human beings should understand themselves, their life realities, and their relationship with God and creation. Indigenous peoples will generally maintain a collection of many myths and folktales that explain the unity of nature and religion, and of nature and culture, and the Creator-human-world relationships. These myths, when understood in the proper context can become an invaluable source for a theology which empowers Indigenous people.

Liberating Rites, Rituals and Ceremonies

Given the preceding explanations and descriptions of an Indigenous worldview, what the West calls religion is the way of living for Indigenous peoples. And living is considered perpetual act of ceremony. By ceremony, I mean here the way the sacred infuses the everyday life of the people through relationships of respect and reciprocity with one another and not the specific ceremonies performed by the people for particular occasions or in a particular place, which are in fact integral to the Indigenous community. Indeed, Indigenous people's existence is filled with both group ceremonies and numerous personal ceremonial acts.[451]

While certain peoples such as American Indians use the term "ceremony" for performative acts which acknowledge the sacreds, others prefer the terms "rite" and "ritual." Rites and rituals play essential roles in the lives of the people and they are integral to human existence. Indeed, human existence might be described as a life of perpetual ceremonies. From birth to death our life is punctuated and accentuated by rites and rituals. In "Liberating Rituals," Tom Driver asserts that, "the performance of rituals is as characteristic of human being as is speaking of language and living in social groups."[452] He goes on to underscore the significance of rituals by noting, "In a very real sense, to study humanity is to study ritual; and this has prompted me to think that to ponder the future of humanity is to consider the future of ritual."[453] This is certainly true with the Naga people who are known for their lavish rituals and ceremonies. Nagas consider rites and rituals as integral for the community because they express and reinforce the message of wholeness and unity. The well-being of the whole community depends on the ceremonies they perform.

---

[451] Silko's Ceremony and Welch's *Fools Crow* among many others reflect the ceremonial life of the American Indians. In both the stories, the life of the protagonists are presented as exemplifying continually the ceremonial life – they are engaged in a series of ceremonies. Leslie M. Silko, Ceremony (New York: Penguin Books, 1986). James Welch, *Fools Crow* (New York: Penguin Books, 1987).

[452] Tom F. Driver, *Liberating Rites: Understanding the Transformative Power of Ritual* (Boulder: Westview Press, 1991), 12.

[453] Ibid., 10.

There are rituals to be performed by individuals and there are those to be performed by the community and the purpose or subject can be oneself, family, or the entire tribe. Even the rituals performed by an individual are done so for the sake of or on behalf of the whole community. Deloria offers this regarding the significance of American Indian ceremonies: "Ceremonies are performed on behalf of the earth, all humans, and other forms of life...."[454] In a similar vein, Tinker observes that the underlying purpose of a particular ceremony called the Sun Dance is, "That the people might live!"[455] He then adds, "The ceremony is sometimes referred to as an annual world renewal ceremony and can be described as a ceremony for maintaining the balance and harmony of life."[456]

In Naga tradition it was usually the village chief or the priest who performed the necessary rituals before any of the work begins in the year.

> For instance at the time of sowing paddy, the village chief offered sacrifices and performed the paddy sowing rites one day ahead of his subjects. If in some rare cases, an individual by mistake did the sowing ahead of the village chief the entire village suffered from failure of crops that particular year and had to face famine."[457]

When a ritual of the community is done incorrectly or actually neglected not only the community suffers, but the animals and plants also suffer. For example, it was a regular practice to perform certain rites when a sow produce a litter or a calf was born, in order to ensure the baby's health, and a story was told of a Tangkhul Naga village in which all the pigs died after contracting a peculiar disease. It was later discovered that a person in the village did not observe the appropriate rites and rituals after his saw bore a litter.[458] As Khayaipam Khamrang points out, "Rites and rituals for the Tangkhuls are the signs that the whole world is inter-related and inter-connected. When one part is subjected to gross misuse the whole order is adversely affected."[459] This situation is evidence to support the belief that all of creation is bound mysteriously and inextricably so that nothing that happens does so in a vacuum.

Indigenous Socio-Cultural Traditions

Tribal life is characterized by communitarianism and the Naga people have a clear and "civilized" set of social and cultural principles based on social justice and

---

[454] Deloria, *God is Red,* 3.

[455] Tinker, *Spirit and Resistance,* 55.

[456] Ibid., 59.

[457] R. R. Shimray, *Origin and Culture of Nagas* (New Delhi: Pamleiphi Shimray, 1985), 227f.

[458] Khayaipam Khamrang, *Towards an Eco-Theology: Resources from the Primal Religion of the Tangkhul Nagas* (An Unpublished M. Th. Thesis, 1992), 67.

[459] Ibid.

kinship relations. The principle of selfless love and concern for the welfare of the community infuses the social and cultural life of the tribe. This governing principle of the society is known as *sobaliba* in Ao-Naga and *tlawmngaihna*[460] in Mizo[461] and this social-ethical principle provides the basis for harmonious communitarian living. This spirit of intimate relationship could very well be considered as the philosophical and ethical foundation of a communitarian society which could be clearly seen in the way tribal people lived out their life in the community. Theirs was a life of sharing and caring, justice and honesty, simplicity and truthfulness because the welfare of the community takes precedence over all other interests.[462]

Another cultural practice of the Naga people that was of paramount importance was the system of the bachelor's dormitory, widely known among the Nagas as *morung* system and *zawlbuk* among the Mizos. In some tribes there was also a separate dormitory for women. This *morung* system had multiple functions with the most important being that it served as a sort of cultural training center where the youngsters were taught tribal ways, traditions, and knowledge. This system also provided the site for learning social etiquette, arts and crafts, and certain social responsibilities. In other words, it was the custodian of culture, traditions, and values of tribal community. Young men and young women even spent their nights in their respective dormitory. It was an institution through which people were instilled with high ethical principles and strict disciplines. It is therefore obvious why K. Thanzauva describes *zawlbuk* as an institution where the principle of *tlawmngaihna* is put into practice.[463]

Traditional values such as the principle of *sobaliba/tlawmngaihna* and socio-cultural structures such as *morung/zawlbuk* systems have a great deal to offer for a new Indigenous theology. If this new theology is to be relevant some of these important cultural resources must be reclaimed and recovered. In his attempt to recover the value of the principle of *tlawmngaihna,* Thanzauva calls for reinterpretation of the concept in light of present circumstances. He proposes that:

> It is necessary to incorporate the universal concern of Christian teaching for love and justice into *tlawmngaihna* to meet the challenges of today. Thus, *tlawmngaihna* in the modern situation is love in action to protect and uphold the marginalized, and a commitment to create

---

460 K. Thanzauva, *Theology of Community: Tribal Theology in the Making* (Aizawl: Mizo Theological Conference, 1997), 120-126; M. Kipgen, *Christianity and Mizo Culture: The Encounter Between Christianity and Zo Culture in Mizoram* (Aizawl: Mizo Theological Confrence, 1997), 64-74.

461 Mizos are another prominent Indigenous peoples in Northeast India.

462 Shimray, *Origin and Cultures of Nagas,* 120.

463 Thanzauva, 122; cf. T. Jacob Thomas, "Indian Tribal Culture: A Rediscovery of Cultural Values." in *Indian Journal of Theology* 35, no. 2, 1993, 64-79.

> a just, harmonious, progressive, participatory and self-reliant society . . . . It requires involvement in the struggle against exploiting systems and structures, which spoil the harmony of community.[464]

This is how one could develop an Indigenous theology of social ethics informed by Indigenous cultural resources. Similarly, one could also reclaim the concept of *morung/zawlbuk* for constructing Indigenous ecclesiology in the context of contemporary Indigenous society. "A zawlbuk ecclesiology suggests that the local church should be an instrument for the well-being, harmony and development of the local community where it exists, without losing its universal nature."[465]

Indigenous People's Experience and History

While it is critically important to reclaim past traditions and values, it is also equally important that any theology we articulate relates to the recent and contemporary experiences. C. S. Song, a leading Thaiwanese theologian, states in no uncertain terms the importance of experience to theological articulation:

> The totality of life is the raw material of theology. Theology deals with concrete issues that affects life in its totality and not just with abstract concepts that engage theological brains. No human problem is too humble or insignificant for theology. Theology has to wrestle with the earth, not with heaven.[466]

Any theology that is divorced from concrete life experience of the people hardly qualifies as a living theology. Contextual theology must arise out of the existing struggle and issues of the people and in the case of Indigenous theology this must be done in the context of the people's suffering and pain. This includes taking seriously the people's emotional welfare and their aspirations and hopes. It is for this particular reason that in chapter 2, I discussed the socio-economic, political and historical experiences of the Naga people. A living and empowering theology could only emerge out of the experiences of the people. We must also reflect on the faith experience of the community as both a producer and product on the lived realities of the people. This will evoke theological questions such as what is God for us? What is Christ to the suffering Indigenous people in Northeast India? The Naga people's experience is a source of theology because they seek to experience and discern God's presence in the midst of their struggle for liberation.

---

[464] Thanzauva, 122; cf. T. Jacob Thomas, "Indian Tribal Culture: A Rediscovery of Cultural Values." in *Indian Journal of Theology* 35, no. 2, 1993, 127.

[465] Ibid., 142.

[466] Choan-Seng Song, *Tell Us Our Names: Story Theology from an Asian Perspective* (Indore: Satorakashan Sanchar Kendra, 1986), 6.

Similarly, a people's history is important because it is in that history that their identity is shaped. Or put it another way, a people without a history are a people without an identity; and to lose one's identity is to lose the meaning of and reason for existence. Theologically, history is important because it is in history that God acts and intervenes. Song expresses this understanding eloquently:

> The frontiers of our theology must move from the history of Israel and the history of Christianity in the West to the history in which we are involved in Asia. With this expansion of our historical horizon, we gain broader and deeper insights into the mystery of God's ways with the nations.[467]

God acts in history and the areas of God's activity include human experience in history, current events and culture. Unfortunately, Naga peoples' history has been marked by suffering and oppression. It is a history of people subjected to genocide, exploitation, discrimination, displacement and alienation in which their very own survival has been and continues to be threatened.

That being said, Naga peoples' history is more, it is Naga people saying no to all forms of exploitation and discrimination; it is their ongoing struggle for liberation; it is their fight for their rights and sovereignty. The Naga's history of struggle for liberation is therefore a valuable source of theology. Kosuke Koyoma, in reflection of his involvement with the farmers of Northern Thailand, asserts that, "Involvement is the only 'soil' from which theology germinates."[468] Likewise, it is in their own history that Naga people have to find their theological interpretation of God's work in the world because that Divine activity is inseparable from their historical experience.

Space, Creation, and Land: Indigenous Theological Point of Reference

In the preceding discussion I have explained how Indigenous worldview serves as the source of knowledge for Indigenous peoples. Additionally, I have illustrated that space, land, and creation are integral to the holistic worldview of Indigenous people. Space, creation, and land together serve as the foundation of Indigenous people's concept of life, relationship and interdependence. The many concepts expressed by "All our relations" articulates succinctly that humans along with other creations are part of this integrated whole. Space, creation and land are representative of relationship, reciprocity, inter-dependence and wholeness.

Given this reality, Indigenous theologians have argued convincingly that an Indigenous theology must begin with space and creation, and not with humans. Tinker explains:

---

[467] Song, *Tell Us Our Names,* 8.

[468] Kosuke Koyoma, *Waterbuffalo Theology* (Maryknoll: Orbis Books, 1989), viii.

> That all American Indian spiritual insights and hence Indian theology must begin with creation is reflected already in the basic liturgical posture of Indians in many North American tribes. Prayers are most often said with the community assembled into some form of circle – a key symbol for self-understanding in these tribes because it represents the whole of the universe and our place and role within it. All see themselves as coequal participants in the circle, standing neither above nor below anything else in creation.[469]

Likewise, Longchar, a Naga theologian, affirms spatiality as the primary datum for doing Indigenous theology. He brings out a clear distinction between dominant Christian theology and Indigenous theology in the following argument.

> The dominant Christian theology looks at space from the point of view of humanity. Humanity is the point of reference and the norm. In this case, the primary datum of doing theology is humanity and their liberation. However, for the tribals, the point of departure is space. Space is the point of reference and the key to understanding human selfhood, God and spirit. The space is the foundation for liberation.[470]

Placing space and creation as theology's starting point is crucial because it affirms the relatedness of all beings and all that is created. Consequently, we are all destined to be together as one universal family in which everyone is a coequal participant. Space and creation centered theology provides an orientation to life which is, again, centered on relationship, reciprocity and wholeness. It conveys the imperative recognition of cosmic oneness. And this idea of space is further rooted in the understanding of land; land is a space and a place.

Theologically, this spatial understanding has a far reaching significance. As Nirmal Minz points out, "Space means that everything is integrally related to one another and therefore, they must treat each other with justice, required and demanded of each other."[471] Additionally, it is land that provides identity and security to the people a part from being the Mother to the people. To this day, the Naga people identify themselves with their village rather than their names.[472]

---

469 Tinker, *Spirit and Resistance*, 91.

470 Longchar, *An Emerging Asian Theology*, 68.

471 Nirmal Minz, "Tribal Perspective on Ecology," in Wati Longchar and Yangkahao Vashum, ed., *The Tribal Worldview and Ecology*, Tribal Study Series no. 2. Jorhat: Tribal Study Center, 1998), 4.

472 Yangkahao Vashum, "Theology of Land: A Naga Perspective," in Wati Longchar and Yangkahao Vashum, ed., *The Tribal Worldview and Ecology*, Tribal Study Series 2 (Jorhat: Tribal Study Center, 1998), 75f.

A stranger on being enquired would tell his or her village name first, followed by his or her name. Land not only holds them together as a community but also it provides them their status as a people in the world. As Tinker explains, "... Indigenous peoples experience their very personhood in terms of their relationship to the land."[473]

This space/creation centered theology enables us to re-evaluate and reconsider the traditional views of God, Christ, Spirit and salvation including our human place in creation. From a spatial perspective, Longchar argues that God is also organically related to the whole of creation. He explains further:

> This understanding of God leads us to conceive Christ in a new way. Christ is no longer conceived as the one who works only in the hearts of the believers. But we are challenged to see Christ as the incarnate one who is organically related to the total eco-system. Jesus shares His Being with the whole created order. Since Jesus Chris is an integral part of creation, all parts of creation are now reconciled to Christ. It rejects a Christ of personalim. The incarnation of God in Jesus represents God's entry into finite space.[474]

In like manner, the space-creation centered theology enables us to conceive of human, creation, and church as organically related to one another and to God.

From an Indigenous point of view, therefore, a space-creation centered theology provides a corrective to the human-centered theology of the dominant Christian tradition.

---

473 Tinker, *Spirit and Resistance,* 102.

474 Longchar, *An Emerging Asian Theology,* 89.

Chapter 5

Dreaming the Future
A Theological Construction of a Naga-Indigenous Christology

The discussion so far has been related to the various elements which are necessary for the construction of a Naga-Indigenous Christology of culture and liberation. In chapter one I first demonstrated that the Naga people's theological understanding and faith expression has been heavily influenced by Western colonization and missionization, and followed that by articulating the need to construct a Naga-Indigenous Christology derived from the people's culture and lived reality. In chapter two I argued for the necessity of situating Naga-Indigenous Christology within the socio-economic, and political context of the people. With chapter three I made the case for locating Naga-Indigenous Christology in the existing bodies of Christological traditions and approaches in history by briefly outlining some background and identifying existing models of contextual theology so that in chapter four I could demonstrate the importance of establishing an appropriate methodology for constructing a Naga-Indigenous Christology.

In this fifth, and final, chapter I will assemble the specific elements I have identified in the previous four chapters so that we are able to construct a Naga-Indigenous Christology that will be meaningful and relevant to the experiences and cultural realities of the Naga people. I will begin by discussing in brief the significant concepts of the extent Indigenous theology in Northeast India.

Indigenous Theology in Northeast India

Indigenous theology in Northeast India, like any other contextual theology, takes seriously the socio-political context of the people. It holds human situatedness as well as Creation as the starting point for theological construction with the aim to develop a theology that is recognizably relevant, meaningful, and empowering to the people. The act of doing theology can be understood as reflections on the faith of our fathers and mothers; however, more often than not, theology reflects the Christian traditions (Bible and Christian traditions) in their strict sense. Very little importance is given to the traditions of our own fathers and mothers except to the degree that they are condemned as evil and devilish. Indigenous theology affirms the value and legitimacy of Indigenous culture. It reiterates the faith that God has been and still is present in the cultural life of the Indigenous people.

The origin and development of Indigenous theology in Northeast India is fairly recent, having taken shape in the late 1980s and early 1990s.[475] As a contextual theology, it seeks to reflect the faith experiences of Indigenous people on the one hand, and to re-appropriate the Indigenous cultural values for theological reflection on the other. Additionally, the critical point of departure for Indigenous theology is the matrix of Indigenous worldview. The Indigenous worldview is characterized by the inter-relatedness of all things and it recognizes and values the harmony that Creation establishes between humanity and nature. Accordingly, the entire reality of life including our understanding of God and spirituality has to be seen within the perspective of our relatedness with all creation. In other words, Creation and not humans must serve as the starting point for Indigenous theology.

Indigenous theology is also a theology of liberation and as a liberation theology it must make use of the liberative messages contained in the Bible for our faith reflection and articulation.[476] God's act of liberation in the Exodus from Egypt and throughout the history of Israel, the prophetic messages of liberation in the Hebrew scriptures and, above all, Jesus' declaration that his ministry was to bring good news to the poor, release to the captives, and sight to the blind, are all witness to the claim that if an Indigenous theology is to be faithful to the liberative acts of God it must be a theology of liberation and healing.

The tribals in Northeast India long for liberation in all dimensions of life – politically, socially, economically, religiously and psychologically. Politically, there are a number of so-called "insurgent" groups[477] whose operations because of the pervasive presence of Indian armed forces, often lead to violence and bloodshed

---

[475] The pioneers of Indigenous theology in Northeast India include Jonathan H. Thumra, Renthy Keitzer, K. Thanzauva, Wati Longchar, among others. The Eastern Theological College, Jorhat, Assam has been in the forefront of developing Indigenous theology. The College has established a Tribal Study Center as part of the ongoing research in tribal cultures and religious traditions.

[476] K. Thanzauva, "Tribal Theological Trends in North East India," in Renthy Keitzar, ed., *Good News for North East India* (Guwahati: Chrsitian Literature Center, 1995), 104-113.

[477] There are over 100 "insurgency" groups operating in Northeast states. While many of them are fighting for their political independence, many others are fighting for their rights and privileges within the Indian constitution. The Naga peoples have been struggling against India for their political independence for over 70 years now.

and human rights abuses;[478] consequently tensions are very high compounding the already volatile situation of the region. Factional violence, ethnic clashes and tribal feuds have brought additional suffering into the lives of the people. Further complicating the region's struggles is the fast spreading infection of HIV/AIDS. The prevalence of HIV/AIDS in the Northeast region is considered to be one of the highest of any region in India. The people in the region need liberation and healing from all these structural, and corporate, and social sins in addition to our personal sins and aggressions. We need the spirit of reconciliation and peace to prevail among our people; therefore, Indigenous theology must be a theology of liberation and healing.

Indigenous theology is also necessary in order to establish and maintain our Indigenous Christian identity; this Indigenous Christian identity can emerge only when we are willing to respectfully reclaim our cultures and histories in conjunction with our expressions of faith. Additionally, an Indigenous theology will challenge Indigenous Christians to engage the scriptures in the light of Indigenous people's circumstances and cultural values, so as a living theology it must bring meaning and relevance to our tribal life and world. As the authors of *Native American Theology* state, "Our argument, however, goes beyond simply 'revisioning' conventional categories of Western systematic theology. It also means considering new categories from Native thought-worlds."[479] Naga-Indigenous theology is committed to such an endeavor in which Naga worldviews and cultures remain at the center-stage of theological enterprise.

Dreaming the Future: A Naga-Indigenous Christology of Culture and Liberation

In this section I will apply this theology to the task of constructing a Naga-Indigenous Christology which is likewise meaningful and relevant to the experience of the Naga people. In constructing a Christology of culture and liberation that is informed by cultural values and priorities, I will employ the following cultural metaphors: Jesus as the Rooster, Jesus as the Elder Brother and the Ancestor, Jesus as the Liberator, and Jesus as the Reconciler. I have chosen these cultural metaphors for a couple of reasons. These metaphors are widely known among the Naga people and so they represent the common beliefs and practices of the people. Additionally, these cultural metaphors provide the necessary cultural resources for constructing a relevant Christology that responds to the contemporary socio-political context of the Naga people.

---

[478] For a detailed information on human rights abuses refer to Luingam Luithui and Nandita Haksar, *Nagaland File: A Question of Human Rights* (New Delhi: Lancer International, 1984); Shimreingam Shimray, *Theology of Human Rights: A Critque on Politics* (Jorhat: Ruth Shimray, 2002).

[479] Clara Sue Kidwell, Homer Noeley, George E. "Tink" Tinker, *A Native American Theology* (Maryknoll: Orbis Books, 2001), 113.

Jesus as the Rooster

Rooster in Naga Traditions

Every society in the world has, in one way or other, identified animal(s) which either represent their national identity or symbolize the religious practices of certain group of people. For example, in India, the peacock is considered the national bird; the Dragon is considered a sacred animal by the Chinese, for American Indians Buffalo is their sacred animal. Likewise, for the Naga people, among others Rooster is their sacred animal.

In their cultural past Naga's religious traditions included many ceremonial activities. There were different kinds of ceremonies for different occasions and purposes, such as: ceremonies for the birth and naming of a child, an individual's sickness and good health, community well-being, the observance of *genna*, and purification ceremonies.[480] There were also a number of ceremonies connected with agricultural activities because agriculture was the main occupation of the Naga people; sacrifices were offered before and after clearing the fields chosen for cultivation, seed sowing, and harvesting of the crops, etc.

In general, the primary occasions involved animals. Different animals were chosen for sacrificial offerings according to the nature and purpose of the ceremony. The most commonly chosen animals included the chicken, rooster, dog, pig, buffalo and *mithun*.[481] Other items such as eggs, rice beer, and cooked rice were also widely used for sacrificial offerings. Of all these, the rooster was by far the most valued sacrificial animal.

The rooster was always regarded as an animal that possessed the particular qualities that the people looked for in a sacrificial animal – purity, aesthetic beauty and physical charm, and more. Describing the beauty of the rooster N. Saleo Mao stated, "A rooster is decorated with beautiful ornaments from head to leg, and top to bottom. He not only looks gorgeous, he also appears very gracious at the same time."[482] In addition to being a most handsome and pure animal, the

[480] Stephen Ankang of Lungpha village, interview by author, 11 August, 2003, Ukhrul, Tape recording. Angkang is the President of Development for Hao Ancient Custom Research Organization (DHACRO); Jessami village Elders: W. Atsilhi, W. Kelhipelo, W. Kanmi, and W., chung, of Jessami village, interview by author, 8 August 2003, Jessami village, tape recording; Italakpe Iheilung of Jalukie Town, interview by author, 17 July 2003, Jalukie Town, tape recording. Italakpe is an elder and an expert on Zeliangrong Naga culture and traditions.

[481] I. Bendangangshi and I. T. Apok Aier, *The Religion of the Ao Nagas,* Second Revised Edition (Guwahati: I. Bendangangshi, 1997), 56. Mithun is a bison-like animal that is indigenous to the region.

[482] N. Saleo of Pudunamai village, interview by author, 27 July 2003, Pudunamai village, tape recording. Similar view is also expressed by Daihrii Akha. Daihrii Akha, of Makhel village, interview by author, 27 July 2003, Makhel village. Tape recording. Both Saleo and Akha are experts in Mao Naga culture and traditions. Saleo is 78 and Akha is 81.

rooster was considered one of the most alert, intelligent, and humble animals.[483] Humility was an especially important trait; a blameless rooster was often chosen for sacrifices.

Rooster Sacrifice: So that the People might Live!

Rooster sacrifice was connected with restoring well-being and ceremony; it could take place for the individual or the community.[484] The individual ceremony usually occurred when a person became (seriously) ill; in certain cases the sickness was considered to be due to the temporary loss of the person's soul. With the help of the *khanong* (in Tangkhul Naga), medicine person, the family members could determine whether the person's soul was in the captivity of a certain spirit. In order to help restore the person's soul a ceremony was conducted; this ceremony was known in Ao Naga as *Tanuja* which means soul-calling ceremony.[485]

The ceremony was conducted with utmost care and seriousness, usually by the village medicine person, and accordingly, a rooster without blemish was preferred. The medicine person accompanied by members of the family, would go to the location of the ceremony, usually at the outskirt of the village.[486] On reaching the spot, the medicine person would conduct the ceremony. He/she would then toss the rooster up into the air releasing it to the jungle reciting these words: "Take this rooster instead of so and so and release the soul immediately."[487] Once the rooster was released it was generally expected that the rooster would never return to the village and that was considered a good sign. The sick person would recover from sickness and his/her health was restored. If the rooster walked back to the village it was understood that the person would never recover from the sickness.

As regards the community one of the prominent ceremonies which also required the use of an unblemish rooster was the purification ceremony. The ceremony usually span for six to eight days. The entire village spent the days

---

[483] According to a Khasi tradition, an Indigenous community in Northeast India, the three main characteristic features of a rooster are: his humility, obedience and self-renunciation. The tradtion says that the rooster was originally naked without any feathers but it was God who clothed him and exalted him because of his humility, obedience and self renunciation. Felix H. Kharkhongor, *The Revealed Christ of the Khasi Religion* (Worthing: Loxwood Press, 1994), 25.

[484] Stephen Angkang of Lungpha village, interview by author, 11 August 2003, tape recording; M. K. Lorin of Phenshünyu village, interview by author, 28 July 2003, Kohima, tape recording.

[485] Bendangangshi and Aier, *The Religion of the Ao Nagas,* 85-86; cf. S. K. Phungthar of Chingjui Ngajaphung village, interview by author, 22 June 2003, Chingjui Ngajaphung village, tape recording.

[486] The actual ceremony proceedings varied from tribe to tribe; while the tribes like the Ao would also kill other animals as part of the ceremony, many other tribes did not.

[487] Bandangangshi and Lipok, 87.

observing *genna*[488] which meant that the people were prohibited from working and traveling and everyone was expected to devote themselves to thinking about the Sacred Other and the ceremony. On the last day the medicine person, accompanied by all members of the village council, would proceed to the venue of ceremony, usually at the outskirts of the village. Here again, the medicine person would throw the rooster up into the air releasing it to the jungle while asking the Sacred Other's blessings upon the village and community. The "releasing" of the rooster meant its imminent death. The purpose of the ceremony was to purify the village from all forms of social evils and impediments: that is, to ask the Sacred Other to take away the ills and sufferings of the community, and to protect the village from future epidemics and calamities. In short, the ceremony was conducted for the well-being of the whole village and community.[489]

Aside from being a sacrificial animal, the rooster was also a mythic figure. According to myths of the Nagas the rooster was responsible for persuading the Sacred Other to provide light (sunlight) to the world, and, he was the animal to whom the Sacred Other entrusted the role of maintaining the proper duration of day and night.

Jesus and the Rooster

The significance of the sacrifice of rooster in Naga tradition is realized in the notion that the unblemish rooster dies on behalf of the person or community on whose behalf the sacrifice was offered. The rooster was sacrificed so that the ills and sufferings of the people might be taken away in order that health and well-being of the community might be restored; in other words, it was a ceremony for purification and restoration. A living animal, in this case the rooster, was sacrificed so that the people might live!

Additionally, the healing power of the ceremony rests on the knowledge that the rooster chosen for the sacrifice was a flawless one so that the people were offering their best and the most fitting sacrifice to the Sacred Other. The

---

[488] In certain tribes, the purification ceremony was carried out by only the male population but was done on behalf of the whole community. There were certain elaborate activities involved in the observance of this ceremony including male folks spending a day or two in the jungle during which they would bath as part of the purification. The Angami and the Chakhesang people usually carried out this purification ceremony during the *Sekrenyi* festival. The purification ceremony of the men was known as *Phousanyi* in Angami. According to D. Kuolie, the Angami tribe would also sacrifice a rooster during the purification ceremony of a child. The sacrificial rooster was known as *Nuobo vü* in Angami. D. Kuolie of Kohima, interview by author, 17 July 2003, Kohima, tape recording. Kuolie is Professor and Chair of the Dept. of Teneidie (Tribal Studies), Nagaland University; Cf. Theysheyi Vero, of Thiphuzu village, interview by author, 21 July 2003, Dimapur, tape recording. Vero is an elder from Chakhesang Naga tribe.

[489] The Khiamniungan Nagas had a tradition of rooster sacrifice during the wedding ceremony. Tipping their fingers in the blood of the rooster, the bride and the groom took vows of marital relationship as husband and wife. Putong Jenko, of Pangsha village, interview by author, 28 July 2003, Kohima.

sacrifice of flawless or blameless animal may be a familiar concept to many of us; the Hebrew Bible is replete with such stories of sacrifice of blameless animal(s) to Yahweh. "Many of the Old Testament [sic] sacrifices are typologically interpreted in the New Testament as referring to the atoning sacrifice of Jesus Christ for the sins of humanity."[490] And indeed, in the New Testament the death of Jesus Christ, a man without sin – a flawless victim – was regarded as a perfect sacrifice. In the words of the writer of the Letter to the Hebrews, "...The blood of Christ, who through the eternal Spirit offered himself without blemish to God...."[491] Further, the sacrifice of Christ is considered permanent and eternal unlike those of Hebrew Scriptures which were regarded as temporary.[492] Like wise, the Naga sacrifices were temporary.

Of course, every metaphor or image has its limitations and I believe the use of a rooster as representative of Jesus has its own limitations. One is, unlike the rooster, Jesus voluntarily gave up his life for the world; however, it should be noted that some theologians, especially the liberation theologians, are critical of the idea that Jesus' death was voluntary. These critics contend Jesus did not give up his life of his own volition; rather, he was left with no other choice but to die. Based on the nature of Jesus' ministry and the events leading up to his crucifixion, they argue that Jesus was forced to his death. He took on the task himself when confronted with the challenges from the religious and worldly powers in Palestine. One might argue that the death of Jesus Christ has universal appeal and significance, whereas the rooster's sacrifice was limited to the community which undertook the ceremony. However, while the primary goal of the people's sacrifice of a rooster was limited to the immediate community, it did nevertheless contribute to the well-being of the rest of the world and the whole earth; put another way, as I explained in chapter four, when a community is at peace and in harmony, the larger world is also improved, if only indirectly. What is of real importance here is that both Jesus and the rooster died so that the people might live!

Sacrifices were normally conducted by a religious priest, the medicine person, or the head of the family, if the sacrifice pertained to the family. The sacrificial ceremony of the rooster likewise was carried out by the medicine person on behalf of the community. The difference is that in the case of Jesus, he was both the priest and the victim but not merely the priest but the high priest par excellence.

---

[490] Renthy Keitzar, "The Indigenization of Naga Christian Theology," in V. K. Nuh, ed., *In Search of Praxis Theology for the Nagas* (New Delhi: Regency Publications, 2003), 43.

[491] Heb. 9:14. All Scripture passages cited are from the New Revised Standard Version (NRSV).

[492] Heb. 9:26.

Jesus the Rooster of the Sacred Other

As I noted above, there are certain similarities between sacrifices described in the Hebrew Scriptures and the Naga traditions of sacrifice: they both offered sacrifices of animals to represent as a substitute to take away sickness, suffering and other calamities. The form and meaning between the two sacrifices were similar. Their biggest differences lay in the choice of sacrificial elements; The Nagas used roosters, chickens, and pigs, while the Jews used lambs, rams, doves, and turtles.

In John 1:29 Jesus is referred to as, "The lamb of God who takes away the sins of the world." In order to understand this text in Naga cultural categories and thought patterns, Renthy Keitzar proposes that a Naga translation of the text would read as, "Behold the cock of God who takes away the sins of the world."[493] Keitzar rightly argues that the Naga people are familiar with the rooster and not the lamb or goat which were not known to the people traditionally. In light of this, sacrificial referent must be adapted to Naga cultural categories to make the message relevant and meaningful to the people. According to Keitzar:

> The prototype and types in Bible and their correspondences in the Naga Christian concepts should undergo certain adaptations in the context of our cultural categories. I do not think the Nagas ever sacrificed a lamb or ram when they never raised sheep. Hence, our use of the sacrifice of the lamb in our Christian vocabulary is rather obscure. Why not use an equivalent term which is relevant? For example, the "Cock of God' instead of the Lamb of God;" the "sacrifices of pig and mithuns; and offering of eggs" instead of doves and turtle doves.[494]

Jesus as the Ancestor and Elder Brother

Ancestor Veneration in Naga Religious Traditions

Just as it is in many places around the world, ancestor veneration is regarded by the Nagas as the oldest religion. A Naga scholar Mashangthei Horam, claims that ancestor veneration was the "real religion of the Nagas."[495] However, with the appearance of Christian missionaries in the mid 19th century, and their subsequent influence, the Naga's attitude toward the ancestors has changed dramatically. Of course, the ancestors are still highly revered and continue to hold a special place in the lives of the people. Ancestor veneration is not exclusive to the Nagas, it was widely known and practiced all over the world, particularly among the indigenous peoples and still is in certain cultures.[496]

---

493 Keitzar, "The Indigenization of Naga Christian Theology," 44.

494 Ibid.

495 M. Horam, *Nagas Old Ways, New Trends* (New Delhi: Cosmo Publications, 1988), 13.

496 Jonathan H. Thumra, "The Naga Primal (Traditional) Religion and Christianity: A Theological Reflection", in V. K. Nuh, ed., *In Search of Praxis Theology for the Nagas* (New Delhi:

Central to Naga religious beliefs was the existence of the spirits as the mediators between the Sacred Other and the world. The Nagas believed that the Sacred Other related to the people and world through the spirits. Nagas also differentiate between malevolent and benevolent spirits such that the malevolent spirits were associated with misfortune, calamities, and illnesses while the benevolent spirits such as the house spirits, fertility spirits, and ancestor's spirits were known for blessing people with good health, good crops, healthy relationships between and among people, and a good family and community life. The benevolent spirits were generally believed to be responsible for the general well-being and prosperity of the people. Above all, the spirits were acknowledged for their roles in creating and sustaining the earth and were therefore revered and venerated. They were appealed to and offered sacrifices, not out of fear or concern but out of reverence and love.

The Nagas believed that their ancestors' spirits never depart from their family and community; that they continued to abide with the living as unseen members of the family. Because, of this, at every family meal a portion of food would always be offered to the spirits; usually on plate or bowl placed with those of the living family members. Foods were also offered to the ancestors in all major festivals and religious ceremonies of the village or community. Ancestors' spirits were believed to surround the living families with their protective care and love. Whenever a baby child smiled or giggled, it was understood that an ancestor's spirit was playing with the child and the child was believed to be under the protective care of the ancestor.

The ancestors were most of all, regarded as both the source and facilitators of family lineage which maintained an unbroken connection back through history and from the present and into the future of a Naga family and community. In other words, the ancestors were the medium that maintained and sustained family and community connections from generation to generation.

For all this, the ancestors were revered and venerated. Unlike other indigenous communities, the Nagas did not have elaborate form of veneration; nor did they have shrines specifically designated for the ancestor. These particularities were consistent with Naga people's notion of the Sacred Other being everywhere and therefore could be acknowledged everywhere and anytime unconstrained by human edifices: for them the whole earth was a temple.

Naga Family: The Role of the Eldest Son/Brother

In Naga society, the eldest son enjoyed unique status in the family and among his siblings. As first born he was successor to the father in the family lineage; also as the first born, he received the largest and best share of family inheritance including

Regency Publications, 2003), 55f; A. Wati Longchar, *The Tribal Religious Traditions in North East India: An Introduction,* Revised Edition (Jorhat: Eastern Theological College, 2003), 19-20.

the moveable and the immovable properties.[497] However, these privileges were not without responsibilities. In the event of the death of his father, the majority of family responsibility would rest on him. He would assume the role of father in taking care of the family and in accordance with the customary duty, he was also required to oversee the distribution of the remaining family inheritances to his siblings, especially his younger brothers. His presence in the new role is felt most readily and often as the final arbiter of the decision making; every member in the family contributes to decision making but the final decision ultimately lies with the oldest son.

Traditionally family inheritances, especially the immovable properties, were not available to the daughters only the sons could inherit family properties. This practice applied even in the cases in which families did not have sons, only daughters.[498] In such case, the nearest and the oldest male kin of the family would inherit the properties upon the death of the parents and all daughters were married off. No daughter could take with her any immovable properties to her husband's place. The rationale behind that practice was that with marriage the woman automatically became the co-custodian of her husband's inherited properties. It should be noted, however, that the daughters/women were also eligible for movable family properties such as cash, clothing, and animals.[499] Of course, in contemporary Naga society, the old systems such as family inheritance are beginning to loose currency to the changes of time. Daughters are being awarded family's immovable properties which was not permissible in the recent past. This is still an exception to the rule and not the norm that is being widely followed; indeed, majority of the Naga people are still opposed to such changes.

Jesus as the Elder Brother and Ancestor

In this section I will explore the image of Jesus as an elder brother and an ancestor. I begin by affirming that Jesus has a close filial relationship with God the Father. In the Gospels we read that Jesus made several references to the heavenly Father

---

[497] Stephen Ankang, *Hau (Tangkhul) Customary law (Hau Shiyan Chikan)* (Ukhrul: Development for Hau Ancient Custom and Research Organization, 1999), 132-133. Among Sumi Nagas, the family inheritance would be equally divided among the sons. Hekhevi Achumi, of Khumshimi village, interview by author, 21 July 2003, Dimapur. In case of the Konyak Naga, the oldest son inherited all family properties – movable and immovable. But, gradually the properties would be also divided among the younger brothers when they married. Generally, the property would be divided into three portions and out of these one of the portions would be given to the brother who decided to begin a married life. Y. Chingang Konyak of Kongan village, interview by author, 28 July 2003, Kohima, tape recording. Konyak is 69 and belongs to a priestly family of Kongan village in Mon district, Nagaland. He is an authority on Konyak culture, history and traditions.

[498] T. Luikham, *Wung (Tangkhul) Naga Okthot Mayonza: Wung (Tangkhul) Naga Traditional Laws* (Ukhrul: By Author, 1961), 212; Cf. Angkang, *Hau (Tangkhul) Customary Law,* 133.

[499] Luikham, *Wung (Tangkhul) Naga Okthot Mayonza,* 212.

and he called him God Abba, demonstrating his love and affection for the Father. In a number of instances, Jesus addressed God as Father: in the garden of Gethsemane,[500] upon dying on the cross.[501] And then we find in the Gospel of John the intimate relationship maintained between Jesus and the Father. Additionally, the Gospel writers describe the status of Jesus as being the "firstborn son."[502] As firstborn son, "He constituted not only the continuation of the family but also the continuity and permanence of Israel's covenant relationship with God."[503]

As the first born son, Jesus can be compared to the eldest son in the Naga family and I will identify some applications in no specific order, in which Jesus is a satisfactory representative for the Naga context. The first possibility for an exchange of Jesus for the oldest son is to be a role model for others, especially his siblings for whom he was expected to set a high standard of behavior to be emulated. Of course, not every elder brother could live up to the expectations of the people; indeed, many fell short of the expectations of the family and community in discharging the tasks they were entrusted with. But there were also many elder brothers, who were genuinely concerned for the well-being of others and they took seriously their responsibilities. Precisely for this reason, the elder brother was usually entrusted with the responsibility of taking care of his siblings; the younger siblings would look up to him for all practical purposes including advise on day to day decision making and apportioning of the family inheritances.

Jesus Christ is truly an "elder brother" whose life demonstrated the qualities that were expected of an elder brother. Jesus is the elder brother *par excellence*, for in him the desires and expectations of an elder brother came into its fulfillment. Jesus, unlike other individual brothers did not become a disappointment of the family and the community. In the words of François Kabasélé, "Christ is a true 'eldest one,' as he has disappointed neither our expectations nor those of his Father. His Father has restored and crowned him (in the resurrection)."[504] Jesus himself expressed that he has been an example for his disciples and he admonished that they follow his example: "For I have set you an example, that you also should do as I have done to you."[505]

The ancestor and elder brother exercised a critical role of being mediators. The elder brother being the eldest son in the family was charged with religious duties including offering sacrifices to the Sacred Other on behalf of the family. On the death of the father the eldest son was expected to carry out all family

---

[500] Matt. 26:39.

[501] Luke 23:46.

[502] Luke 2:7; Matt. 1:25.

[503] Peter C. Phan, *Christianity with an Asian Face: Asian American Theology in the Making* (Maryknoll: Orbis Books, 2003), 136.

[504] François Kabasélé, "Christ as Ancestor and Elder Brother" in Robert J. Schreiter, ed., *Faces of Jesus in Africa* (Maryknoll: Orbis Books, 2000), 122.

[505] John 13:15.

ceremonies and sacrifices. On the other hand, the ancestor played a mediating role between the spiritual world and the living. In the worldview of the Nagas, the notion of the community encompassed not only the living but also the dead and the spiritual beings; the ancestors were an integral part of the community. Additionally, as a life giving source in the sense that through the ancestors generations of human societies have come to exist, the ancestors were closer to the Source. "It is their relation to the Supreme Being and to the living on earth that places them in this special intermediary position."[506]

Jesus Christ is the mediator between God the Father and the world including human beings and creation. In and through Jesus we have access to the Father. Jesus made it amply clear when he declares that, "He is the way to the Father." St. Paul also talks about Jesus as the advocate – advocating for us to the Father. Perhaps, the "Word becoming flesh" in and through Jesus Christ is the ultimate revelation of the Mystery, God the Father to the world. The mystery of the invisible is made known through Jesus Christ. Thus Jesus said that by knowing him his followers can know the Father, for the "Father and I are one." In Naga tradition, the ancestors represented the mystery of the invisible.[507] In adapting the role of Jesus to the Naga cultural context, one can substitute Jesus as the Ancestor who represents the mystery of the invisible God.

In addition to serving as role models and mediators, the ancestors were the "makers and teachers of the present; they represent the past of the race, and all its sacrifices . . . . They represent the moral experience of the race . . . . They represent the unwritten law, the traditions of the commune, the duties of all to all."[508] These descriptions go on to show how much the ancestors meant in the lives of Naga people; indeed, their existence as a community depended a great deal on their ancestors. They not only represented the laws and traditions of the people, they were actually the foundation on which the community life is built and sustained. In sum, the identity of the community was founded and shaped by and on the ancestors.

Jesus Christ is our sure foundation; our life and faith rest on him. He is our moral teacher; he is the exemplar of how believers ought to live. In Christ we have a new tradition and law, a law that is written not on the stones or papers but on the heart; he represents the unwritten law of the community of believers. Furthermore, the identity of a believer or community of faith rests on Jesus Christ and in this sense, Jesus Christ is the ancestor in whom we find the meaning of our existence. He not only represents the moral experience of the people of faith but the future also rests in his hands. In Christ, the past, the present, and the future come together.

---

[506] Kabasélé, "Christ as Ancestor and Elder Brother," 124.

[507] Horam, *Nagas Old Ways, New Trends,* 19.

[508] Ibid., 19.

One of the significant functions for which the ancestors were highly regarded among the Naga people was that they were sensitive to people's hardships and problems so that they shared the joys and sorrows of the family and community.[509] They were always there for the people, in times of joy and sorrow.

The idea of ancestors being there for the people fits very well with the image of Jesus Christ as Emmanuel, "God who is with us." Jesus is the ancestor who understands the longings and anxieties of the people, who is always there for the people in times of sorrows and joy. He suffers and weeps with those who are suffering; he cares for the people and shares their deepest longings and aspirations. In Jesus people find their solace and comfort. Jesus lives near the people and he is concretely present in their lives. Like the ancestors and neighbors, Jesus lives in the community sharing with them their sorrows and joys.[510] In the words of Leonardo Boff:

> Christ is our brother since he participated in the anonymity of almost all human beings and assumed the human situation that is identical for all.... Jesus is our elder brother, since within this human life, assumed both in obscurity and publicly, he lived in such a human manner that he revealed God, by his death and resurrection, realized all those dynamisms of which we are capable.[511]

Finally, one might ask how did Jesus get the status of being an ancestor? Jesus earned the status of an ancestor through his death and resurrection-exaltation, as it was said of the ancestors. One has to die first to be ultimately venerated as an ancestor by the descendents. According to Phan, "Jesus acquired his status as an ancestor through four events: his descent among the dead, his resurrection-exaltation, his becoming the new Adam, and the worship rendered by his followers."[512] Phan goes on to add that Jesus "is no longer dead but alive and dwells among his own family of spiritual descendents, his adopted brothers and sisters, just as the ancestors are truly alive and present in the memory of their descendents."[513] Of course, in trying to equate the significance of the resurrection of Jesus Christ with ancestor veneration, the limitations must be recognized. The resurrection of Jesus cannot and should not be "reduced to this aspect of being made the ancestor alone."[514]

---

509 Horam, *Nagas Old Ways, New Trends,* 19.

510 Similarly, Luis G. Pedraja speaking from Hispanic context said, "Just like my neighbors, relatives, and friends, Jesus also lived in our community. *Jesus is My Uncle: Christology from a Hispanic Perspective* (Nashville: Abingdon Press, 1999), 15.

511 Leonardo Boff, *Jesus Christ Liberator: A Critical Christology for Our Time* (Maryknoll: Orbis Books, 1986), 342-343.

512 Phan, *Christianity with an Asian Face,* 142.

513 Ibid., 142.

514 Ibid., 142.

Ancestor Christology and Feminist Theology

An Ancestor Christology which is constructed and informed by concepts derived from the patriarchal system of Naga society also will have its shortcomings. Although the ancestors were inclusive of male and female, grandpas and grandmas, fathers and mothers, the rites of ancestor veneration were usually conducted by male member of the family. The role of the male was critical in order for the practice and perpetuation of ancestor veneration; therefore this articulation of ancestor Christology can be seen to be affirming and reifying the valorized status of men.

Every metaphor has its limitation in the sense that a metaphor as representative of a person, object or action must never be taken literally. Metaphor, in other words is a form of figurative language used to illustrate the meaning and significance of another subject or object. The issue is the appropriateness of the metaphor in the cultural context of a people. The ancestor used here as a metaphor for Jesus is helpful in so far as it helps the reader or listener to relate to Jesus Christ in a meaningful manner. At the same time the feminist critique which claims ancestor and elder brother metaphors reflect patriarchal values has validity and for this reason, a feminist theology could function effectively as a critical corrective while also enriching the ancestor Christology. In other words, to be kept in the proper perspective, an empowering ancestor Christology would benefit if understood in the light of feminist theological perspectives. Phan rightly observes that:

> Such a liberationist Christology need not and does not abolish ancestor veneration; as part of an Asian theology, it will purify the practice of ancestor veneration of elements that privilege the male, both as an ancestor and a minister of the cult of ancestors. Thus purified, ancestor worship remains, I submit, a rich resource for painting a portrait of Christ that make sense to billions of Asians.[515]

Jesus as the Liberator

The image of Jesus as liberator resonates powerfully in the lives of the Naga people; indeed, a primary reason Naga people embraced the Christian faith was the message of liberation in Jesus Christ; a liberation not only from spiritual bondage, but from physical, mental, cultural and social bondage as well. For Naga people the image of Jesus as liberator becomes very real in the context of their historical struggle for self-determination and political freedom they have waged for over half a century. In the Naga people's quest for political identity and freedom, despite the powerful forces working against them, their faith in Jesus the liberator has kept their hopes alive.

---

[515] Phan, *Christianity with an Asian Face,* 145.

Today in the writings of feminist theologians, social and political activists, and liberation theologians the call for liberation is felt more emphatically within Northeast society. In their search for identity and liberation, women have looked to Jesus as their source of empowerment and liberation. They appeal to the transforming and empowering ministry of Jesus Christ; hence Jesus is seen as the radical transformer[516] as well as the liberator. The themes of liberation and equality have figured prominently in the works of female Indigenous theologians vis-à-vis the patriarchal oppressions in the tribal society; theologians such as , R.L. Hnuni, a Mizo, and Limatula Longkumer, an Ao Naga, have advocated for the liberation of women from all forms of exploitation, injustice and discrimination they have suffered in the patriarchal system.[517] While women in Northeast Indigenous societies enjoy much more social freedom than the rest of Indian society, "It is an unbalanced freedom and womenfolk suffer to the maximum the pain of injustice and discrimination, though free they are not liberated."[518] Women do not have the same privileges as men do particularly in inheritance, leadership and decision making, or generally in social, political and religious affairs. This is true even in the case of matrilineal/matriarchal societies of Khasis and Garos in the region; while women in these societies are entitled to family inheritance, in fact only women are entitled to family inheritance, the ultimate decision making power rests with the maternal uncle of the family. Women's experience of marginalization, oppression and discrimination, and their determination to fight for their rights and equality in church and society were clearly articulated in the first ever conference of theologically trained Naga women held recently in Dimapur, Nagaland.[519] The conference ended with this powerful affirmation:

---

[516] H. Wanda Kharlukhi, "Jesus: A Radical Transformer", in *Journal of Tribal Studies,* vol. 7, no. 1 (January – June 2003), 203-209; Zakali Shohe, "Protest with a Cause: A Study of the Temple Act of Jesus for Empowering Naga Women in their Struggles", in Longkumer and Longkumer, ed., *Side by Side,* 127-139.

[517] R. L. Hnuni, *Transforming Theology for Empowering Women,* Tribals Study Series, no. 4 (Jorhat: Women's Studies ETC, 1999); "Women in the Context of the Bible and Mizoram," in K. Thanzauva, ed., *Towards Tribal Theology: The Mizo Perspective* (Aizawl: Mizo Theological Conference, 1989), 80ff; Limatula Longkumer, "Rediscovering Women's Role and Status in Society," in A. Wati Longchar and Larry E. Davis, ed., *In Doing Theology with Tribal Resources: Context and Perspective,* Tribal Study Series, no. 3 (Jorhat: Tribal Study Center, 1999), 77-90; "Naga Women in Theological Education", in Limatula Longkumer and Talijungla Longkumer, ed., *Side by Side: Naga Women Doing Theology in Search of Justice and Partnership* (n. p.: CCA –EGY Unit & Naga Women Theological Forum, 2004), 18ff; cf. Nungshitula, *The Nnaga Images of the Human Bieng: A Resource for a Contemporary Theological Anthropology* (Jorhat: Tribal Study Center, 2001).

[518] R. L. Hnuni, "Women in the Context of the Bible and Mizoram", in K. Thanzauva, ed., *Towards a Tribal Theology: The Mizo Perspective* (Aizawl: Mizo Theological Conference, 1989), 80ff.

[519] The conference held in May 28-30, 2003 in Dimapur brought together a group of theologically trained Naga women under the theme "Doing Feminist Theology from Naga Women Perspective." The papers read and presented in the conference have been put together in a book

> We, the theologically Trained Naga Women, hereby affirm that the Creator God has created human beings in His image with equal rights.... Therefore, we disapprove of any demeaning human made distinctions on the basis of any gender.... We furthermore affirm that "everyone" has the inherent rights as human beings and as Christians to service, in solidarity and partnership for the uplift of the people and towards building an egalitarian community of the Naga Church and Society.[520]

In the context of Naga people's struggle for political freedom, a political theology of liberation has inevitably come to play an essential role in Naga theological thinking. While the majority of Naga Christians are still quite conservative theologically, when the issues are political sovereignty and freedom they are prepared to shed their conservatism in favor of a liberative theology. The struggle for political freedom is a grass roots movement inspired by the spirit of nationalism that burns within every Naga. The church, along with other civil groups has not only supported the movement for independence, it has also taken an active role in the struggle. In *The Relevance of the Theological Motif of Exile* Noulezhalie R. Medom attempts to appropriate the significance of the exilic motif and then applies it to Naga people's struggle for political freedom.[521] While the Israelites' exile took place within a specific historical and social setting, Nagas and Israelites have both experienced oppression at the hands of foreign rulers. Medom argues that in a paradoxical manner, Nagas too experience exile; they are rendered strangers in their own homeland. The exilic motif can be related to the Nagas because, "it serves as an analogous model of struggle for identity."[522]

Of course liberation must not be confined to the political dimension alone; it entails release from all forms of injustice and exploitation – social, economic, spiritual, psychological and physical as well. Liberation encompasses all forms of unfreedom which prevent people from enjoying the fullness of God-given life at both individual and communal levels. Contemporary Naga society is experiencing social and moral breakdown at all levels; there is corruption in political and civil administration, institutionalized injustice and oppression, and organized crime and violence. According to Wati Aier contemporary Naga society is characterized by:

---

recently published: Limatula Longkumer and Talijungla Longkumer, ed., *Side by Side: Naga Women Doing Theology in Search of Justice and Partnership* (n. p.: CCA – EGY Unit & Naga Women Theological Forum, 2004).

[520] Limatula Longkumer and Talijungla Longkumer, ed., *Side by Side,* 154.

[521] Noulezhalie Ricky Medom, *The Relevance of the Theological Motif of Exile to the Naga's Struggle for Sovereignty as a People* (Delhi: ISPCK, 2002), 84-105.

[522] Ibid., 103.

> Economic corruption, stagnation and the deflation of natural resources.... The unprecedented phenomenon of extortionism in every nook and corner, the attraction to the vigilante styles in order to curb and punish crime, these bear witness . . . to the utter weakness and failure of the "status quo" and to political, moral, ethical and intellectual bankruptcy of the so called "responsible heads and keepers" of the nation, and the Church.[523]

He goes on to assert that the unfortunate state of Naga society is not merely the consequence of the sociological theories of change as others have suggested, but is instead, a largely systemic problem exemplified and exacerbated by the weakness of the established authorities. In the light of these conditions, Aier makes a clear and most challenging call for liberation in the lives of the people and church. He calls for "radical allegiance to Christ that is totally opposed to 'principalities and powers' which have enslaved and dehumanized" the people.[524]

In a similar manner, another church leader and theologian makes a pointed critique against the church for its apathy toward social issues confronting Naga society today. Tuisem A. Shishak queries:

> What does the Bible have to say to those who exploit illiterate poor villagers, to capitalist abuses, to corrupt government officials who accept bribery, to dishonest politicians? What about the comfortable indifference in our churches towards the suffering of the masses? What about the many Baptist churches . . . . Have believers in Christ raised a prophetic voice against these?[525]

He goes on to challenge that, "A church that is not the victim of the class struggle has nothing credible to say about the issue of violence. To sanctify 'non-violence' while silently condoning society's institutionalized forms is hypocrisy."[526]

Both Shishak and Aier concur that in order to receive full liberation Naga Christians must profess total allegiance to Christ because it is only in and through

---

[523] Wati Aier, "Nagas at Present (From a Theological Perspectives)", in http://www.nscnonline.org/webpage/Articles/Nagas_at_present.htm

[524] Ibid.; Aier makes similar challenges in some of his other writings. A Cry from the Rice fields: A call of Freedom for the Nagas (Mokokchung: By the Author, 1989), 56ff; "The Thrust of Theology to Naga Society", in V. K. Nuh, ed., *In Search of Praxis Theology for the Nagas* (New Delhi: Regency Publications, 2003), 1-6.

[525] Tuisem A. Shishak, "Liberation Theology and the Naga Church", in V. K. Nuh, ed., *In Search of Praxis Theology for the Nagas,* 12.

[526] Ibid., 13.

Christ that one can receive total liberation and participate in the liberation of others.[527]

People's longings and aspirations for liberation are also expressed through art and song. What could perhaps be termed the strongest expression of a Naga theology of liberation is found in the lyrics of *Songs of Liberation* composed and sung by Takatemjen. Just some of the lyrics are reproduced here:[528]

Liberation

Liberation, oh, liberation
How long is the road to liberation?
You can't pretend not to see
You can't pretend not to hear
You can feel the groanings of the people
And hear them pray all day long

I saw my people marchin' on
The exodus has just begun
We do not know how long is the road
But we're going to the promised land
Oh my brothers let's march on with the Lord

Let My People Go

Let my people go
To serve the living God
We don't wanna stay

In Egypt anymore
Let my people go

Let freedom ring
From every hill and plain
Let the whole world know
We have been liberated
To serve the living God

[527] Tuisem A. Shishak, "Liberation Theology and the Naga Church", 14; Wati Aier, "Nagas at Present"; Cf. V. K. Nuh, *Nagaland Church and Politics* (Kohima: V. Nuh & Bro., 1986), 11-39. For Nuh the Nazareth Manifesto of Jesus Christ (Luke 4: 18-19) is the basis for total liberation from all forms of injustices including from political domination.

[528] Takatemjen, *Songs of Liberation, A Cassette Recording* (Mokokchung: Logos Cassettes, 1989).

Integrity of Creation and Liberation

While the talk of liberation from socio-economic and political oppression and injustice is critical, that in itself is inadequate unless we relate it to the issues of Creation and ecology. In other words, it is simply unthinkable from the perspectives of Indigenous people to talk about justice as if the only concern is human beings. It is critically important to recognize the interconnectedness of all Creation so that we are able to address and engage the issues in an informed and holistic manner. For Indigenous people issues of justice and peace cannot be meaningfully addressed without first addressing the problems of land and Creation; after all, most human problems are connected to earth and its resources. One of the most articulate spokespersons for such an approach is George E. "Tink" Tinker. In keeping with Indigenous people's orientation to space and creation, Tinker argues that the World Council of Churches (WCC) program of Justice, Peace, and the Integrity of Creation (JPIC) needs a reversal of order in which Creation should be first followed by justice and peace. Tinker offers this reasoning:

> ...I consistently argued in the World Council of Churches that their conciliar process titled "Justice, Peace and the Integrity of Creation" (JPIC) should have been titled "Creation, Justice, Peace." I believe that such a theological prioritizing of creation expands the scope of our possibilities and responsibilities far beyond the existing boundaries of environmental concerns. Rather than the extant and relatively narrow focus on ecology, a theological prioritizing of creation must provide a spiritual and theological foundation for justice. Respect for creation must necessarily result in justice – justice for all creation, as well as justice for all humans – even as genuine justice necessarily will result in peace.[529]

Speaking from the context of African Indigenous and rural communities, Edward P. Antonio argues that, "The environment is the specific conjuncture of relationships between people, their local knowledge, the social structures in which these subsist and the outside world of rivers and trees, soil and land, space and time."[530]

There are other contemporary theologians who have raised similar concerns and the need to recognize the critical connection that exists between ecological problems and the suffering of the poor. In "Social Ecology: Poverty and Misery," Leonardo Boff explains that, "Ecological injustice is transformed into social

---

[529] George E. Tinker, *Spirit and Resistance: Political Theology and American Indian Liberation* (Minneapolis: Fortress Press, 2004), 111.

[530] Edward P. Antonio, "Letting People Decide: Towards an Ethic of Ecological Survival in Africa", in David G. Hallman, *Ecotheology: Voices from South and North* (Geneva: WCC Publications, 1994), 233.

injustice by producing social oppression, exhaustion of resources, contamination of the atmosphere and the deteriorating quality of life that touches all human beings."[531] Boff thus calls for developing a new socio-environmental ethic that is based on an "attitude of benevolence and mutual belonging" toward the earth. K.C. Abraham, an Indian liberation theologian, argues that, "We shall not be able to achieve social justice without justice for the natural environment; we shall not be able to achieve justice for nature without social justice."[532] Jürgen Moltmann is another theologian who sees the inter-related nature of Creation and human problems. He rightly argues that authentic liberation can be experienced only when we take into account the multiple levels of struggles: the struggles for economic justice; the struggles for human dignity and human rights; the struggles for peace with nature, and; the struggles for hope against apathy in asserting the significance of the whole in personal life.[533]

The importance of acknowledging the connections between Creation and human problems is further reinforced by the feminist theologians, especially in the Third World. As Kwok Pui-lan rightly observes, "Feminist theologians in the Third World also look for cultural and religious principles and resources to overcome a mechanistic, capitalist, and Darwinian mind-set."[534] Pui-lan then describes the works of some of the women theologians. While Aruna Gnanadason "lifts up the principle of Shakti, the feminine and creative source of the universe characterized by harmony between humans and nature," Anne Pattel-Gray, an Aboriginal and Pacific feminist theologian, "have emphasized a profound reverence for nature, communal ownership, and women's roles in ceremonies and in providing sustenance for life."[535]

It is in the light of this holistic perspective that we need to interpret the salvafic work of Jesus Christ; the liberative significance of Jesus Christ is for the whole of creation, not humans alone. There is a biblical tradition which speaks of God entering into a "personal pact" with the whole of creation which derives from the idea of a covenantal family of the whole of Creation.[536] God established a covenant not only with Noah and his family but with every living creature – birds,

---

[531] Leonardo Boff, "Social Ecology: Poverty and Misery," in David G. Hallman, ed., *Ecotheology: Voices from South and North,* 244.

[532] K. C. Abraham, *Liberative Solidarity: Contemporary Perspective on Mission* (Thiruvalla: Christava Sahtiya Samithi, 1996), 114.

[533] Jürgen Moltmann, *The Future of Creation* (London: SCM Press, 1979), 110-112.

[534] Kwok Pui-lan, *Postcolonial Imagination and Feminist Theology* (Louisville: Westminster John Knox Press, 2005), 165.

[535] Ibid. Aruna Gnanadason, Toward a Feminist Eco-Theology for India," in Rosemary Radford Ruether, ed., *Women Healing Earth: Third World Women on Ecology, Feminism, and Religion* (Maryknoll: Orbis Books, 1996), 79; Anne Pattel-Gray, *Through Aboriginal Eyes: The Cry from the Wilderness* (Geneva: World Council of Churches, 1991), 1-12.

[536] Genesis 9:8-17;cf. Hosea 2:20.

cattle, and every animal, every living thing on earth and the earth itself. In his letter to the Romans, St. Paul writes about the groaning of the whole of Creation and their hope for freedom from the bondage of decay.[537] This holistic view of liberation is further exemplified in the messianic vision of the new heaven and the new earth.[538] This messianic kingdom will be characterized by the peaceful coexistence between domestic animals and wild beasts, and of humans with all of nature. According to a tradition of the Naga people, the relationship between human beings and the whole of creation does not end with this earthly life, the same relationship continues to exist even in the life after death, in the village of the dead (*Kazeiram* in Tangkhul Naga).[539] The Nagas did not believe in hell or heaven; what they believed was the extension of the present life to the life after death. In *Kazeiram* all animals, fowl, and other creatures continue to live together with human beings as they were in this earthly life. This seems to suggest that human beings and the rest of the creatures have the same destiny; their relationship is eternally bound.

The Bible speaks of liberation in terms of life in abundance and relationship. A. Wati Longchar summarizes the biblical concept of liberation as follows:

> Liberation implies abundance of life in terms of abundant harvest, physical and mental healing, harmonious relationship between humans, beasts and a new stewardship of all earth's resources (Lev. 26: 3-7, Is. 35:1-10). Liberation embraces all aspects of life.... The testimony of the NT is centered around "the Son of God with a human body on earth" and thus the NT writers interpret liberation in terms of the total renewal of cosmic order. St. Paul testifies that God's redemption in Jesus Christ, the reconciliation achieved through the life, death, and resurrection of Christ extends to all creation.[540]

The liberative significance of the suffering, death and resurrection of Jesus Christ encompasses the whole cosmos – humans and the creation.

Jesus as the Reconciler

Peacemaking and Reconciliation in Naga Traditions

The village was and still is the constant of the Naga people. The village was always the center of the community, around which all communal life revolved.

---

[537] Rom. 8:19-21.

[538] Isa. 11:9; 65:17-25; Rev. 21:1-4.

[539] Jonathan H. Thumra, "The Primal Religious Traditions," in P. S. Daniel, et al, ed. *Religious Traditions of India* (Serampore: Indian Theological Library, Senate of Serampore College, 1988), 72.

[540] A. Wati Longchar, "Jesus Christ in Tribal Theology: A Critique", in *Journal of Tribal Studies*, vol. 7, no. 2 (July-December, 2003), 259.

In a socio-political sense, the village served as the kingdom and state of the Naga people in that each village was independent and democratic. Being independent from each other meant that it was critically important for each village to learn to maintain peaceful and friendly relationships with neighboring villages. At the same time, any infringement on or interference in the matters or interests of another village would result in conflicts and possibly even war between or among the effected villages. The conflicts or rivalries generally took place on one or a combination of three distinct levels: inter-clan, inter-village, and inter-tribal. The Naga people were known for their bravery and for the art of war making. In the same manner, the Naga people were also known for their abilities in peacemaking and reconciliation as well as their hospitality, welcoming spirit, and generosity.

There were a number of rich and profound traditions of peacemaking and reconciliation practiced and transmitted from generation to generation by each of the Naga tribes. Different tribes have different names for peacemaking and reconciliation. The Sumi tribe calls it *Alu Pekili* which means reconciliation; the Chakhesang people know it as *Küchene* meaning the feast of peacemaking. To this day, despite the strong influence of modern legal and judicial systems, most Naga tribes prefer to settle their conflicts and disputes according to customary laws and traditions. The February 2, 2006 headline of *The Morung Express*, news online issued daily from Dimapur, Nagaland read as, "Kidima peace model inspires Rio: customary law is best for dispute settlement."[541] This headline refers to the resolution of the "two-decades old confrontation over differences arising out of the usage of – Kedima and Kidima – by the villagers" of Kidima. The villagers decided unanimously in favor of using Kidima for all purposes. Certainly, this is just one of many disputes settled in accordance with the age-old peacemaking traditions.

The peacemaking traditions varied from tribe to tribe. While some tribes had an appointed mediator, many other tribes worked through the collective leadership of the village council or the elders. The Angami, Ao, Tangkhul, Mao, Zeliangrong, Rengma, Lotha as well as others relied primarily on the collective efforts for peacemaking normally through their respective village council or elders. It is possible, even likely, that some of these tribes made use of both an individual mediator and the village council in the reconciliation process. A few tribes such as the Konyak, Chakhesang, and Sumi had their appointed mediators; they were known as *Lampu,*[542] *Demi*[543]*, and Chochomi*[544] respectively. A person

[541] "Kidima peace model inspires Rio: Customary Law is best for dispute settlement," available from http://www.morungexpress.com/

[542] According to Y. Chingang Konyak, there are two types of Lampus: General or village Lampu and Khel (locality) Lampu. Y. Chingang Konyak of Mon, interview by author, 28 July 2003, Kohima, tape recording.

[543] V. K. Nuh of Thesulomi village, interview by author, 28 July 2003, Kohima. Nuh is an authority on Chakhesang culture, history and traditions. He is 70.

[544] Hekhevi Achumi of Dimapur, interview by author, 21 July 2003, Dimapur. Achumi is 61 and comes from a Chief clan of Khumshimi village. He is an authority on Sumi culture, history

of high integrity was chosen to act as the mediator in the Chakhesang and Sumi tribes, while the *Lampu* was a hereditary position for the Konyaks. It should be noted that even in the case of the appointed mediator he or she had to work under the close supervision of the village council or chief. Most Naga peacemaking was carried out collectively through the efforts of the community.

The typical peacemaking tradition always included the exchange of gifts,[545] exchange of visits between the villages, and sharing of community meals which meant lots of eating, drinking and celebrating marked the joyous occasion. The richness and the depth of peace making can be gauged from the peace treaty pledge entered between Kezoma and Pfosemei villages. The peace treaty pledge reads as follows:

1) Whatever we've done upon one another before coming to know each other shall be forgiven.
2) Our friendship will not be broken and we shall not forsake one another until the heavens and the earth, the sun and the moon are no more.
3) On the day of your trouble, I will be of your help and on the day of my trouble, you will be of my help.
4) On the day people oppress you, I will stand behind you and on the day people oppress me, you will stand behind me.
5) If you violate the treaty we have made, all harm shall be fall upon you and if I violate them, all harm shall be fall upon me.
6) This treaty made shall not be altered.[546]

For the purposes of this discussion, I have chosen two traditions that best demonstrate the Naga's rich traditions of peacemaking: they are the traditions of *Pukreila* and *Aksü*. While the former is identified with the Tangkhul people, the latter comes from the Ao tribe and they also represent the mediator/council dichotomy. The *Pukreila* demonstrates peacemaking through the initiative of the mediator and is in fact unique because *Pukreila* is a woman.[547] The *Aksü* is a

---

and traditions.

[545] The most common but also highly significant gifts exchange includes spear and dao. Dao is a traditional Naga sword that can be used for all practical purposes. The exchange of gifts means much more than a ceasefire. Both spear and dao are made of iron; iron is generally known for its cool and serene quality. Spear and dao therefore signify serenity and tranquility, peacefulness and equanimity.

[546] S. K. Hockey, "The Benefit of Peace Treaty: Peace and Reconciliation," in *Pfosemei Peace Treaty Reaffirmation Feast, 1800-2001 Souvenir* (Pfosemei: Pfosemei Peace Treaty Reaffirmation Committee, 2001).

[547] Of course, even in the case of Pukreila, she had to act in behalf of the village under the watchful eyes of the people and the Tangkhul Long which is the apex body of the Tangkhul civil organization. Therefore, it is also a case of collective efforts of peacemaking.

distinctive example of peacemaking and reconciliation effected through collective efforts.

Pukreila the Peacemaker

In Tangkhul Naga society, a girl/woman married to a man from another village was called *Pukreila.*[548] *Pukreila* is not the name of a person, rather it is a title conferred on a girl/woman married to a man from a village other than her own. This girl/woman was given a specific role to serve in the community – peacemaker. Since she was identified with the role of peacemaker, *Pukreila* is also the name of an office, the office of mediation or peacemaking.

As I noted above, Nagas were known for their war-making. However, war was always the last resort and their efforts to secure justice. Justice for the Nagas was a relational term so it cannot be understood outside the Naga cultural context. There were a variety of reasons for going to war. People went to war when there was boundary encroachment, a woman divorced unreasonably, denying customary courtesy and right, breaking the observance of *genna* by one village, etc.[549] Additionally, it was against the tribal value of land ownership to forcibly claim or encroach the land of another person or village; such an action was treated a serious crime. These are all related issues of justice and human equality.

Naga war making was generally a declared war.[550] This was a war fought between two or more villages or tribes at an agreed upon time in an agreed upon location, and included a neutral party, acceptable to the participants, who would oversee the battle. In the case of the Tangkhul Nagas, this neutral party was the Tangkhul Long, the ranking social-political organization of the tribe, who usually monitored the event.[551] When the defeated camp retreats or surrenders, the victorious group must not pursue and attack them from behind. In the event that none of the parties could command a victory, *Pukreila* had the right to intervene and neutralize the fight. Holding the *Zeithing*, a traditional iron staff, she would

---

[548] Y. K. Shimray, "Tangkhul Customary Law and Women", TMs, 2; T. Luikham, Wung (Tangkhul) Naga Okthot Mayonza, 127; cf. Elungkebie, Women in Peacemaking: North East India Perspective," in *Women's Issues in 21st Century*. Women Study Series no. 1, ed. Narola Imchen (Jorhat: Tribal Study Center, 2001), 121-134.

[549] M. Horam, *Social and Cultural Life of Nagas: The Tangkhul Nagas* (Delhi: Low Price Publications, 1992), 91f; Cf. Yangkahao Vashum, "Tangkhul Naga-Christian Theology of Human Rights," M. Th. Thesis, 58.

[550] Besides the declared war which is known in Tangkhul Naga as *rairei pharei*, there were undeclared wars and the war of hostages. While the secret or undeclared war followed hide and attack tactics and was usually protracted, the war of hostages had a person taken and held in the village until a ransom was paid by the guilty party. The hostage cannot be killed under any circumstance. Ako Shaiza of Ukhrul, interview by author, 12 August 2003, Ukhrul, tape recording. Shaiza, a former Tangkhul Long President, is an authority on Tangkhul culture and traditions. Cf. Ankang, *Hau (Tangkhul) Customary Law, 168; Luikham, Wung (Tangkhul) Naga Okthot* Mayonza, 124-16.

[551] Ankang, *Hau (Tangkhul) Customary Law*, 168.

step in between the two enemies and shout "Enough"! "Enough"! The intervention of *Pukreila* ultimately led to the end of the war and the dispute was settled. Under customary law *Pukreila* enjoyed special protection from both the villages. The provision of the law said, "You shall not harm a *Pukreila*."[552] Consequently, no one dared harm her; indeed, to harm *Pukreila* was to dig one's own grave.

Aksü: Feast of Goodwill and Friendship

As it was with other Nagas, the Ao people were known for their tradition of peacemaking called *Aksü* which when translated literally means "pig dead or killed."[553] *Aks*ü is generally observed as a feast meal of pork in celebration of the settlements reached between opposing groups. Additionally, *Aksü* also means reconciliation arrived through exchange of pigs between the parties. According to Takatemjen, "The practice of *Aksü*, i.e. the giving of pigs as a present was both frequent and valued."[554] *Aksü* could be observed between friends, families, clans, and villages. The observance of *Aksü* between villages, known as *Yimden Aksü*, was considered the highest form of *Aksü* and would be observed by the respective village councils on behalf of their people, to promote goodwill and diplomatic relations.[555] In its most broad use *Aks*ü signifies the breaking down of distrust, hatred, and hostility while affirming acceptance, forgiveness, peace and harmony between or among the villages; *Aksü* also served to re-new and reaffirm their commitments for peaceful co-existence between or among villages, and the frequent exchange of gifts symbolized these enduring relationships. Through such continuous observance of *Aksü*, the people could feel that "the spirit of *Aksü* was everywhere."[556] According to Takatemjen, the spirit of *Aksü* is comprised of the following:

> The spirit of *Aksü* is a spirit of friendship.
> The spirit of *Aks*ü is a spirit of sharing.
> The spirit of *Aksü* is a spirit of forgiveness.
> The spirit of *Aksü* is a spirit of healing.
> The spirit of *Aksü* is a spirit of peace.
> The spirit of *Aksü* is a spirit of harmony.
> The spirit of *Aksü* is a spirit of recognition.

---

552 Shimray, "Tangkhul Customary Law," 3. This was true also in the case of the Konyak and Chakhesang tribes; the Lampu and Demi (mediators) respectively could not be harmed in any way.

553 Lipok Jamir, "Table Fellowship: A Model for Naga Reconciliation: A Contextual Theology of Reconciliation in Light of the Concept and Practice of Aksü among the Ao Nagas," in *Journal of Tribal Studies*, vol. 9, no. 2 (July-December 2005), 3.

554 Takatemjen, *Studies on Theology and Naga Culture* (Delhi: ISPCK, 1998), 117.

555 Ibid.; Cf. Panger Imchen, *Ancient Ao Naga Religion and Culture* (Delhi: Har-Anand Publications, 1993), 92.

556 Takatemjen, *Studies on Theology and Naga Culture*, 121.

The spirit of *Aksü* is a spirit of goodwill.
The spirit of *Aksü* is a spirit of brotherhood.
The spirit of *Aksü* is a spirit of neighborliness.
The spirit of *Aksü* is a spirit of unity.
The spirit of *Aksü* is a spirit of acceptance.
The spirit of *Aksü* is a spirit of co-existence.
The spirit of *Aksü* is a spirit of reconciliation.[557]

Jesus as the Reconciler

The image of Jesus as reconciler is an image often used to describe the significance of the salvific work of Jesus Christ. The Christian idea of reconciliation stems from and is rooted in the death of Jesus Christ. Through death on the cross, all people are brought "at-one-ment" with God. New Testament writings are replete with this image of Jesus as the reconciler. In many of his letters to the new converts, Paul testifies to the redeeming work of Jesus Christ in terms of God reconciling the world in and through the death and resurrection of Jesus Christ. Not only is the world reconciled to God, but the world is reconciled to itself. Paul writes, "In Christ God was reconciling the world to himself . . . ."[558]; and in the letter to the Ephesians Paul refers to Jesus as our peace: "For he is our peace; in his flesh he has made both groups into one and has broken down the dividing wall, that is, the hostility between us."[559] Mercy Amba Oduyoye, an African woman and theologian affirms that Christ is "the one who has broken down the barriers we have created between God and us as well as among us . . . thereby saving us from isolation and alienation, which is the lack of community that is the real experience of death."[560]

The work of reconciliation in Hebrew Scripture is shown to take place in a ceremonial context; sacrifices are offered to atone for the wrongs of the individual and nation. One example is Israel's annual Day of Atonement[561] during which "Elaborate ceremonies were performed and these were designed to expiate the sins of the whole nation."[562] In other words, reconciliation is primarily the restoration of the broken relationships between God and the world and the restoration of relationships between and among humans.

[557] Takatemjen, *Studies on Theology and Naga Culture*, 120-121.

[558] 2 Corinth. 5:19.

[559] Eph. 2:14.

[560] Mercy Amba Oduyoye and Elizabeth Amoah, "The Christ for African Women", in Virginia Fabella and Mercy Amba Oduyoye, ed., *With Passion and Compassion: Third World Women Doing Theology* (Maryknoll: Orbis Books, 1994), 44.

[561] Lev. 23:26ff.

[562] F. W. Dillistone, "Atonement," in Alan Richardson and John Bowden, *A New Dictionary of Christian Theology* (London: SCM Press Ltd., 1983), 50.

Peacemaking and reconciliation in Naga context is also understood in this sense of mending broken relationships. As Aküm Longchari rightly points,

"A paradigm of restorative justice was characteristic of traditional Naga jurisprudence where the central concern was to heal the wounds, address the imbalances, and restore the broken relation."[563] The goal of peacemaking is then to create a condition of *shalom*[564] at the individual and corporate levels; where every form of brokenness is mended, every wound is healed, and peace and harmony prevail at all levels and places.

Jesus exemplified the art of peacemaking through his teaching and day to day interactions with the people. He associated freely and identified with those persons society judged to be sinners including women, tax collectors, lepers, and the poor.[565] He shared food with them and acknowledged their inherent dignity as fellow beings created by God. We are told that Jesus dined with a sinner woman in the house of a Pharisee[566] and that he accepted the hospitality of sisters Mary and Martha;[567] Luke notes that Jesus did not shun tax collectors as he shared a meal with Levi,[568] he extended an unconditional invitation to another tax collector named Zacchaeus.[569] Though tax collectors were assumed wealthy, they were among the most despised individuals/groups in Roman occupied Palestine. The Bible thus speaks of "God's preference for the poor." Gustavo Gutierrez explains:

> Such then is the preferential option: the dismantling of anonymity to give a name and a face. In general, Jesus has opted for the poor; but also, concretely, he has opted for people like the hemorrhaging woman....When we speak of preferential love, and the love of God, preferably for the poor, we are speaking of giving the loved ones an identity, of making them feel like people.[570]

---

[563] Aküm Longchari, "Challenges and Opportunity of Church for Nation Building," in http//:nscnonline.org/nscn/index-2.html

[564] Shalom is a Hebrew term for peace which means wholeness or well-being. Peace in this sense, imply not merely a cessation of armed conflicts but a state of well-being of a person or community physically, materially, spiritually, and socially.

[565] For a comprehensive understanding of who the poor are in the Bible refer to Gustavo Gutierrez, *The Power of the Poor in History*, trans. Robert Barr (Maryknoll: Orbis Books, 1988), 12-22; Luise Schottroff and Wolfgang Stegemann, *Jesus and the Hope of the Poor*, trans. Matthew J. O'Connell (Maryknoll: Orbis Books, 1986), 6-16.

[566] Lk. 7: 36-50.

[567] Lk. 10: 38-42.

[568] Lk. 5: 25-32.

[569] Lk. 19: 1-10.

[570] Gustavo Gutierrez, "Renewing the Option for the Poor," in David Batstone and others, eds., *Liberation Theologies, Postmodernity, and the Americas* (London: Routledge, 1997), 75.

By identifying himself with the poor and the downtrodden, Jesus was breaking down the existing social norms and recreating a community that is characterized by respect, acceptance, and interpersonal relationship.

Reconciliation and Table Fellowship

The Christology we ultimately determine is most meaningful and life-affirming for Naga Christians must express in no uncertain terms the liberation from all oppression which Jesus offered the people in Palestine who suffered under Roman rule and the chains of poverty, illness, and alienation; put another way, the Naga Indigenous Christology we formulate must be capable of bringing peace to the people and communities of Nagaland. Jesus was the master of peacemaking and this was illustrated in his relationship with the people. He lived peace in his involvement with the poor, the downtrodden, and the outcast; indeed one could say peacemaking was his way of life. By sharing a table and food with the marginalized and forsaken, Jesus demonstrated his message that in God's Kingdom everyone is welcome irrespective of occupation, gender or status. His actions spoke loudly that those who are seen as somehow less than worthy in the patriarchal hierarchy of Roman-occupied society were in fact valuable and worthy in the eyes of God, and they could be freed by the love of Jesus. At the same time he was also showing the people that service to the least among society is a prerequisite for the Kingdom. Joachim Jeremias makes a poignant observation on the reports of these activities of Jesus:

> In the East, even today, to invite a man to a meal was an honor. It was an offer of peace, trust and brotherhood, and forgiveness: in short, sharing a table meant sharing life.... Jesus' meals with the publicans and sinners, too, are not only events on a social level, not only an expression of his unusual humanity and social generosity and his sympathy with those who were despised, but had an even deeper significance. They are an expression of the mission and message of Jesus' (Mk. 2:17) eschatological meals, anticipatory celebrations of the feast in the end-time (Lk. 13:28 f; Mt. 8:11-12).[571]

Jeremias concludes that, "The inclusion of sinners in the community of salvation, achieved in table-fellowship, is the most meaningful expression of the message of the redeeming love of God."[572] As exemplified by the traditional Naga feast of *Aksü* as well as Jesus' sharing meals with those of the least, table fellowship signifies acceptance and the spirit of sisterhood and brotherhood between and

[571] Joachim Jeremias, *New Testament Theology: The Proclamation of Jesus* (New York: Charles Scribner's Sons, 1971), 115-116.

[572] Joachim Jeremias, *New Testament Theology: The Proclamation of Jesus* (New York: Charles Scribner's Sons, 1971), 115-116.

among the people; it signifies cordiality, friendship, and goodwill. Both the feast of *Aksü* and the stories of Jesus sharing food with the least of society offer strong and tangible images that will inform and enliven a Naga Indigenous Christology. These are powerful images which can guide and strengthen Nagas as they seek to reestablish mutual respect among themselves and will also serve to encourage the people's sense of self worth. Table fellowship is meant to be joyous and a celebration of the positive relationships people share with one another. It is a demonstration of persons or people being at-one with one another.

The traditional Naga feast of *Aksü* reminds us the significance of sharing our meals with one another in this time when Naga society is being torn by disagreement and factionalism, this time when Naga society suffers from fratricidal violence and death. In Nagaland today, a theology of reconciliation would mean applying the biblical concept of reconciliation in addition to the spirit of *Aksü*.[573] It would mean following the examples of Jesus Christ in letter and spirit and learning to lead a life that is informed by the spirit of *Aksü*. Jesus admonished his disciples to be doers of the word, rather than passive listeners. Jesus said, "Blessed are the peace makers, for they will be called children of God."[574] The thrust of Jesus' message is very clear: "Go and do likewise." Be the agent of peace. Peace and peacemaking is future oriented and they demand aggressive pursuance. Speaking in the context of American Indian struggle for liberation, Taiaiake Alfred, a leading Kanienkeha (Mohawk) scholar and activist, states:

> Peace is hopeful, visionary, and forward-looking; it is not just the lack of violent conflict or rioting in the streets. . . . Reconceptualized for our struggle, peace is being Onkwehonwe, breaking with the disfiguring and meaningless norms of our present reality, and recreating ourselves in a holistic sense. This conception of peace requires a rejection of the state's multifaceted oppression of our peoples simultaneously with and through the assertion of regenerated Onkwehonwe identities.[575]

The challenge in applying this admonition to the Naga context is that, individually and collectively we must assume the roles of a *Pukreila*. *Pukreila* was a powerful agent of peace in the society; her words were respected by one and all.

Today, by following the tradition of *Pukreila,* Naga women are actively involved in the peacemaking process. Women's organizations such as the Naga Mother's Association (NMA), and the Naga Women's Union of Manipur (NWUM) have taken a leading role particularly, in the ongoing negotiations between the Naga national leaders and the Government of India. They are also

---

[573] Takatemjen, *Studies on Theology and Naga Culture,* 127.

[574] Matt. 5: 9.

[575] Taiaiake Alfred, *Wasáse: Indigenous Pathways of Action and Freedom* (Peterborough: Broadview Press, Ltd., 2005), 28.

actively working to forge unity between and among the various Naga political factions and insurgency movements. They have spoken out against the violence and killings perpetrated by both Indians and Nagas. Apart from their peace efforts Naga women are working for social recovery and regeneration as well. They have taken initiative to address the problems of drug and alcohol addiction among the youth, and they are providing essential care to persons afflicted with HIV and AIDS. These women are indeed the *Pukreilas* of our time.

While the *Pukreila* primarily symbolizes the role of women in peacemaking, the call to be an agent of peace is for everyone, male and female, young and old. We are all called to be peacemakers wherever we may be; we can all be *Pukreilas* of our time.

Naga Indigenous Christology: Liberation, Reconcilation, and Healing

Liberation, reconciliation, and healing are the gifts and graces of the living Jesus just as they are the values and strengths of the best of Naga traditions; they are interrelated and inseparably linked. There cannot be true liberation without reconciliation, just as there cannot be true reconciliation without freedom; they are like the two sides of the same coin. Liberation will encompass all that constitute a condition of *shalom*, where justice, peace, and harmony prevail. Jesus' declaration that he came into the world so that people might have life in fullness speaks of a liberated life, a life also reconciled in Christ.

Having said this, it must be pointed out that there is no easy way to reconciliation and freedom. The notion of forgive and forget does not work unless the persons who are responsible for the wrongs committed are ready to own up their responsibility. There can be no genuine reconciliation and freedom without the recognition and acknowledgement by the perpetrators of the wrongs committed. There can be no reconciliation without first coming to terms with the realities of the past. Confronting the past is never easy, it is an agonizing and painful process but the healing that comes about through such process is real and worthwhile. The perpetrators must not only recognize the wrongs committed, they must also claim their culpability and express sincerely their intention to improve their ways. In the Naga's search for freedom and healing it is critical that India recognize and accept the wrongs she has inflicted during decades of aggression against and domination of the Naga people. It is true that healing within and among the Naga people must be sought and dealt with by the Naga people themselves in ways consistent with their culture and values. However, given the fact of Naga peoples' suffering and loss are linked directly to India's aggression and occupation, the Naga people's healing must be accompanied by the healing of the Indians. Speaking in the context of American Indian people, Tinker argues convincingly that:

> While the internal healing of American Indian communities may be Indian business at one level, any real healing or liberation in the world of American Indians must be paralleled by healing in the world of euro-americans in order for the healing of Indian peoples to be sustained.[576]

This is very true in the case of the Naga people vis-à-vis decades of Indian colonization. In order for the healing to take place, India must not only recognize the identity of the Nagas as a people with a unique history as a sovereign nation, but they must also take responsibility for the decades of Naga peoples' suffering.

The 2001 recognition of the unique history of Naga people, important as that is, cannot ameliorate the genocidal crimes committed against the Naga people for over 70 years. It is critically important for the healings of both the Naga communities and Indians that India own up its aggression rather than resorting to the usual denials and subsequent intimidation.

A vital and affirming belief in Christ makes for not only a liberated life, it also provides for a life at its fullest. The goal of liberation is to make possible the wholeness of life but this wholeness is dependent on the Naga people being free from the reality of oppression they endure under India's occupation. Freedom must be experienced in the real physical world as well as in the spiritual life of the Naga people. The Naga people must be allowed to reclaim their past with a view to dreaming their own future. There is indeed power in naming and reclaiming; the healing process then must begin with naming and reclaiming. Winona LaDuke asks:

> How does a community heal itself from the ravages of the past? . . . I found an answer in the multifaceted process of recovering that which is "sacred." This complex and intergenerational process is essential to our vitality as Indigenous peoples and ultimately as individuals.[577]

In a similar manner, Taiaiake Alfred, reminds Indigenous communities the importance of reclaiming their traditional values for their survival and future.

> The only way we can survive is to recover our strength, our wisdom, and our solidarity by honoring and revitalizing the core of our traditional teachings. Only by heeding the voices of our ancestors can

---

[576] Tinker, *Spirit and Resistance,* 5.

[577] Winona LaDuke, *Recovering the Sacred: The Power of Naming and Claiming* (Cambridge: South End Press, 2005), 11. For LaDuke "Sacred" means the whole web of relationship with the land, Creation, and nature, it means the freedom to practice one's own spirituality in sacred lands.

> we restore our nations and put peace, power, and righteousness back into the hearts and minds of our people.[578]

Alfred concludes saying, "The challenge for us is to commit ourselves to those teachings and to walk those indigenous paths."[579] Speaking in the context of Naga people' search for healing and recovery, Longchari also expresses the importance of reclaiming their stories.

> I believe to move forward, we must first begin to understand where we came from and where we are today! In order to do so, we must reclaim our heritage, reclaim our stories, erase the myths that have distorted our identity and begin addressing our history in a way that embraces the richness of our cultures and one that will liberate us from the parochial systems that continue to suffocate us.[580]

The healing process for the Naga people must begin with the naming and reclaiming of neglected stories and traditions. Reclaiming their history and regaining the vision to dream their own future are essential to any efforts to bring wholeness back to the Naga people. In this sense the construction of a Naga-Indigenous Christology is an important dimension of dreaming the future in light of the Naga people's past and present experiences. The image of Jesus as the rooster conveys the significance of the sacrificial death of Jesus in a way that is culturally recognizable and relevant to the Naga people. Similarly, the portrayal of Jesus as the ancestor and elder brother enables Naga Christians to relate to Jesus in a familiar and meaningful way: Jesus as the ancestor is "God with us", who is there for the people in times of sorrows and joy; the past, present, and future come together in Christ; and Jesus as elder brother represents a much needed role model for all. The image of Jesus as the liberator resonates with considerable power in the lives of the Naga people as they strive to persevere in their struggle for political, social, and economic freedom. However, the significance of Jesus' liberative work goes far beyond human freedom; it encompasses the whole of Creation in which humanity and the rest of Creation constitute the community in need of liberation. Our examination of two peacemaking traditions of the Naga people, the traditions of *Pukreila* and *Aksü*, demonstrates in direct contradiction of colonizer's insistence that Nagas were and are warmongering savages, they were and are a peace-loving people who place great value in friendship and harmonious co-existence. These traditions of peacemaking and reconciliation enrich our understanding of the significance of the role of Jesus as reconciler.

---

[578] Taiaiake Alfred, *Peace, Power, and Righteousness: An Indigenous Manifesto* (Ontario: Oxford University Press, 1999), xii.

[579] Alfred, *Wasáse: Indigenous Pathways of Action and Freedom,* 236.

[580] Longchari, "Challenges and Opportunity of Church for Nation Building."

The Naga people deserve the freedom to determine the kind of future they want without any interference from outside forces. St. Paul says in Galatians, "For freedom Christ has set us free. Stand firm, therefore, and do not submit again to a yoke of slavery."[581] Freedom for which Christ has set us free includes the Naga people's freedom to reclaim their histories and the ability to dream their own future. The liberation and healing of the Naga nation must take place on two fronts: reconciliation between and among the Naga people, and the reclamation of their stories and subsequent opportunity to dream their own future in a way that is consistent with their culture and values. It is fundamental that the Naga people unite themselves for the just cause of their struggle and to keep alive in themselves the right to dream their own future.

Finally, the physical and psychological effects of the oppression, domination, and genocide inflicted on the Naga people by the British and India require a power that can only be provided by a Christological belief and understanding which is infused with the reconciling and healing potential of the combined values of Naga tradition and the living Jesus.

[581] Gal. 5: 1.

Conclusions

A living and meaningful Christology does not arise in a vacuum; it must always emerge out of a peoples' historical experience. This Christology must be grounded in the socio-economic and political realities in which the people live, and also incorporate the best of the people's values and traditions. A Naga-Indigenous Christology will likewise be done in the context of the historical realities of the Nagas and will be informed and guided by Naga-Indigenous values and traditions. A Naga-Indigenous Christology will be a reflection of the people's experience of oppression, loss, suffering; it will identify and express the concerns and longings that Nagas live with each day; and, it will embody their aspirations to be a sovereign people able to dream and shape their own future. Indeed, I believe that this affirming and liberating Christology will provide the substance for a Naga-Indigenous theology that Naga Christians can claim as their own as they seek to restore their self worth and tribal identities. The historical reality under Indian occupation and their struggle for political independence serve as critical elements for their theological articulation and reflection. Also, as I have noted in the preceding chapters, a significant aspect of a postcolonial theological methodology is the reclamation of the past stories and traditions which had sustained the people for tens of generations so that those traditional resources in combination with the people's contemporary experiences can be applied to construct a relevant and meaningful Christology of culture and liberation.

Further more the construction of Naga-Indigenous Christology is an important dimension of dreaming the future in light of the Naga people's past and present experiences. In the process of identifying the factors necessary to the formulation of an empowering Naga-Indigenous Christology, I have relied a great deal on the cultural resources of Indigenous peoples, but primarily I have enlisted the resources of the Naga people in order to produce a critical Christology built on and around four cultural images: 1) Jesus as the Rooster 2) Jesus as Elder Brother and Ancestor 3) Jesus as Liberator, and 4) Jesus as Reconciler. These four images were chosen not only because each is widely known among the Nagas, but also because each metaphorical image offers specific but rich resources that transfer easily to the affirming image of Jesus.

With my first choice of cultural image of the rooster, I have demonstrated that both the rooster and Jesus died so the people might live! The purpose of the ceremony in which the rooster sacrificed was for the purification and restoration of the community. Although the effect of Naga rooster sacrifice was directed primarily toward the well-being of the immediate community on whose behalf the ceremony was conducted, it is important to remember that the rest of the world and Creation also benefited. As noted in chapter four, when a community is at peace and in harmony, the larger world is also effected, if only indirectly. The image of Jesus as the rooster conveys the significance of the sacrificial death of Jesus in a way that is culturally appropriate and relevant to the Naga people.

My portrayal of Jesus as the ancestor and elder brother enables the Naga Christians to relate to Jesus in a culturally familiar and meaningful way. Jesus as the ancestor fulfils the longings and expectations of the family members and community while Jesus as elder brother represents the much needed role model for all believers. Jesus as ancestor is God with us in that he not only understands our problems but also shares the joy and pain of the family and community. Additionally, Jesus as both ancestor and elder brother not only advocate on our behalf before the Father, it is in and through him the community of faith finds its meaning for existence. Christ represents the new tradition and law of the community which are written on our hearts. In him the past, the present, and the future come together.

I also chose the image of Jesus as the liberator because this resonates powerfully in the lives of the Naga people in their ongoing struggle for political, social, and economic freedom. Jesus' message of liberation provides the necessary hope and sustaining power the people require in their journey toward freedom; however, the significance of Jesus' liberative work goes far beyond human freedom, it liberates the whole of Creation in which humanity and the rest of Creation constitute the liberated community. In other words, our human liberation is incomplete until and unless the rest of Creation is liberated as well. Both the biblical and Naga Indigenous traditions are very clear on this holistic view of liberation as I have demonstrated in the preceding chapter.

Our examination of Naga people's peacemaking traditions, particularly the traditions of *Pukreila* and *Aksü*, constitute the fourth cultural tradition which I identified and it demonstrates that, quite contrary to the colonizer's repeated description of the Nagas as warmongering savages, Nagas were and are people with rich peacemaking traditions, and that they were and are a peace-loving people who value friendship and harmonious co-existence. Nagas, just as other Indigenous peoples in the world, recognize that all Creation is interconnected and their survival is dependent on the connections they maintain with others. Put another way, Nagas understand that maintaining harmonious relationship with the rest of the world is critical to their own peaceful existence. Examination of these traditions of peacemaking and reconciliation enriches our understanding of the significance of the role of Jesus as reconciler. Additionally, it enables the people to relate the message of Jesus' work of reconciliation in a way that is culturally appropriate and meaningful. All of this serves to demonstrate that Naga-Indigenous culture and values are compatible for their faith profession and appropriation. Jesus the reconciler is a part of the Naga culture as much as he is present in people's culture.

It must be further reiterated that liberation, reconciliation, and healing must be understood as elements of one larger vision and must not be seen in isolation from each other. Naga people's liberation and healing must begin by naming and reclaiming their lost stories and histories, and by reclaiming their ability to dream their own future without any interference from outside powers. The illegal occupation of Nagaland must stop so the Naga people can dream their future in accordance with their desires and consistent with their culture and values.

At the end, the physical and psychological effects of the oppression, domination, and genocide inflicted on the Naga people by the British and India require a power that can only be provided by a Christological belief and understanding which is infused with the reconciling and healing potential of the combined values of Naga tradition and the living Jesus.

Bibliography

Books

Alem, O. *Tsüngremology*. Mokokchung: Clark Theological College, 1994.

Alemchiba, M. *A Brief Historical Account of Nagaland.* Kohima: Naga Institute of Culture, 1970.

Alfred, Taiaiake. *Wasáse: Indigenous Pathways of Action and Freedom*. Peterborough: Broadview Press, Ltd., 2005.

________. *Peace, Power, and Righteousness: An Indigenous Manifesto*. Ontario: Oxford University Press, 1999.

Althaus-Reid, Marcella. *Indecent Theology: Theological Perversions in Sex, Gender and Politics*. New York: Routledge, 2000.

Angkang, Stephen. *Hau (Tangkhul) Customary Law* (Hau *Shiyan Chikan).* Ukhrul: Development for Hau Ancient Custom and Research Organization, 1999.

Ao, A. Bendang. *History of Christianity in Nagaland: A Source Material.* Mokokchung: Shalom Ministry, 1998.

________. *History of Christianity in Nagaland: The Ao Naga Tribal Christian Mission Enterprise,* 1872-1972. Mokokchung: Shalom Ministry Publication, *2002.*

Ao, A. Lanunungsang. *From Phizo to Muivah: The Naga National Question in North- East India.* New Delhi: Mittal Publications, 2002.

Ao, Tajenyuba. *British Occupation of Naga Country.* Mokokchung: Naga Literature Society, n.d.

Aquino, Maria Pilar. *Our Cry for Life: Feminist Theology from Latin America.* Maryknoll: Orbis Books, 1993.

Aschroft, Bill, Gareth Griffiths, and Helen Tiffin, ed. *The Post-Colonial Studies Reader*. London: Routledge, 1995.

Azam, Kousar J. *Ethnicity, Identity, and the State in South Asia.* New Delhi: South Asian Publishers, 2001.

Babha, Homi K. *The Location of Culture*. London and New York: Routledge, 1994.

Balasurya, Tissa. *Planetary Theology*. Maryknoll: Orbis Books, 1984.

_________. *Mary and Human Liberation: The Story and the Text*. Edited by Helen Stanton. Harrisburg: Trinity Press International, 1997.

Baruah, Sanjib. *Durable Disorder: Understanding the Politics of Northeast India*. New Delhi: Oxford University Press, 2005.

Batstone, David, Eduardo Mendieta, Lois Ann Lorentzen, and Dwight N. Hopkins, eds., *Liberation Theologies, Postmodernity, and the Americas*. London: Routledge, 1997.

Bendangangshi, I. and I. T. Apok Aier. *The Religion of the Ao Nagas*. 2nd rev. ed. Guwahati, Assam: by the authors, 1997.

Bhowmick, P. K. *Rethinking Tribal Culture in India*. Kolkota: R. N. Bhattacharya, 2001.

Boff, Leonardo. *Cry of the Earth, Cry of the Poor*. Translated by Phillip Berryman. Maryknoll: Orbis Books, 1997.

_________. *Jesus Christ Liberator: A Critical Christological Essay for Our Time*. Translated by Patrick Hughes. Maryknoll: Orbis Books, 1978.

_________. *Ecology and Liberation: A New Paradigm*. Translated by John Cumming. Maryknoll: Orbis Books, 1984.

Bonino, José Miguez. *Faces of Jesus: Latin American Christologies*. Translated by Robert R. Barr. Maryknoll: Orbis Books, 1984.

_________. *Doing Theology in a Revolutionary Situation*. Philadelphia: Fortress Press, 1975.

Bosch, David J. *Transforming Mission: Paradigm Shift in Theology of Mission*. Maryknoll: Orbis Books, 1991.

Broke, Rita N. *Journeys* By *Heart: A Christology of Erotic Power*. New York: Crossroad Publishing Company, 1984.

Cajeti, Gregory. *Native Science: Natural Laws of Interdependence*. Santa Fe: Clear Light Publishers, 2000.

Carr, Anne. *Transforming Grace: Christian Tradition and Women's Experience*. San Francisco: Harper, 1988.

Cesaire, Aime. *Discourse on Colonialism*. Translated by P. Joan. New York: Monthly Review Press, 1972.

Chambers, Iain and Lidia Curti., ed. *Postcolonial Questions: Common Skies, Divided Horizons*. London: Routledge, 1996.

Chana, Subhadra Mitra, ed. *Nagaland, a Contemporary Ethnography*. New Delhi: Cosmo Publication, 1992.

Chomsky, Noam. *Hegemony or Survival: America's Quest for Global Dominance*. New York: Henry Holt and Company, 2003.

Christ, Carol P. and Judith Plaskow, ed. *Womenspirit Rising: A Feminist Reader in Religion*. San Francisco: HarperSanFrancisco, 1992.

Churchill, Ward. *Fantasies of Master Race: Literature, Cinema and the Colonization of American Indian Liberation.* Boulder: City Lights Books, 1998.

________. *Acts of Rebellion: The Ward Churchill Reader*. New York: Routledge, 2003.

________. *Kill the Indian, Save the Man: The Genocidal Impact of American Indian Residential Schools*. San Francisco: City Lights Books, 2004.

Clarke, Sathianathan. *Dalits and Christianity: Subaltern Religion and Liberation Theology in India.* Delhi: Oxford University Press, 1998.

Cleage, Albert. *The Black Messiah.* Kansas City: Sheed and Ward, 1969.

Cone, James H. *A Black Theology of Liberation.* 20th Anniversary ed. Maryknoll: Orbis Books, 1990.

________. *God of the Oppressed.* rev. ed. Maryknoll: Orbis Books, 1997.

Cone, James H. and G. S. Wilmore, ed. *Black Theology: A Documentary History*, 2 vols. Maryknoll: Orbis Books, 1993.

Cox, Jeffrey. *Imperial Fault Lines: Christianity and Colonial Power in India, 1818-1940.* Stanford: Stanford University Press, 2002.

Csapo, Eric. *Theories of Mythology*. Malden and Oxford: Blackwell, 2005.

Daly, Mary. *Beyond God the Father: Toward a Philosophy of Women's Liberation: With an Original Reintroduction by the Author*. Boston: Beacon Press, 1985.

Daniel, P. S, and David C. Scott, ed. *Religious Traditions of India.* Serampore: Indian Theological Library, 1988.

Das, N. K, and C. L. Imchen, ed. *People of India: Nagaland.* Vol. 34. General editor, K. S. Singh. Anthropological Survey of India. Calcutta: Seagull Books, 1994.

Davis. *Census of Assam,* 1891, Part II.

Deloria Jr, Vine. *The World We Used to Live In: Remembering the Powers of Medicine Men*. Golden: Fulcrum Publishing, 2006.

________. *Evolution, Creationism, and Other Modern Myths. A Critical Inquiry.* Golden: Fulcrum Publishing, 2002.

________. *Spirit and Reason: The Vine Deloria Jr. Reader.* Edited by Barbara Deloria, Kristen Foener, and Sam Scinta. Golden: Fulcrum Publishing, 1999.

________. *Red Earth, White Lies: Native Americans and the Myth of Scientific Fact.* Golden: Fulcrum Publishing, 1997.

________. *God is Red: A Native View of Religion,* 2nd ed. Golden: North American Press, 1992.

Dena, Lal. *Christian Missions and Colonialism: A Study of Missionary Movement in Northeast India with Particular Reference to Manipur and Lushai Hills,* 1894-1947. Shillong: Vendrame Institute, 1988.

Diamond, Irene and Gloria F. Orenstein, ed. *Reweaving the World: The Emergence of Ecofeminism.* San Francisco: Sierra Club Books, 1990.

Douglas, Kelly Brown. *The Black Christ.* Maryknoll: Orbis Books, 1994.

Downs, Frederick S. *Christianity in North East India: Historical Perspectives.* Delhi: International Society for Propagation of Christian Knowledge, 1983.

________. *The Mighty Works of God: A Brief History of the Council Baptist Churches in North East India: The Mission Period 1836-1950.* Gauhati: Christian Literature Center, 1971.

Driver, Tom F. *Liberating Rites: Understanding the Transformative Power of Ritual.* Boulder: Westview Press, 1991.

Dubey, S. M., ed. *North East India: A Sociological Study.* Delhi: Concept Publishing Company, 1978.

________. ed. *Tribal Heritage of India. Vol.* 1. *Ethnicity, Identity and Interaction.* New Delhi: Vikash Publishing House Pvt. Ltd., 1977.

Dunn, Edmond J. *Missionary Theology: Foundations in Development.* Foreward by Richard P. McBrien. Washington D. C.: University Press of America, 1980.

Eliade, Mircea. *Myth and Reality.* Translated by Willard R. Trask. New York: Harper & Row, 1975.

Elwin, Verrier, ed. *The Nagas in the Nineteenth Century.* Bombay: Oxford University Press, 1969.

________. *The Tribal World of Verrier Elwin: An Autobiography.* New York and Bombay: Oxford University Press, 1964.

Eusebius. *Life of Constantine.* Translated and Commentary by A. Cameron and S. G. Hall. Oxford: Clarendon Press, 1999.

Fabella, Virginia, and Mercia A. Oduyoye, ed. *With Passion and Compassion: Third World Women Doing Theology.* Maryknoll: Orbis Books, 1988.

Fabella, Virginia, and Sergio Torres, ed. *The Irruption of the Third World: Challenge to International Economic Order, Challenge to Theology: Papers from the Fifth International Conference of the Ecumenical Association of the Third World Liberation Theologians, August 17-29, 1981, New Delhi, India.* Maryknoll: Orbis Books, 1981.

Fanon, Frantz. *The Wretched of the Earth.* Preface by Jean-Paul Sartre. New York: Grove Press, 1963.

________. *Black Skin, White Mask.* New York: Grove Press, 1967.

Fiorenza, Elisabeth Schüssler. *In Memory of Her: A Feminist Theological Reconstructions of Christian Origins.* New York: Crossroads Publishing Company, 1983.

________. *Jesus: Miriam's Child, Sophia's Prophet: Critical Issues in Feminist Christology.* New York: Continuum, 1994.

Foucault, Michel. *Power/Knowledge: Selected Interviews and Other Writings,* 1972-1977. Edited by Colin Cordon. Hertfordshire: Harvester Press, 1980.

Fürer-Haimendorf, Christopher von. *Return to the Naked Nagas: An Anthropologist's View of Nagaland, 1936-1970.* New edition. London: J. Murray, 1976.

________. *The Konyak Nagas: An Indian Frontier Tribe.* New York: Holt, Rinehart and Winston, 1969.

Gachui, Maiya. *Hao Miun Ngashan kala Tangkhul Khararchan (History of Tangkhul).* Imphal, Manipur: by the author, 1986.

Grant, Jacqueline. *White Women's Christ: Black Women's Jesus.* Atlanta Scholars Press, 1989.

Grim, John A., ed. *Indigenous Traditions and Ecology: The Interbeing of Cosmology and Community.* Cambridge: Harvard University Press, 2001.

Gutierrez, Gustavo. *A Theology of Liberation: History, Politics and Salvation.* 15th Anniversary ed. Translated and edited by Carida Inda and John Eagleson. Maryknoll: Orbis Books, 1999.

________. *The Power of the Poor in History.* Translated by Robert Barr. Maryknoll: Orbis Books, 1988.

Haight, Roger. *Jesus Symbol of God.* Maryknoll: Orbis Books, 2002.

Hansen, Holger Bernt and Michael Twaddle, ed. *Christian Missionaries and the State in the Third World.* Athens: Ohio University Press; Oxford: James Currey, 2002.

Harvey, Graham, ed. *Indigenous Religions: A Companion.* London and New York: Cassel, 2000.

Hayward, Isabel Carter. *Speaking of Christ: A Lesbian Feminist Voice.* New York: Pilgrim Press, 1989.

Hazarika, Sanjoy. *Strangers of the Mist: Tales of War and Peace from India's Northeast.* New Delhi: Viking, 1994.

Hennelly, Alfred T., ed. *Liberation Theology: A Documentary History.* Maryknoll: Orbis Books, 1990.

Hnuni, R. L. *Transforming Theology for Empowering Women: A Theological and Hermeneutical Reflection in the Context of North East India.* Tribal Study Series, no. 4. Jorhat: Women's Studies ETC, 1999.

Hodson, T. C. *The Naga Tribes of Manipur.* London: Macmillan and Company Limited, 1911.

Hoogvelt, Ankie. *Globalization and the Postcolonial World: The New Political Economy of Developmet.* Baltimore: John Hopkins, 1997.

Hopkins, Dwight N. *Introducing Black Theology of Liberation.* Maryknoll: Orbis Books, 1999.

________. *Down, Up, and Over: Slave Religion and Black Theology.* Minneapolis: Fortress Press, 2000.

Horam, Mashangthei. *Social and Cultural Life of Nagas: The Tangkhul Naga.* New Delhi: Cosmo Publications, 1977.

________. *Nagas Old Ways New Trends.* New Delhi: Cosmo Publications, 1988.

________. *Naga Insurgency: The Last Thirty Years.* New Delhi: Cosmo Publications, 1988.

Horsley, Richard A. *Hearing the Whole Story: The Politics of Plot in Mark's Gospel.* Louisville: Westminster John Knox Press, 2001.

Howard, Bradley R. *Indigenous People and the State: The Struggle for Native Rights.* Dekalb: Northern Illinois University Press, 2003.

Hutton, J. H. *The Angami Nagas, with some Notes on Neighboring Tribes.* 2nd ed. London: Oxford University Press, 1969.

________. *The Sema Nagas.* 2nd ed. London: Oxford University Press, 1968.

Imchen, Panger. *Ancient Ao Naga Religion.* Delhi: Har-Anand Pubilcation, 1993.

Isasis-Diaz, Ada Maria. *Mujerista Theology: A Theology for the Twenty-first Century.* Maryknoll: Orbis Books, 1996.

Jacobs, Julian. *The Nagas: Hill Peoples of Northeast India: Society, Culture, and the Colonial Encounter.* New York: Thames and Hudson, 1990.

Jajo, Champhang. *Christian Life in a Tribal Context: In Manipur.* Imphal, Manipur: by the author, 1990.

Jameson, Fredric. *Postmodernism or, the Cultural Logic of Late Capitalism.* Durham: Duke University Press, 1999.

Jeremias, Joachim. *New Testament Theology: The Proclamation of Jesus.* New York: Charles Scribner's Sons, 1971.

Kamei, Gangmumei. *Ethnicity and Social Change: An Anthology of Essays.* Imphal: Smt. Pouganglu Gangmei, 2002.

Karotemprel, Sebastian, and Deepali Nanda. *The Tribes of Northeast India.* Calcutta: Fira KLM Private Limited, 1984.

Karotemprel, Sebastian, ed. *The Catholic Church in Northeast India, 1890-1990.* Shillong: Vendrame Institute, 1993.

Kasper, Walter. *Jesus the Christ.* London: Burns and Oates, 1976.

Keitzar, Renthy. *In Search of a Relevant Gospel Message.* Guwahati: Christian Literature Centre, 1995.

________. *Triumph of Faith in Nagaland.* Kohima: NBCC, 1987.

________. ed. *Good News for North East India: A Theological Reader.* Guwahati: Christian Literature Center, 1995.

Keller, Catherine, Michael Nausner, and Mayra Rivera, ed. *Postcolonial Theologies: Divinity and Empire*. St. Louis: Chalice Press, 2004.

Khamuiwo, Wungyao. *Wung (Yang) Tangkhul Naga Wurtam kala Mayonza.* Ukhrul, Manipur: by the author, 1999.

Khan, Haider A. *Technology, Development and Democracy: Limits of National Innovation Systems in the Age of Postmodernism.* Cheltenham: Edward Elgar, 1998.

Kharkongor, Felix H. *The Revealed Christ of the Khasi Religion.* Worthing: Loxwood Press, 1994.

Kidwell, Clara Sue, Homer Noeley, and George E. "Tink" Tinker, *A Native American Theology*. Maryknoll: Oris Books, 2001.

Kipgen, M. *Christianity and Mizo Culture: The Encounter Between Christianity and Zo Culture in Mizoram.* Aizawl: Mizo Theological Conference, 1997.

Konyak, A. Yanang. *From Darkness to Light: A Story of the Baptist Work among the Konyak Nagas.* Guwahati: Christian Literature Center, 1986.

Koyama, Kosuke. *Water Buffalo Theology.* 25th Anniversary edition, Revised and Expanded Maryknoll: Orbis Books, 1999.

Kumar, B. B. *The Tribal Societies of India: A Macro Perception.* New Delhi: Omsons Publications, 1998.

Kumar, Ram Narayan, and Laxmi Murthy. *Four Years of the Ceasefire Agreement between the Government of India and National Socialist Council of Nagalim: Promises and Pitfalls.* New Delhi: Civil Society Initiatives on the Naga Peace Proces, 2002.

Kyung, Chung Hyung. *Struggle to be the Sun Again: Introducing Asian Women's Theology.* Maryknoll: Orbis Books, 1990.

LaDuke, Winona. *Recovering the Sacred: The Power of Naming and Claiming.* Cambridge: South End Press, 2005.

Lakeland, Paul. *Postmodernity: Christian Identity in a Fragmented Age*. Minneapolis: Fortress Press, 1996.

Lanunungsang Ao, A. *From Phizo to Muivah: The Naga National Question in North East India.* New Delhi: Mittal Publications, 2002.

Longchar, A. Wati. *The Tribal Religious Traditions in North East India: An Introduction.* Jorhat: Eastern Theological College, 1991.

________. *An Emerging Asian Theology: Tribal Theology Issue, Method and Perspective.* Tribal Study Series, no. 8. Jorhat: Tribal Study Center, 2000.

________. ed. *An Exploration of Tribal Theology.* Tribal Study Series no. 1. 6 Jorhat: Tribal Study Center, 1997.

________. ed. *In Search of Identity and Tribal Theology: A Tribute to Dr. Renthy Keitzar.* Tribal Study Series no. 9. Jorhat: Tribal Study Center, 2000.

________. ed. *No more Guns! People's Struggle for Justice: Focus on North East India.* Tribal Study Series, no. 7. Jorhat: Tribal Study Center, 2000.

________. ed. *Encounter between Gospel and Tribal Culture.* Tribal Study Series, no. 5. Jorhat: Tribal Study Center, 1999.

Longchar, A. Wati, and Yangkahao Vashum, ed. *The Tribal Worldview and Ecology.* Tribal Study Series no. 2. Jorhat: Tribal Study Center, 1998.

Longchar, A. Wati, and Larry Davis, ed. *Doing Theology with Tribal Resources: Context and Perspective.* Tribal Study Series no. 3. Jorhat: Tribal Study Center, 1999.

Longvah, S. *Nagawui Kharing-Kharak (The Life Style of the Nagas).* Imphal, Manipur: by the author, 2001.

Lotsuro, Angeline. *The Nagas: A Missionary Challenge.* Shillong: Vendrame Institute Pubilcations, 2000.

Luikham, Ramayo. *Folklore and Tales of the Nagas.* New Delhi: Emmanuel Publishers and Printers, 1983.

Luikham, T. *Wung (Tangkhul) Naga Okthot Mayonza: Wung Tangkhul Naga Traditional Laws.* Vol. I & II. Imphal, Manipur: by the author, 1961.

Luithui, Luingam, and Nandita Haksar. *Nagaland File: A Question of Human Rights.* New Delhi: Lancer International, 1984.

Mackenzie, Alexander. *The North-East Frontier of Assam.* Delhi: Mittal Publications, 1979.

Mann, Michael, ed. *Colonialism and Civilizing Mission: Cultural Ideology in British India.* London: Wimbledon Publishing Company, 2004.

Mao, Ashiko-Daili. *Nagas: Problems and Politics.* New Delhi: Ashish Publishing House, 1992.

Martey, Emmanuel. *African Theology: Inculturation and Liberation.* Maryknoll: Orbis Books, 1993.

Maxwell, Neville. *India, the Nagas and the North-east.* New Edition. London: Minority Rights Groups, 1980.

McFague, Salie. *Models of God: Theology for an Ecological, Nuclear Age.* Minneapolis: Fortress Press, 1987.

McLeod, John. *Beginning Postcolonialism.* Manchester and New York: Manchester University Press, 2000.

Medom, Noulezhalie Ricky. *The Relevance of the Theological Motif of Exile to the Naga's Struggle for Sovereignty* as a *People.* Delhi: Indian *Society* for Promoting Christian Knowledge (ISPCK), 2002.

Meier, John P. *A Marginal Jew: Rethinking the Historical Jesus, Vol. 1: The Roots of the Problem and the Person.* New York: Doubleday, 1991.

Memmi, Albert. *The Colonizer and the Colonized.* Expanded ed. Introduction by Jean-Paul Sartre. Boston: Beacon Press Books, 1967.

Mills, J. P. *The Ao Nagas.* With a Foreword by Henry Balfour and supplementary notes and bibliography by J. H. Hutton. London: Macmillan, 1926. Reprint, Bombay: Oxford University Press, 1973.

________. *The Lhota Nagas.* With an introduction and supplementary notes by J. H. Hutton. London: Macmillan, 1922. Reprint, New York: AMS Press, 1979.

________. *The Rengma Nagas.* London: Macmillan, 1937. Reprint, New York: AMS Press, 1979.

Miri, Sujata. *Liangmai Nagas, Legends and Stories.* New Delhi: Har-Anand Publication in Association with Vikas Publishing House, 1991.

Misra, Udayan. *The Periphery Strikes Back: Challenges to the Nation State in Assam and Nagaland.* Shimla: Indian Institute for Advanced Study, 2000.

Moltmann, Jürgen. *Jesus Christ for Today's World.* Translated by Margaret Kohl. Minneapolis: Fortress Press, 1994.

________. *The Way of Jesus Christ: Christology in Messianic Dimensions.* Translated by Margaret Kohl. Minneapolis: Fortress Press, 1993.

________. *The Crucified God: The Cross of Christ* as *the Foundation and Criticism of Christian Theology.* Translated by R. A. Wilson and John Bowden. Minneapolis: Fortress Press, 1993.

Murry, Ezamo. ed. *Thus Said the Missionaries: A Collection of Valuable Records of the Early American Missionaries on the Early Naga Church in General, and the Kyong (Lotha) Church in Particular Including Important Information on the Social, Economic, Political and Ecclesiatical State of the Nagas in the Last Quarter of the 19'h Century.* Wokha, Nagaland: by the author, 1979.

________. *Tribal Spirituality Reconsidered: A Psychological Study of Religion.* Delhi: ISPCK, 1995.

Nag, Amit Kumar. *Rani Gaidinliu: A Study of the Jadonang Movement of the Nagas.* Guwahati: United Publishers, 1976.

Naga Peoples Movement for Human Rights, ed. *The Nagas: Truth and Hope for the Living.* Kohima: Naga Peoples Movement for Human Rights, n.d.

Nagaland Baptist Church Council. *From Darkness to Light: A Publication of the Nagaland Baptist Church Council on the Occasion of the Celebration of* 125 *Years of Christianity in Nagaland.* Kohima: Nagaland Baptist Church Council, 1997.

Nagaland Pradesh Congress Committee, ed. *Bedrock of Naga Society.* Kohima: NPCC, 2000.

Nandy, Ashis. *The Intimate Enemy: Loss and Recovery of Self under Colonialism.* Delhi: Oxford University Press, 1983.

Ngareophung, N. G. *Wung Rampan Khangacha Yan (Tangkhul Customary Law).* Ukhrul, Manipur: by the author 1998.

Noël, Lise. *Intolerance: A General Survey*. Translated by Arnold Bennett. Montreal & Kingston: McGill-Queen's University Press, 1994.

Nuh, V. K., ed. *In Search of Praxis Theology for the Nagas.* New Delhi: Regency Publications, 2003.

Nungshitula. *The Naga Images of the Human Being: A Resource for* a *Contemporary Theological Anthropology.* Jorhat: Tribal Study Centre, 2001.

Nyamity, Charles. *Christ as Our Ancestor: Christology from an African Perspective.* Gweru: Mambo Press, 1984.

Oduyoye, Mercy Amba. *Daughters of Anowa: African Women and Patriarchy.* Maryknoll: Orbis Books, 1997.

O'Grady, John F. *Models of Jesus.* Garden City: Images Books, 1982.

Olupona, Jacob K., ed. *Beyond Primitivism: Indigenous Religious Traditions and Modernity.* New York and London: Routledge, 2004.

Ortiz, Alfonso. *Tewa World: On Time, Space, Being and Becoming in* a *Pueblo Society.* Chicago: University of Chicago, 1982.

Pachuau, Lalsangkima. *Ethnic Identity and Christianity: A Socio-Historical and Missiological Study of Christianity in Northeast India with Special Reference to Mizoram.* Frankfurt am Main: Peter Lang, 2002.

Pakem, B., ed. *Nationality, Ethnicity, and Cultural Identity in North-East India.* New Delhi: Omsons Publications, 1990.

Parratt, J., ed. *A Reader in African Theology.* London: SPCK, 1987.

Pattel-Gray, Anne. *Through the Aboriginal Eyes: The Cry from the Wilderness.* Geneva: World Council of Churches, 1991.

Pedraja, Luis G. *Jesus is My Uncle: Christology from a Hispanic Perspective*. Nashville: Abingdon Press, 1999.

Pelikan, Jaroslav. *Jesus through the Centuries: His Place in the History of Culture.* New Haven and London: Yale University Press, 1985.

Pettigrew Centenary Celebrations Committee. *Rev. William Pettigrew (A Pioneer Missionary of Manipur).* Imphal: Centenary Celebration Committee, 1996.

Phan, Peter C. *Christianity with an Asian Face: Asian American Theology in the Making.* Maryknoll: Orbis Books, 2003.

Philip, E. G. *Educational Work among the Garos, Jubilee Report 1886.*

Pieris, Aloysius. *An Asian Theology of Liberation.* Maryknoll: Orbis Books, 1993.

Presler, H. H. *Primitive Religions in India.* Madras: Christian Literature Society, 1971.

Pui-lan, Kwok. *Postcolonial Imagination and Feminist Theology.* Louisville: Westminster: John Knox Press, 2005.

Ramunny, Murkot. *The World of the Nagas,* 2nd rev. & enl. ed. New Delhi: Northern Block Centre, 1993.

Rayan, Samuel. *Ecological Dimensions of Our Faith: To Care for the Earth – Towards A Theology of Nature.* Kunchala Rajaratnamand Endowment Lectures. Madras: Gurukul Lutheran Theological College and Research Institute, 1991.

Roy, Arundhati. *An Ordinary Person's Guide to Empire.* Cambridge: South End Press, 2004.

Roychowdhury, Prafulla. *The North East: Roots of Insurgency.* Calcutta: Firma KLM Pvt. Ltd., 1995.

Ruether, Rosemary Radford. *Sexism and God-Talk: Toward a Feminist Theology.* Boston: Beacon Press, 1983.

________. *To Change the World: Christology and Cultural Criticism.* New York: Crossroad Publishing Company, 1981.

Rustomji, Nari. *Imperilled Frontiers: India's North-Eastern Borderlands.* Delhi, Oxford, New York: Oxford University Press, 1983.

Said, Edward. *Orientalism.* New York: Vintage Books, 1979.

________. *Culture and Imperialism.* New York: Vintage Books, 1993.

Sangma, Milton S. *History of American Baptist Mission in North-East India (1836-1950).* Vol. 1. New Delhi: Mittal Publications, 1987.

________. *History of American Baptist Mission in North-East India,* vol. 2. New Delhi: Mittal Pubilcations,1992.

Sanneh, Lamin. *Whose Religion is Christianity: The Gospel Beyond the West.* Grand Rapids: William B. Eerdmans Publishing Company, 2003.

Sarin, V. I. K. *India's North-East in Flames.* Ghaziabad: Vikas Publishing House Pvt. Ltd., 1982.

Schottroff, Luise and Wolfgang Stegemann. *Jesus and the Hope of the Poor.* Translated by Matthew J. O'Connell. Maryknoll: Orbis Books, 1986.

Schreiter, Robbert J., ed. *Faces of Jesus in Africa.* Maryknoll: Orbis Books, 1991.

Segundo, Juan L. *Liberation of Theology.* Translated by John Drury. Maryknoll: Orbis Books, 1976.

________. *The Historical Jesus of the Synoptics.* Translated from the Spanish by John Drurry. Maryknoll: Orbis Books, 1985.

________. *Signs of the Times.* Edited by T. H. Alfred. Translated by Robert R. Barr. Maryknoll: Orbis Books, 1994.

Sema, Hokishe. *Emergence of Nagaland.* New Delhi: Vikas Publishing House Pvt. Ltd., 1986.

Sharma, Suresh, *Tribal Identity and Modern World.* New Delhi: Sage Publications, 1994.

Shimmi, Y. L. Roland. *Comparative History of the Nagas: From Ancient Period Till 1826.* New Delhi: Inter-India Publications, New Delhi, 1988.

Shimray, A. S. W. *History of the Tangkhul Nagas.* New Delhi: Akansha Publication House, 2001.

Shimray, M. K. *Tangkhul Miwurlung.* Imphal, Manipur: by the author, 1967.

Shimray, R. R. *Origin and Culture of Nagas.* New Delhi: Pamleiphi Shimray, 1985.

Shimray, Shimreingam: *Theology of Human Rights: A Critique on Politics.* Jorhat: Ruth Shimray, 2002.

Silko, M. *Ceremony*. New York: Penguin Books, 1986.

Singh, Kanwar Randip. *The Nagas of Nagaland: Desperadoes and Heroes of Peace.* New Delhi: Deep & Deep Publications, 1987.

Sittler, Joseph. *Evocations of Grace: Writings on Ecology, Theology, and Ethics.* With a Foreword by Martin E. Marty. Edited by Steven Bouma-Prediger and Peter Bakken. Grand Rapids: William B. Eerdmans Publishing House, 2000.

Smart, Ninian. *Worldviews: Crosscultural Exploration of Human Beliefs.* Third Edition. Upper Saddle: Prentice Hall Inc., 2000.

Smartha, Stanley J. *One Christ – Many Religions.* Maryknoll: Orbis Books, 1991.

Smith, Linda Tuhiwai. *Decolonizing Methodologies: Research and Indigenous Peoples.* New York: Zed Books Limited, 1999.

Smith, W. C. *The Ao Naga Tribe of Assam: A Study in Ethnology and Sociology.* London; Macmillan and Company Limited, 1925.

Snaitang, O. L. *Christianity and Social Change in Northeast India (A Study of the Role of Christianity in Social Change among the Khasi-Jaintia Tribes of Meghalaya).* Shillong: Vendrame Institute; Calcutta: Firma KLM Pvt. Ltd., 1993.

Sobrino, Jon. *Jesus the Liberator: A Historical-Theological Reading of Jesus of Nazareth.* Translated by Paul Burns and Francis McDonagh. Maryknoll: Orbis Books, 1993.

________. *Jesus in Latin America.* Maryknoll: Orbis Books, 1987.

Solo, Jonah M, and K. Mashangthei, ed. *Forty Years in Manipur Assam: An Account of the Wok of Rev. William Pettigrew March,* 1939. Imphal: M. Asinath and K. Ruth, 1986.

Song, Choan-Seng. *Third-Eye Theology: Theology in Formation in Asian Setting,* rev. ed. Maryknoll: Orbis Books, 1979.

________. *Theology from the Womb of Asia.* Maryknoll: Orbis Books, 1986.

________. *Tell Us Our Names: Story Theology from an Asian Perspective.* Indore: Santorakashan Sanchar Kendra, 1986.

Spivak, Gayatri Chakravorty. A *Critique of Postcolonial Reason: Toward a History of the Vanishing Present.* Cambridge: Harvard University Press, 1999.

________. *The Spivak Reader: Selected Works of Gayatri Chakravorty Spivak*. Edited by Donna Landry and Gerald Maclean. New York: Routledge, 1996.

Stanley, Brian, ed. *Christian Mission and the Enlightenment*. Grand Rapids: William B. Eerdmans Publishing Company, 2001.

Stanton, Elizabeth Cathy. *The Woman's Bible*. New York: Arno Press, 1972.

Stevens, Maryanne, ed. *Reconstructing the Christ Symbol: Essays in Feminist Christology*. New York: Paulist Press, 1993.

Sugirtharajah, R. S., ed. *Asian Faces of Jesus*. Faith and Cultures series. Maryknoll: Orbis Books, 2001.

________. *Postcolonial Reconfiguratons: An Alternative Way of Reading the Bible and Doing Theology*. St. Louis: Chalice Press, 2003.

Sumi, Akheto, ed. *Perspectives: Current Issues* in *Theological Thinking: Essays* in *Commemoration of 30th Anniversary Clark Theological College Aolijen Mokokchung, Nagaland.* Mokokchung: Clark Theological College, 2002.

Takatemjen. *Studies on Theology and Naga Culture*. Mokokchung: CTC; Delhi: ISPCK, 1998.

Tamez, Elsa, ed. *Through Her Eyes: Women's Theology from Latin America*. Maryknoll: Orbis Books, 1989.

Thangaraj, M. Thomas. *The Crucified Guru: An Experiment in Cross-Cultural Christology*. Nashville: Abingdon Press, 1994.

Thanzauva, K. *Theology of Community: Tribal Theology in the Making*. Aizawl: Mizo Theological Conference, 1997.

Thiong'o, Ngũgĩ wa. *Decolonizing the Mind: The Politics of Language in African Literature*. Oxford: James Currey Ltd., 1986.

Tinker, George E. *Missionary Conquest: The Gospel and Native American Cultural Genocide*. Minneapolis: Fortress Press, 1993.

________. *Spirit and Resistance: Political Theology and American Indian Liberation*. Minneapolis: Fortress Press, 2004.

Trivedi, Haris and Meenakshi Mukherjee. *Interrogating Postcolonialism Theory, Text and Context*. Shimla: Indian Institute of Advanced Study, 1996.

Tungoe, Merithung. *Administrators Missionaries and a World Turned Upside Down*. Jorhat: ETC; Delhi: ISPCK, 2000.

Vansina, Jan. *Oral Tradition as History*. Madison: University of Wisconsin Press, 1985.

Vashum, Reisang. *Nagas' Right to Self Determination: An Anthropological-Historical Perspective*. New Delhi: Mittal Publications, 2000.

________. *Indo-Naga Conflict: Problem and Resolution*. New Delhi: Indian Social Institute, 2001.

Vuola, Elina. *Limits of Liberation: Feminist Theology and the Ethics of Poverty and Reproduction*. London: Sheffield Academic Press, 2002.

Walls, Andrew F. *The Cross-Cultural Process in Christian History: Studies in the Transmission and Appropriation of Faith*. Maryknool: Orbis Books, 2002.

Welch, James. *Fools Crow*. New York: Penguin Books, 1987.

West, Andrew. *The most Dangerous Legacy: The Development of Identity, Power and Marginality* in *the British Transfer to India and the Nagas.* Hull: Centre *for* South-East Asian Studies, 1999.

Williams, Delores S. *Sisters in the Wilderness: The Challenge of Womanist God-Talk.* Mryknoll: Orbis Books, 1993.

Wilmer, Franke. *The Indigenous Voice* in *World Politics: Since Time Immemorial.* Violence, Cooperation, Peace: An International Series, ed. Francis A. Beer and Ted Robert Gurr. Newbury Park: Sage Publications, Inc., 1993.

Yonuo, Asoso. *The Rising Nagas: A Historical and Political Study.* Delhi: Vivek Publishing House, 1974.

Published Articles, Essays, and Reports

Aleaz, K. P. "Gospel and Culture: Some Indian Reflections." *Indian Journal of Theology* 36, no. 2 (1993): 64-79.

Alemchiba, M. "Problems of Readjustment to New Situation with Special Reference to Naga Tribes." In *Highlander* 4, no. 1 & 2 (March-April, 1973): 35-43.

Antonio, Edward P. "Letting People Decide: Towards an Ethic of Ecological Survival in Africa." In *Ecotheology: Voices from South and North*, ed. David G. Hallman, 227-234. Geneva: WCC Publications, 1994.

Appiah-Kubi, Kofi. "Jesus Christ – Some Christological Aspect from African Perspectives." In *Voices from the Third World* 16, no. 2 (December 1993): 7-28.

Assam Mission of the American Baptist Missionary Union, Papers and Discussion of the Jubilee Conference held in Nowgong, December 18-29, 1886. The Assam Mission of the American Baptist Missionary Union, 1887.

Balfour, Henry. "Foreword." In *The Sema Nagas*, J. H. Hutton, xv-xvii. London: Macmillan and Co. Ltd., 1921.

Barpuraji, S. K. "Early Christian Missions in the Naga Hills: An Assessment of their Activities." *Journal of Indian History* 48, no. 143 (1970): 427-435.

Baruah, Sanjib. "Confronting Constructionism: Ending India's Naga War." *Journal of Peace Research* 40, no. 3 (May 2003): 321-338.

Batteste, Marie. "Maintaining Aboriginal Identity, Language, and Culture in Modern Society." In *Reclaiming Indigenous Voice and Vision*, ed. Marie Battiste. Vancouver: UBS Press, 2000.

Bear, Leroy Little. "Foreword." In *Native Science: Natural Laws of Interdependence*, Gregory Cajete, ix-xii. Santa Fe: Clear Light Publishers, 2000.

Bishop, Allan J. "Western Mathematics: The Secret Weapons of Cultural Imperialism." In *The Postcolonial Studies Reader*, ed. Bill Aschroft, Gareth Griffiths, and Helen Tiffin, ed., 71-76. London and New York: Routledge, 1995.

Blaufuss, Mary Schaller. "De-centered and De-centering Missiology: A Search for New Relationships and New Terminology." *Asian Journal of Theology* 16, no. 2 (October 2002): 428-448.

Carson, Penny. "The British Raj and the Awakening of the Evangelical Conscience: the Ambiguities of Religious Establishment and Toleration, 1698-1833." In *Christian Missions and the Enlightenment*, ed. Brian Stanley, 45-70. Grand Rapids: William B. Eerdmans Publishing Company, 2001.

Christ, Carol P. "Rethinking Theology and Nature." In *Reweaving the World: The Emergence of Ecofeminism*, ed. Irene Diamond and Gloria F. Orenstein, 58-69. San Francisco: Siera Club Books, 1990.

Croatto, J Severino. "The Political Dimension of Christ the Liberator." In *Faces of Jesus: Latin American Christologies*, ed. José Míguez Bonino. Translated from Spanish by Robert R. Barr, 102-122. Eugene: Wipf and Stock Publishers, 1998,

Delatavo, Alan J. "Images of Christ in Filipino Culture and Atonement Experiences - A Case in the Contextualization of the Gospel Message." *Asian Journal of Theology* 15, no. 1 (April 2001): 140-150.

Dillistone, F. W. "Atonement." In *A New Dictionary of Christian Theology*, ed. Alan Richardson and John Bowden. London: SCM Press Ltd., 1983: 44.

Dirlik, Arif. "The Postcolonial Aura: Third World Criticism in the Age of Capitalism." In *Critical Inquiry* 20, 1994: 328-356.

Downs, Frederick S. "Christianity as a Tribal Response to Change in Northeast India." *Missiology: An International Review* 8 (October 1980): 407-416.

________. "Identity: The Integrative Principle." *Asian Journal of Theology* 6 (1992): 238-249.

________. "Tribal Ecumenism in North East India: The Christian Role in Solidarity Movements." In *Good News for North East India: A Theological Reader*, ed. Renthy Keitzar, 8-21. Guwahati: Christian literature Center, 1995.

________. "Vision for Tribal Churches in North East India: Historical Perspective." In *Encounter between Gospel and Tribal Culture.* Tribal Study Series, no. 5, ed. A. Wati Longchar, 116-126. Jorhat: Tribal Study Center, 1999.

Dunch, Ryan. "Beyond Cultural Imperialism: Cultural Theory, Christian Missions, and Global Modernity." *History and Theory* 41, no. 3 (2002): 301-325.

Eaton, Richard M. "Conversion to Christianity among the Nagas, 1876-1971." *Indian Economic and Social History Review* 21, no. 1 (1984): 1-44.

Elungkiebe. "Women in Peacemaking: A North East India Perspective." In *Women's Issues in the 21st Century.* Women Study Series, ed. Narola Imchen, no. 1. 121- 134. Jorhat: Women's Study Centre, ETC, 2001.

Gnanadason, Aruna. "Toward a Feminist Eco-Theology for India." In *Women Healing Earth: Third World Women on Ecology, Feminism, and Religion*, ed. Rosemary Radford Ruether, 74-81. Maryknoll: Orbis Books, 1996.

Gutierrez, Gustavo. "Renewing the Option for the Poor." In *Liberation Theologies, Postmodernity, and the Americas,* eds., Batstone, David, Eduardo Mandieta, Lois Ann Lorentzen, and Dwight N. Hopkins, 69-82. London: Routledge, 1997.

Hall, Stuart. "When was 'the Post-Colonial?' Thinking at the Limit." In *Postcolonial Question: Common Skies, Divided Horizons.* London: Routledge, 1996.

________. "The Emergence of Cultural Studies and the Crisis of the Humanities." In *October* 53, (Summer, 1990): 11-23.

Hinga, Teresa M. "Jesus Christ and the Liberation of Women." In *The Will to Arise: Women, Tradition, and the Church in Africa*, ed. Mercy Amba Oduyoye and Musimbi R. A. Kanyoro, 184-197. Maryknoll: Orbis Books, 2002.

Hnuni, R. L. "Vision for Women in North East India." In *Equipping the People of God for Ministry.* ed. C. Wallu Walling and A. Wati Longchar, 36-52. Impur: Ao Theological Kaket Adoksuba Rogo, 2001.

Hockey, S. K. "The Benefit of Peace Treaty: Peace and Reconciliation." In *Pfosemei Peace Treaty Reaffirmation Feast, 1800-2001 Souvenir.* Pfosemei: Pfosemei Peace Treaty Reaffirmation Committee, 2001.

Iralu, Kaka. "16 Point Agreement – The Greatest Betrayal in Naga History." Available from *http//:www.nscnonline.org/nscn/index-2.html.*

Jamir, Lipok. "Table Fellowship: A Model for Naga Reconciliation: A Contextual Theology of Reconciliation in Light of the Concept and Practice of *Aksü* among the Ao Nagas." *Journal of Tribal Studies* 9, no. 2 (July-December 2005): 1-18.

Jo, Yong-Hun. "A Christian Environmental Perspective on the View of Nature in Asian Thought." *Asian Journal of Theology* 16, no. 2 (October 2002): 396-408.

Johari, J. "Creation of Nagaland: Triumph of Ebulient Infranationalism." *Indian Journal of Political Science* 36, no. 1 (January-March 1975):13-38.

Johnson, Elizabeth. "Jesus the Wisdom of God: a Biblical Basis for Non-Androcentric Christology." In *Ephemerides Theologicae Lovanienses* 61, no. 4 (1985): 261-294.

Jones, Gordon. "Good News for North-East India." In *Good News for North East India*, ed. Renthy Keitzar, 1-7. Guwahati: Christian Literature Center, 1995.

Kabasele, François. "Christ as Chief." In *Faces of Jesus in Africa,* ed. Robert Schreiter, 103-115. Maryknoll: Orbis Books, 1991.

________. "Christ as Ancestor and Elder Brother." In *Faces of Jesus in Africa, ed. Robert Schreiter, 116-127.* Maryknoll: Orbis Books, 1991.

Keitzar, Renthy. "Importance of Tribal Religion in Theological Curriculum." *Baptist News* 42 (October-December 1993): 3-7.

________. "A Study of the North-East India Tribal Christian Theology." In *Good News for North East India,* ed. Renthy Keitzar, 32-40. Guwahati: Christian Literature Center, 1995.

________. "The Indigenization of Naga Christian Theology." In *In Search of Praxis Theology for the Nagas,* ed, V. K. Nuh, 34-52. New Delhi: Regency Publications, 2003.

Keller, Catherine, et al. "Introduction: Alien/Nation, Liberation, and the Postcolonial Underground." In *Post Colonial Theologies: Divinity and Empire,* ed. Catherine Keller, Michael Nausner, and Mayra Rivera, 1-19. St. Louis: Chalice Press, 2004.

Kharlukhi, H. Wanda. "Jesus: A Radical Transformer." *Journal of Tribal Studies* 7, no. 1 (January-June 2003): 203-209.

Kikon, Dolly, "Destroying Differences, Schooling Consent: A Critical Analysis of Education Policy in Indian-administered Nagaland." Available from *http//:www.nscnonline.org/webpage/Articles/dolly_kikon.htm.*

King, Robert H. "Introduction: The Task of Theology." In Peter C. Hodgson and Robert H. King, ed. *Christian Theology: An Introduction to its Traditions and Tasks.* Newly Updated Edition. Minneapolis: Fortress Press, 1994, Kolie, CeCe. "Jesus as Healer?" In *Faces of Jesus in Africa,* ed. Robert Schreiter, 128-151. Maryknoll: Orbis Books, 1991.

Koyama, Kosuke. "Doing Theology with Creation in Asia." *PTCA Bulletin* 13, no. 1 & 2 (June & December 2000): 17-23.

Kwasikwakye-Nuako. "The Akan People, Ancestors and Christmas: Towards Indigenizing Christianity in Africa." *Voices from the Third World* 19, no. 1 & 2 (December 2002): 175-204.

Levison, John R, and Levison-Pope, Priscilla. "Jesus in Latin America." *Bible Today* 33 (January 1995): 43-46.

Longchar, A. Wati. "Lijaba - The Earth Entering Supreme Being: The Ao-Naga Concept of God and Ecology." In *The Tribal Worldview and Ecology.* Tribal Study Series, ed. A. Wati Longchar and Yangkahao Vashum, no. 2, 24-33. Jorhat: Tribal Study Center, 1998.

________. "Doing Creation Theology with Tribal Culture of India." *PTCA Bulletin* 13, no. 1 & 2 (June & December 2000): 37-43.

________. "A Creation Poem of the Ao-Naga: A Theological Exploration." In *The Tribal Worldview and Ecology.* Tribal Study Series, ed. A. Wati Longchar and Yangkahao Vashum, no. 2, 53-68. Jorhat: Tribal Study Center, 1998.

________. "The Need for Studying Tribal Theology." In *An Exploration of Tribal Theology.* Tribal Study Series, ed. A. Wati Longchar, no. 1, 1-20. Jorhat: Tribal Study Center, 1997.

________. "Myth: A Source for Conceptualizing Tribal Theology." In *An Exploration of Tribal Theology.* Tribal Study Series, ed. A. Wati Longchar, no. 1, 78-95. Jorhat: Tribal Study Center, 1997.

________. "Jesus Christ in Tribal Theology: A Critique: A Response." *Journal of Tribal Studies* 7, no. 2 (July-December 2003): 248-249.

Longkumer, N. Limatula. "Rediscovering Women's Role and Status in Society." In *Doing Theology with Tribal Resources: Context and Perspective.* Tribal Study Series, ed. A. Wati Longchar, and Larry E. Davis, no. 3, 77-90. Jorhat: Tribal Study Center, 1999.

________. "Naga Women in Theological Education." In *Side By Side: Naga Women Doing Theology in Search of Justice and Partnership*, ed. Limatula Longkumer and Talijungla Longkumer, 16-29. n. p.: CCA-EGY Unit & Naga Theological Forum, 2004.

Madera Vargas, Ignacio. "The Faces of Oppression and Marginality." In *Latin American Documentation* 28 (July-August 1998): 24-28.

Magessa, Laurenti. "Christ the Liberator and Africa Today." In *Faces of Jesus in Africa*, ed. Robert J. Schreiter, 151-163. Maryknoll: Orbis Books, 2000.

Mann, Michael. "'Torch Bearers Upon the Path of Progress:' Britains Ideology of a 'Moral and Material Progress' in India. An Introductory Essay." In *Colonialism as Civilizing Mission: Cultural Ideology in British India*, ed. Herald Fischer-Tine and Michael Mann, 1-26. Grand Rapids: William B. Eerdmans Publishing Company, 2001.

Marty, Emmanuel. "Theology and Liberation: The African Agenda." In *Voices from the Third World* 28, no. 1 (June 2005), 38-53.

Maxwell, Ian Douglas. "Civilization or Christianity? The Scottish Debate on Mission Methods, 1750-1835." In *Christian Mission and the Enlightenment*, ed. Brian Stanley, 123-140. Grand Rapids: William B. Eerdmans Publishing Company, 2001.

McDonald, H. D. "Nestorius." In Sinclair B. Ferguson and David F. Wright, ed. *New Dictionary of Christian Theology*. Leicester: Inter-Varsity Press, 1988: 457-458.

Mills, James Philip. "The Effect on the Naga Tribes of Assam of their Contact with Western Civilization." *Pacific Science Congress. Sh, Victoria and Vancouver,* 1993. *Proceedings, Toronto* 4 (1934): 2871-2882.

Minz, Nirmal. "Tribal Perspectives on Ecology." In *The Tribal Worldview and Ecology.* Tribal Study Center, ed. A. Wati Longchar and Yangkahao Vashum, no. 2,1-10. Jorhat: Tribal Study Center, 1998.

________. "Cultural Identity of Tribals in India." In *Equipping the People of God for Ministry*, ed. C. Walu Walling and A. Wati Longchar, 8-17. Impur: Ao Theological Kaket Adoksuba Rogo, 2001.

Mohammed, Ovey N. "Jesus and Krishna." In *Asian Faces of Jesus,* ed. R. S. Sugirtharajah, 9-24. Maryknoll: Orbis Books, 1993.

Mukherjee, Meenakshi. "Interrogating Postcolonialism." In *Interrogating Postcolonialism: Theory, Text and Context*, ed. Haris Trivedi and Meenakshi Mukherjee, 3-11. Delhi: Indian Institute of Advanced Studies, 1996.

Nasimyu-Wasike, Anne. "Christology and an African Experience." In *Faces of Jesus in Africa*, ed. Robert J. Schreiter, 70-81. Maryknoll: Orbis Books, 1991.

Natar, Asnath Niwa. "Creation on Sumbanese Perspective: An Attempt of Doing a Contextual Theology." *PTCA Bulletin* 13, no. 1 & 2 (June & December 2000): 49-54.

Nyamiti, Charles. "African Christologies Today." In *Faces of Jesus in Africa*, ed. Robert J. Schreiter, 3-23. Maryknoll: Orbis Books, 2000.

Oduyoye, Amba Mercy, and Elizabbeth Amoah. The Christ for African Women. In *With Passion and Compassion: Third Women Doing Theology*, ed. Virginia Fabell and Mercy Amba Oduyoye, 35-46. Maryknoll: Orbis Books, 1994.

Pettigrew, William. "Report for the Years 1907-1909." In *Rev. Pettigrew's Mission Reports and Letters, 1891-1932*, Compiled and reproduced by Champhang Jajo, 20-29. Ukhrul: Phila Jajo, n,d.

Pieris, Aloysius. "The Buddha and the Christ: Mediators of Liberation." In *Asian Faces of Jesus,* ed. Robert Schreiter, 46-61. Maryknoll: Orbis Books, 1993.

________. "The Place of Non-Christian Religions and Cultures in the Evolution of Third World Theology." In *The Irruption of the Third World: Challenge to International Economic Order, Challenge to Theology: Papers from the Fifth International Conference of the Ecumenical Association of Third World Theologians, August 17-29, 1981, New Delhi, India*, ed. Virginia Fabella and Sergio Torres, 113-139. (Maryknoll: Orbis Books, 1983).

Ray, Niharranjan. "Introductory Address." In *The Tribal Situation in India*, ed. K. Suresh Singh, 3-24. Shimla: Indian Institute of Advanced Study, 1972.

Rev. William Pettigrew's Mission Reports and Letters, 1891-1932. Compiled and reproduced by Champhang Jajo. Ukhrul: Phila Jajo, n. d.

Ritchie, Nelly. "Women and Christology." In *Through Her Eyes: Women's Theology from Latin America*, ed. Elsa Tamez, 85-95. Maryknoll: Orbis Books, 1989.

Sanon, Ansleme T. "Jesus, Master of Initiation." In *Faces of Jesus in Africa,* ed. Robert Schreiter, 85-102. Maryknoll: Orbis Books, 1991.

Sanyu, Visier. "What Nagaland State did to the Nagas: A Historical Perspective." In *Nagaland: A Contemporary Ethnography*, ed. S. M. Channa, 265-278. New Delhi: Cosmo Publications, 1992.

Shishak, Tuisem. A. "The Impact of Pettigrew's Educational Ministry upon the Tangkhul Naga Society." In *Souvenir: TBL Centenary*. Ukhrul: TBL Centenary, 1996: 30-37.

Shohe, Zakali. "Protest with a Cause: A Study of the Temple Act of Jesus for Empowering of Naga Women in their Struggles." In *Side by Side: Naga Women Doing Theology in Search of Justice and Partnership*, ed. Limatula Longkumer and Talijungla Longkumer, 127-139. n. p.: CCA-EGY Unit & Naga Women Theological Forum, 2004.

Singh, K. Brahma. "Early British Manoeuvers in the Naga Hills." *Journal of the United Service Institution of India* 114, no. 476 (1984): 176-186.

Singh, Sarabjit. "Juristic Ethnology of the Meiteis and the Nagas." *Calcutta University Anthropological Papers,* no. 5 (1938): 45-69.

Snaitang, O. L. "Ecumenism and Hill People's Culture in North East India." In *Equipping the People of God for Ministry,* ed. C. Wallu Walling and A. Wati Longchar, 29-35. Impur: Ao Theological Kaket AdoktsOba Rogo, 2001.

Statistical Hand Book of Nagaland 2001. Kohima: Directorate of Economic & Statistics, Government of Nagaland, 2001.

Sumi, Akheto, "Current Issues in Christian Education and their Relevance for Theological Education. A North East India Perspective." In *Advancing with Christ: Souvenir of the Eastern Theological College Centenary Celebration 2005*. Jorhat: Eastern Theological College, 2005: 77-102.

Swu, Isak C. "Announcement of Cease-fire Agreement between the Government of India and National Socialist Council of Nagalim." In *The Nagas: Truth and Hope for the Living*, Naga Peoples Movement for Human Rights, 33. Kohima: Naga Poeples Movement for Human Rights, n. d.

Takatemjen. "Theology of Reconciliation: A Naga Perspective." In *Doing Theology with Tribal Resources: Context and Perspective.* Tribal Study Series, ed. A. Wati Longchar, and Larry E. Davis, no. 3, 105-116. Jorhat: Tribal Study Center, 1999.

Taylor, Mark L. "Spirit and Liberation: Achieving Postcolonial Theology in the United States." In *Postcolonial Theologies: Divinity and Empire*, ed. Catherine Keller, Michael Nausner, and Mayra Rivera, 39-55. St. Louis: Chalice Press, 2004.

Thanzauva, K. "Tribal Theological Trends in North East India." In *Good News for North East India,* ed. Renthy Keitzar, 104-113. Guwahati: Christian Literature Center, 1995.

________. "A Theology of Development in the Context of Hill Tribes in North East India." In *Doing Theology with Tribal Resources: Context and Perspective.*

Tribal Study Series, ed. A. Wati Longchar, and Larry E. Davis, no. 3, 43-59. Jorhat: Tribal Study Center, 1999.

Thistlethwaite, Susan B. "Christology and Postmodernism: Not Everyone Who Says to me, 'Lord, Lord.'" In *Interpretation* 49, no. 3 (July 1995), 267-280.

Thumra, Jonathan H. "Impact of Christianity on the Socio-cultural Ethos of the Tangkhul Nagas." In *Souvenir: TBL Centenary 1996*. Ukhrul: TBL Centenary, 1996, 44-50.

________. "The Naga Primal (Traditional) Religion and Christianity: A Theological Reflection." In *In Search of Praxis Theology for the Nagas*, ed. V. K. Nuh, 53 -76. New Delhi: Regency Publications, 2003.

Tinker, George E. "Jesus, Corn Mother, and Conquest: Christology and Colonialism." In Native *American Religious Identity: Unforgotten* Gods, ed. Jace Weaver, 134-154. Maryknoll: Orbis Books, 1998.

________. "Integrity of Creation, Restoring Trinitarian Balance." In *Constructing Christian Theology* in *the Worldwide Church,* ed. William R. Barr, 56-74. Grand Rapids: William B. Eerdmans Publishing Company, 1997.

________. "The Full Circle of Liberation: An American Theology of Place." In *Eco-Theology: Voices from South and North*, ed. David G. Hallman, 218-224. Geneva: WCC Publications, 1994.

________. "American Indians and Jesus: Reflections Towards an EATWOT Christology." *Voices from the Third World* 18, no. 2 (December 1995): 115-134.

________. "EA TWOT and Theological Methodology: Struggle, Resistance, Liberation and Indigenous Peoples." In *Search for* a new *Just World Order: Challenges to Association of Third World Theologians* held in Tagayaty, Phillipines December 1996. A Special Issue of Voices *from the Third World, edited by K. C. Abraham, 59-78*. Bangalore: EATWOT, 1999.

United Naga Council. "Naga Peace Process and the Response of the Neighboring Communities." In Naga People's Movement for Human Rights, ed. *The Nagas: Truth and Hope for the Living*. Kohima: NPMHR, n.d.: 96-116.

Vashum, Yangkahao. "Sources for Studying Tribal Theology." In *An Exploration of Tribal Theology*. Tribal Study Series, ed. A. Wati Longchar, no. 1, 63-77. Jorhat: Tribal Study Center, 1997.

________. "Theology of Land: A Naga Perspective." In *The Tribal Worldview* and *Ecology*. Tribal Study Series, ed A. Wati Longchar and Yangkahao Vashum, no. 2, 69-94. Jorhat: Tribal Study Center, 1998.

________. "Towards a Tribal Theology of Eco-Human Rights: Resources from the Tangkhul Tradition." *Journal of Tribal Studies:* A *Theological, Cultural* and *Sociological Reflection on Tribal Life* 3, no. 1 (January-June 1999): 47-68.

________. "The Pertinence of Ethics in Development Debates." In *Naga Journal of Indigenous Affairs* 2, no. 1 (December-May, 2003): 56-61.

Dissertation, Academic Thesis and Unpublished Materials

French, Walter Thomas. "Northern Naga: A Tibeto-Burman Mesolanguage." (Vol. 1 and 2). Ph. D. diss., City University of New York, 1983.

Khamrang, Khayaipam. "Towards an Eco-Theology: Resources in the Primal Religion of the Tangkhul Nagas." M. Th. Thesis, Gurukul Lutheran Theological College and Seminary, 1992.

Shimray, Y. K. "Tangkhul Customary Law and Women." TMs: 1-14.

Smith, William Carlson. "Conflict and Fusion of Cultures as Typified by the Ao Nagas of India." Ph. D. diss., University of Chicago, 1920.

Tinker, George E. "The Stones Shall Cry Out": Consciousness, Rocks and Indians." TMs, 1-18.

________. "Lost Bloods: Biological Claims to Indianness in the Postcolonial Conquest." TMs, 1-4.

Vashum, Yangkahao. "Tangkhul Naga - Christian Theology of Human Rights." M. Th. Thesis, Gurukul Lutheran Theological College and Research Institute, 1994.

Interviews

Achumi, Hekhevi, of Khumshimi village. Interview by author, 21 July 2003, Dimapur.

Akha, Daihrii, of Makhel village. Interview by author, 27 July 2003, Makhel village. Tape recording.

Angkang, Stephen, of Lungpha village, Interview by author, 11 August 2003, Ukhrul. Tape recording.

Elders of Jessami village, Athsilhi, W., Kelhipelo, W., Kanmi, W., Achung, W. Interview by author, 8 August 2003. Tape recording.

Gwangting, Namputkung, of Jalukie Town. Interview by author, 17 July 2003, Jalukie Town. Tape recording.

Iheilung, Italakpe, of Jalukie Town. Interview by author, 17 July 2003, Jalukie Town. Tape recording.

Jengko, Putong, of Pangsha village. Interview by author, 28 July 2003, Kohima.

Konyak, Y. Chingang, of Kongan village. Interview by author, 28 July 2003, Kohima. Tape recording.

Koulie, D., of Kohima. Interview by author, 17 July 2003, Kohima. Tape recording.

Lorin, M. K., of Phenshünyu. Interview by author, 28 July 2003, Kohima. Tape recording.

Nuh, V. K., of Thesulomi village. Interview by author, 28 July 2003, Kohima.

Phungthar, S. K., of Chingjui Ngajaphung village. Interview by author, 22 June 2003, Chingjui Ngajaphung village. Tape Recording.

Saleo, N., of Pudunamei village. Interview by author, 27 July 2003, Pudunamai village. Tape recording.

Shaiza, Ako, of Ukhrul. Interview by author, 11 August 2003, Ukhrul. Tape recording.

Vero, Theyesheyi, of Thiphuzu village. Interview by author, 21 July 2003, Dimapur. Tape recording.

Appendix - 1

Declaration of Naga Independence

Naga National Council declared Naga Independence on 14th August, 1947. Cable to United Nations Secretary General

CABLE RUNS:

To

SECRETARY GENERAL
UNITED NATIONS.

BENIGN EXCELLENCY,

* KINDLY PUT ON RECORD .THAT NAGAS WILL BE INDEPENDENT

* DISCUSSION WITH INDIA ARE BEING CARRIED ON TO THAT EFFECT

* NAGAS DO NOT ACCEPT INDIAN CONSTITUTION

* THE RIGHT OF THE PEOPLE MUST PREVAIL REGARDLESS OF SIZE

* NAGA NATIONAL COUNCIL

Note (This message was acknowledged by UN and record is both in UN and Naga National Council files).

Appendix - 2

The Stand of the Naga Civil Society on Naga Integration

In the century of conflicts, the driving force of the Nagas has been **"to bring together all the Nagas and the areas inhabited by them into one common political roof."** This is the **fundamental rights** and the **aspiration** of the Naga people. Through the centuries, various attempts of solution have been formulated with a view to containing the rise of nationalism. Instead of solving the problems, all these piece-meal dealings have increased the problems and motivated the Nagas into stronger determination.

The Naga Hoho once again re-emphasizes the urgent need for the Naga Integration because it has people's aspiration and mandate, historical admission of splitting the Nagas, validity of the political processes, and now the Naga Integration is the Naga people's movement for the solution of Naga problem.

Naga Peoples Movement for Human Rights

The Naga peoples Movement for Human Rights (NPMHR) was formed on September 9, 1978 at Delhi to initiate organized struggle against the violation of our rights as peoples and for achieving certain specific goals. And amongst other, in the 11 point Declaration, number 3 declared the issue of integration which reads as,

> ***"3. the right to live together as a people, and unification of all Naga Lands."*** (NPMHR Declaration)

Naga Students Federation (NSF)

On January 8, 1995 the NSF launched a booklet entitled **"For a Unified Naga Lim."** It clearly outlined the aspiration of the Naga people to live together under one political roof in spite of the "diversified Naga Tribes." It also stated, "Nagas belong to one single race with a common interest and goal. This is a workable, practical basis for a unified Naga Lim." In addition, while writing on the Capsule of Naga history, its status, origins and landmarks it prophetically mentioned,

> ***"Today the Nagas are fighting for a unified Naga Land. The 21st Century will be the Century in which the fulfillment and emergence of this dream is tested."***

Naga Week, December 1- 5, 1993.

In commemoration of International Year of the World's Indigenous People in 1993, the NPMHR and NSF organized the Naga Week at Kohima from Dec 1-5, 1993 and all Naga tribes in India and Myanmar participated in the Week celebration. After careful deliberation, the **7- Point Naga Week Declaration** was made and it showed the wounds inflicted upon the Nagas and they are as under:

1. The right to live together as a people through unification of all Naga inhabited areas.
2. The right to be free from the clutches of occupational forces.
3. The right to have the United Nation's recognition of the Naga country as a sovereign nation.
4. The right to practice and revitalize their cultures, traditions, and customs.
5. The right to manifest, develop, and practice their spiritual and religious traditions, customs, and ceremonies.
6. The right to revitalize develop, use, and transmit to the present and the future generations, their history, languages, art and literature.
7. The right to freedom of movement, assembly, and access to all places of learning, faith, belief, and worship.

   (Source: issued by the Organizing Committee, Naga Week 1993)

Decision of the United Naga Council, Manipur

The political stand taken by the Nagas living in the present state of Manipur through the United Naga Council unanimously resolved for Integration thus:

> ***"That our identity and history have to be defended and preserved at all cost, and the firm political stand of the Nagas of Manipur is to uphold the resolution of the Naga people for integration of all Naga areas under one administration."***
>
> (UNC Headquarters, Senapati Dt., August 09, 2001)

UNC Submission of Memorandum (Sept. 2001)

In pursuance of the decision of UNC, a Memorandum for merger with the Nagas of Nagaland has been submitted to,

1. The President of India, New Delhi.
2. The Prime Minister of India, New Delhi.
3. The Opposition Leader Mrs. Sonia Gandhi, New Delhi.
4. The Convener - NDA, New Delhi.

Declaration Made on the l5th August 2001, Kohima at the Meeting of Naga Peoples convened by the Naga Hoho

The Naga Peoples representatives from Assam, Arunachal Pradesh, Manipur and Nagaland States met on the 18th August 2001 for a Consultative Meeting at Kohima and discussed the various issues confronting the Nagas today and made the following declarations:

1. ***"The members reaffirmed that the Nagas, no matter wherever they are, are one. It also declared that the problems of the Nagas no matter where they are, are because of historical circumstances and that they should be comprehensively addressed by the Naga People as a whole."***
2. ***"The meeting welcomes the decision taken by the Nagas in the present state of Manipur during the Naga Peoples Convention from 8-9th August 2001 upholding the Naga Hoho resolution calling for integration/unification of all Naga areas. It also declared that no Naga would remain a silent spectator to the issues being faced by the Nagas in Manipur and to initiate immediate action in response to the UNC Declaration."***

7th General Assembly of the Naga Hoho May 20-22, 2002.

The Naga Hoho reaffirmed its political stand to work for integration of all the Naga areas in its 7th General Assembly by passing the following resolution,

> ***"The Naga Hoho must reach out and fetch the different Naga tribes under its ambit. It must also work towards the involvement of the larger Naga audience including the Naga intellectuals, bureaucrats, professionals and others."***

Appendix - 3

Announcement of Cease-Fire Agreement Between the Government of India and the National Socialist Council of Nagaland

The Hague, 25th of July 1997

I hereby announce this day the 25th of July 1997, to every citizen of Nagaland wherever they may be, that a Cease-fire Agreement has been entered into between the Government of India and the National Socialist Council of Nagaland, to bring about a lasting political solution to the long drawn-out Indo-Naga issue. The Agreement reads:

1. ***The talks shall be unconditional from both sides;***
2. ***At the highest level; that is, at the Prime Ministers' level; and***
3. ***The venue of the talks shall be anywhere in the world, outside India.***

"For securing a peaceful political solution, discussion has been held between the Government of India and the NSCN leadership. It has been mutually decided to cease fire for a period of three (3) months with effect from the 1st August 1997 and embark upon political level discussions."

Sd/-
Isak C. Swu
Chairman,
National Socialist Council of Nagalim

Appendix - 4

Declaration Adopted at the Launching Ceremony of the Naga National Reconciliation at Kohima on December 20, 2001

WHEREAS, in course of the Naga People's struggle for self-determination, our society has borne witness to and experienced brutalization of human life by forces both within and without; we cannot ignore how profoundly we have hurt one another thereby creating a culture of suspicion and misgivings. There is need for us to come together and heal as a Nation so that we can collectively walk towards our envisioned future based on the principles of justice, freedom, truth and peace.

AND WHEREAS, the first territorial division of Naga country took place by the signing of the Treaty of Yandabo in 1826 without the knowledge and consent of the Naga people and without any reparation/restoration thereafter, even while the British India Government admitted the fact that despite their long years of colonial rule in "India", there were still "free Nagas" in the "un-administered areas" by the time they left India in 1947;

AND WHEREAS, the Naga people submitted their Memorandum to the Simon Commission in 1929 asking the British India Government to leave them alone, and not to lump them together with the rest of India, once the British left, and this resulted in the Naga Hills Excluded Area in the Government of India Act, 1935, which took effect in 1937;

AND WHEREAS, the 9-Point Hydari Agreement with the transitional Indian representatives failed because it was unilaterally abrogated by the Government of India, the Naga people declared their Independence on August 14, 1947 and reaffirmed it by a plebiscite in May 1951 through the banner of the Naga National Council under the leadership of A.Z. Phizo;

AND WHEREAS, further disintegration of Naga country into different administrative units within India took place without a referendum and despite

Naga demands, at various times, for integration of all Naga areas into a single political entity;

AND WHEREAS, the Naga people unitedly launched their Struggle for Political Freedom, the signing of the 16-Point Agreement with the Naga Peoples Convention that led to the formation of the Nagaland state within the Indian Union on December 1, 1963, further deepened the differences of opinion among the Naga people. The Naga struggle nevertheless carried on.

AND WHEREAS, at the initiative of the Naga Baptist Churches, commendable efforts were made by Jayaprakash Narayan, Bimala Prasad Chaliha and Reverend Michael Scott, among others, to settle the Naga Political Issue that resulted in the first Cease-fire in the 1960s, thereby earning the eternal gratitude of the Naga people for their objectivity and breadth of vision as well as their care and concern for Nagas;

AND WHEREAS, the formation of the Revolutionary Government of Nagaland in the late 1960s saw further differences of opinion among the Nagas and later, representatives of the "Underground Organizations" signed the Shillong Accord of 1975, further exacerbating the sense of mistrust, fear and bitterness;

AND WHEREAS, the late 1970s to early 1990s saw the fragmentation of the Naga National Movement into four political organizations, and, a second Cease- fire coming into effect on 1 August 1997 between Government of India and the NSCN led by Isak Swu and Th. Muivah based on mutually agreed principles, -that the talks will be unconditional, that it will be held at the highest level and in a third neutral country - followed later by a separate Cease Fire Agree-ment on 28th April 2001 with NSCN led by S.S. Khaplang, ushering in, for the second time, the thought-process of peace and the search for an honourable solution instead of bitterness and conflict;

AND WHEREAS, the Naga people cannot give up our Struggle with-out an honourable settlement and an adequate acknowledgement of our history, we also know that division, bitterness and armed confrontation will not solve the Naga Political Issue;

We therefore feel the imperative need for Nagas to come together to share, discuss and consult with the grace to absolve our past mistakes and the need to begin building anew future of hope, truth and just peace through a process of healing and compassion.

The Naga Hoho, Churches and the social organizations feel the urgent need to initiate a process to acknowledge the wrongs and the pains of the past that must be put right for the sake of the future. The Naga people as a Nation must have the courage to tell the truth, own the truth and to heal our wounds so that we can move on together at peace with ourselves.

We, therefore, as people to commit ourselves to take this first step of journey towards healing as one nation to collectively express our sorrows to victims of injustice and oppression with the grace to forgive. We call upon all low Nagas to come together and walk with us on this journey. The journey will not be an easy one.

We believe that for any healing to take place we must clean our wounds which by itself is a painful process. Nevertheless we trust that we can go on together recognizing the gift of one another's presence and contributions that can empower us with the courage to walk through this painful but liberating journey of healing so that we can grow together to enrich our understanding, opportunities and responsibilities that can enable us to fulfill our aspirations.

And, hence, as a nation speaking with one voice, we, the Naga people pledge ourselves to transform injustice to justice, inequality to equality, violence to non-violence; to respect one another and all other peoples, to recognize the dignity of all other cultures and to reaffirm our commitment to our values that respect this land and the people and to provide justice and equality for all.

NOW, THEREFORE, at this Launching Ceremony of Naga National Reconciliation, we acknowledge, recognize and pledge the following:-

We confess that we have dishonoured God by our divisions, our pride and our disobedience to Him. We also confess that we have ignored the cries of people for just peace, unity and reconciliation.

Reconciliation is a critical process towards a lasting peace, development, growth and prosperity.

The most urgent need for our people at this moment is to recognize and understand our history and to heal the wounds of the past and to learn to forgive be forgiven. Naga reconciliation will thus reflect the richest fruit of our common heritage from God.

Nagas are one. Every Naga is important and needed. And all Naga tribes, and all sections of Naga society, need to contribute in the search for an honourable Settlement.

Nagas targeting Nagas can not solve the Naga Political Issue. So, all Naga casualties by fellow Nagas and other provocative actions, which are an affront to our Creator, must stop forthwith.

Those who represent the Nagas must be willing to listen to the voice of the Naga people represented through the Village Council, the Regional bodies and the Tribe Hohos, besides the Churches and other mass-based organizations.

After so many years of violence and oppression, the Naga people today deserve peace and a serious search for an honourable settlement of the Naga Political Issue. To this end, all Naga leaders, especially of the conflicting groups, must come together and start a consultation process.

We hereby pledge that from today the 20th of December 2001, we will unitedly work ceaselessly to bring peace, unity and harmony among the Nagas beginning from the grassroots to all sections of the Naga society.

In acceptance and commitment to the above we hereby append, and attest, our signatures on this day the twentieth of December, in the year two thousand

and one. We do this because our people are the foundation and the basis of our Naga Nationhood.

(M. VERO)

President,
Naga Hoho.

Presidents/Representatives of Tribe Hohos.
Convenor and Coordination Committee Members.
Church Leaders
Mass-based Organizations

Appendix - 5

Recognition of the Naga Unique History and Sitation by the Government of India Through the Communiqué of July 11, 2002

In the latest round of talks at Amsterdam between the GOI and the NSCN, came out with a **Joint Communiqué** that indicates a positive progress in the Peace Process. The GOI besides responding to the proposal of the substantive issues given by the NSCN and renewing the invitation of the Indian Prime Minister to the NSCNs Chairman and General Secretary the GOI has also agreed to recognize, **"The Unique history and situation of Nagas."**

> ***"The GOI recognizes the unique history and the situation of Nagas. It is agreed that talks should proceed in an accommodative and forward-looking manner so that a lasting and honorable solution can be arrived at."***

The Naga people are greatly encouraged with the political will shown by the GOI and the Naga civil society are wholehearted in their support for the Peace dialogue which will bring about a genuine negotiated political settlement between the GOI and the Nagas. This support has been expressed without any reservation in all the joint consultative meetings of the Naga civil society and the NSCN for "Strengthening Peace Strategy." Moreover, there is a need on the part of the GOI to stand firm without wavering from its stand.

Appendix - 6

In Search of a Theological Statement "Righteousness exalts a nation, but sin is a disgrace to any people" (Prov. 14:34)

Preface

Having witnessed all the turmoil (political, social, and economic) in Naga society, we the concerned theological people, have been compelled to come together humbly and prayerfully to formulate a theological stance.

Looking at the Naga predicament, confidence among the Nagas has fallen to low ebb today. There is despair in every sphere of our lives. Achievement in the governmental level is almost non-existent. Rather an economic fiasco, a lack of professionalism in all fields ranging from education to politics, and the lack of honesty and integrity in all areas of society, have produced a mood of pessimism at all levels of Naga society as people lose faith in their leaders.

The haunting memories of Matikhru massacre, the abominable and sacrilegious act of the 1st Maratha Regiment and the 8th Mountain Division at Yangki Baptist Church, the nightmares of Oinam, where hundreds of men and women were tortured in the monsoon rain, with two women giving birth in front of the Indian Army jawans (Assam Rifles), untold tortures, rapes and burning of the villages, the use of Christian Churches as camps by the Indian Army, and burning of Mokokchung by the 16th Maratha Regiment, the burning of Akuluto by the 15 Assam Rifles and the indiscriminate firing of Rashtriya Rifles at Kohima have left damage in all Naga inhabited areas.

Facing the Truth is painful for many, while a few others may shun reality and disseminate the facts and happenings by fiction and distortion, the seriousness of the situation brought us as theological people to try to discern and understand the theological significance of facing the truth about the Nagas.

Crises

The State Government and its leaders have lost credibility and accountability. Dueto large-scale political corruption and moral and spiritual bankruptcy, the government today has lost both the capacity and the will to rule and administer justly and efficiently. The people have lost confidence in government and its leadership.

The Naga Churches and their leaders, by and large have also become spiritually and morally bankrupt. They have for the most part aligned themselves with the corrupt State. They have made peace with the established and institutionalized system, that is the "power that be." This unholy and worldly alliance between the church and the state government has given rise to civil or state religion, resulting in the loss of people's faith in the church and its leadership. The church is guilty of misplaced allegiance to the extend that she has failed to acknowledge the Lordship of Jesus Christ in faith and practice. As a consequence, the church has ceased to be prophetic in her mission in that she speaks visions from her own mind, not from the mouth of God.

The Naga freedom fighters now enter into a process of self-elimination as they fight for supremacy among themselves more then for the national cause. Our freedom fighters are violating human rights by killing innocent civilians and meddling with villages' internal affairs, rather than struggling for national cause, creating a sense of confusion, fear and despair among fellow Nagas everywhere.

The military forces, supposedly the custodian of order and security have left un-repairable psychological scars upon our people which amount to violation of human rights in various aspects of life. The army, with its often erratic behaviour whenever confrontation between them and freedom fighters takes place in and around Naga villages, has created fear psychosis in the minds and hearts of the Naga populace. The Indian Army and other para-military units (Assam Rifles included) have done their share of killing, torturing and raping innocent Nagas. The security forces, supported by the Armed forces Special Power Act of 1958, have let loose a reign of terror upon the Naga people and every sort of violence is inflicted against innocent civilians.

Nagaland, once known for its green tropical forests with rich fauna and flora, is seeing today semi-desert on its hill-tops due to wanton exploitation and destruction of forest and water resources.

A Theological Stance

We believe that the Bible is a divine revelation given by God to men, and is a complete and infallible guide and standard of authority in all matters of religion and morals. Whatever it teaches is to be believed; whatever it commands is to be obeyed; whatever it commands is to be accepted; we believe it to be the Word of God and we believe in its power to transform society. "All Scripture is God's breathed and is useful for teaching, rebuking, correcting and training in righteousness, so that the man of God may be thoroughly equipped for every good work" (2 Tim. 3:16, 17). We, therefore, in affirming our faith in the infallibility of the Bible, resolved to declare the following theses as our theological stance:

Thesis I. Holistic Salvation

Salvation is of the whole man-body, soul, and spirit-through personal faith in Jesus Christ. The holistic notion of salvation does not divide the body from the soul, the material from the spiritual, and the personal from the social. Our personal faith in Christ and commitment to Him compel us to love others and to be involved in their welfare. The same faith and commitment should compel us to participate intelligently in the political process. We affirm our faith in God and are deeply moved by our failure to fulfill our mission of bringing peace and justice to the "world" around us, but especially in the Naga-inhabited areas.

Thesis II. Political Salvation

We affirm that Nagas are a nation and that we have every right to exist as a free nation. We believe that Yahweh is a God of freedom and that it is His will that His people should live in freedom. The exodus event in the Bible stands as a living example of how God willed that His people Israel should be liberated from the bondage of foreign rule in order that they might live as a free people and decide their own destiny.

Our faith and commitment to Jesus Christ compel us to denounce the path of violence in our struggle for freedom. Jesus was not a man of violence. Rather He preached love and peace and demanded that His followers should be peacemakers.

And so in obedience to the commands of our Lord we affirm that it is our duty to fight for freedom through non-violent means.

Thesis III. The State

We affirm our faith that the State is ordained by God for the good of the people. However, when the state goes wrong we will obey God rather than men. We affirm our commitment to Christ that calls for a radical struggle against the present state of affairs: corruption, bribery, violence, killings, favoritism, nepotism, factionalism, and faction patronising, extortions and lawlessness, etc.

Thesis IV. Human Rights

We affirm our obedience to God's command: "You shall not murder" (premeditated killing) Exodus 20:13. We affirm that we have no right to take away anyone's life, (particularly that of the innocent) which is given by God. We condemn violations of human rights in any form and affirm the sanctity and integrity of life in its fullness.

Thesis V. Ecology/Creation

The ecological crisis is urging us to affirm our interrelatedness with nature and to commit ourselves to honour the integrity of God's creation. Every inhabited part of the world, and every piece on earth is, and remains, God's. "In the beginning God created heavens and the earth" (Gen. 1:1). "The earth is the lord's and everything in it, the world, and all who live in it" (Ps. 24:1). God has given the earth to the whole human family to till it and to keep it. We affirm that our responsibility as stewards of God's earth is to participate with love and care in His continuing act of creation.

Thesis VI. Naga Churches

The Church is a people called out from the world, elected, chosen, separated, and called to be saints. It constitutes the Kingdom of Christ, a peculiar people sanctified to God Himself. And therefore, we affirm that the church, true to her calling, should act as the salt of the earth and the light of the world, committed to participate in the suffering struggle for the transformation of society through the exercise of active faith in Jesus Christ.

Thesis VII. Theological Critiques and Reflection

By and large, the Naga Churches have made its peace with the established and the institutionalised system. We have lost the fine cutting edge of theology by justifying the sham and counterfeit of the State with the designs of economic and political style of life. The church pulpits are devoid of theology which calls for absolute allegiance to the claims of the gospel and living it out in the socio-political arena of life. Ours is a religion of flight from historical happenings to the spheres of religious subjectivism. This formless religion values personal success in the secular world and all one can accumulate from it and keep their brand of subjective religion justifying their action, more than faithfulness and radical obedience to the demands of the gospel. Its message is harmless and non-prophetic to the corrupt status quo and to the dehumanising demagogues and its agents. Therefore, such a religion enjoys the blessing, and even the sanction of Caesar. This alignment namely, the Church and the State has given rise to civil religion, which blesses the established status quo instead of calling it into question when it is due. The Church is therefore, guilty of misplaced allegiance to the extend that we have failed to distinguish the God of the Bible revealed in Jesus Christ.

We also realise the government and movements of both left and right, seek to bring the Church into political struggle to support their ideology, schemes and interests and to give a theological rationale for their partisan stance. Theological distortion occurs in such a process, and the cutting edge and critical corrective theology of truth are sold on the satanic alter of ideological necessity. Our theology does not permit us to wed Christ and Caesar. Our concern is that the Nagas and the lands inhabited by them must have a just and a right order.

Conflict, fragmentation, mistrust and enmity are at the centre of the Nagas. Our divisions and conflicts are complex. Theologically this means that no unity and reconciliation, no forgiveness and pardon will take place without sincere personal and collective national repentance.

We advocate a theology that is biblical and seek to bring out the truth than reconciliation with sin and selfishness. Nagas are today morally and spiritually bankrupt, politically corrupt, economically dependent and socially unproductive. Deculturalisation, dehumanisation and alienation cannot be our goal and destiny. The quest for factional supremacy with communal clash will lead us to self-elimination. We are at a difficult cross-road in our history and here is a challenge to our people to struggle with their minds rather than with their guns.

Let it be known by every Naga that we have no right to take away anyone's life which is given by God. In spite of the deep chasm of differences, we immediately appeal in the name of Christ our leader to refrain from killings. Let God be the judge and the final decision maker in the struggle for truth and justice.

Our theology informs us that personal commitment and faith in Christ divorced from an active commitment to love, truth and justice is a mockery of the gospel. Our churches need to make a radical turn from the present pattern and must reaffirm our allegiance to the coming reign of God's kingdom among the Nagas.

As an exodus community, the Naga churches must outline the people's hope. The departure from Egypt is much more than a mere image designed to enrich theological representations. The exodus comes to constitute the prototype of divine revelation, the opportune time and privileged moment in which God manifested Himself and continues to do the same. At the same time exodus of history did not just signify a withdrawal from political and social roles. It was liberative revolution from oppression and exploitation. In Christian understanding, the import of exodus is to encourage the abandonment of older immobilist attitude and structures. We are courageous enough to move out of the paralysing structures of the present. God Himself will furnish us with new ones.

Christ brought a beginning to humanity and the whole creation. This is a biblical teaching often overlooked by Christian individualists. Everything that is affected by sin is now affected by redemption. The disintegrating power of sin and evil manifestation in our society have been reversed by redemption, redemption is not only a salvation that lies beyond the present world but a salvation that begins in the present time and history.

Those who are redeemed and belong to the body Christ are to live their lives from a different viewpoint - grounded in God and His revelation, and not in themselves and their selfish desires. For this reason their societal and political unfolding will be different. Instead of oppression, injustice, hatred, greed and dishonesty and the like, the person seeks to bring liberation, justice and love which reflect the "new creation."

Liberation is a precondition for a new society but this is not all of it. While liberation is implemented in liberating historical events, it also denounces their limitations and ambiguities, proclaims their fulfillment and impels them effectively toward total communion. Without liberating historical events, there could be no growth of the Kingdom. We are committed to apply this biblical understanding of salvation and hence call on the Naga churches to contribute to liberation. The responsibility for liberation is placed on our churches as result of God's summon and support.

Conclusion

The present Naga situation calls for a responsive action from churches that are prophetic. We need a bold incisive resolute response that is prophetic because it speaks to particular context to Naga history, a response that does not give the impression of being "neutral" but is clearly taking a stand. In the war' between right and wrong, there are no neutrals, we are either dead or alive.

We are committed to participate in the struggle for transformation towards a just and finite good society. The present situation of the Naga socio-political order challenges the churches to move beyond mere neutral theological stance to a radical theology or transformation, involvement and participation. It is the solidarity of the Naga churches and the people of God to invite all to join in the struggle for God's reign and His Kingdom among us, and that is a challenge to our beloved people.

Today, more than ever, the churches must be prepared to give an answer and guidance in the context. We are called not to remain neutral and cautious. We place ourselves on the threshold of the battle line in order to inspire and motivate Naga churches to reflection and action. The message of the crucified Christ inspires us to sacrifices for justice and liberation. The message of the resurrection gives us hope in the midst of hopelessness challenges us to wake up to action with courage and confidence. This message should be preached not only in words and statements, but also through programmes, actions and campaigns. The hour is at hand!

Signatories

A Group of Naga Theologically Trained Concerned People

1. Rev. K. Lasuh
2. Rev. N. Chiero
3. Mr. L. Sato
4. Dr. Takatemjen
5. Mr. Yangkahao Vashum
6. Mr. I. Mar Imsong
7. Rev. Dr. Wati Aier
8. Mr. Kavito
9. Rev. Pughoto
10. Mr. Khehovi Sema
11. Rev. Dr. V.K. Nuh
12. Rev. Dr. Tuisem A. Shishak
13. Rev. L. Bizo
14. Rev. R.P. Murry
15. Rev. R. Terhuja
16. Mr. Huzo Meru
17. Dr. (Miss) K. Kapfo
18. Rev. K. Somi
19. Fr. Joe Ngakhuchung
20. Rev. L. Mhasi
21. Mr. Suitei
22. Rev. M. Savino
23. Rev. Bikau
24. Mr. Loli Kape
25. Mr. A. Temjen Jamir
26. Mrs. Khrieleno Terhuja
27. Rev. Candid Sareo
28. Mr. K. Kughato Sumi
29. Mr. Neiwete Chirhah
30. Rev. S. Thong
31. Mr. Sentsing Tep
32. Mr. James Longkumer
33. Mr. Shinglo Khing
34. Mr. Neigukuolic Kehie
35. Mr. Pinglang
36. Mr. Weyiete Lohe
37. Mr. K. Koda
38. Mr. Muvoeho

39. Mr. Vitsilhoutuo Dolie
40. Rev. Z. Terhuja
41. Rev. K. Luruo
42. Rev. V. Tetseo
43. Mr. Ashuli Akamo
44. Mr. K. Joshua
45. Mr. Nungoi Khusoh
46. Mr. Imli Wabang
47. Mr. Joshua Loring
48. Rev. Yankey Patton
49. Rev. R.L. Tennyson
50. Rev. Piano Pani
51. Rev. K. Hokey
52. Mr. L. Kholi
53. Mr. Viloshe
54. Rev. Dr. K. Imotemjen Aier
55. Mr. Mesewete Puro
56. Mr. Z. Thsankiu
57. Mr. Tiatoshi Jamir
58. Rev. Dr. I. Ben
59. Mr. L. Yanger Sangtam
60. Rev. R.S. Kishio
61. Mr. L.C. Puli
62. Mr. Kevy V. Sumi
63. Mr. Vesapa Puro !od:
64. Mr. Kedoungulo Mero
65. Mr. krope Chiero
66. Mr. Ezanpemo Odyuo
67. Mr. K. Mhathung Ngullie
68. Mr. Alemba Kikon
69. Mr. Lithiru Pfithu
70. Mr. T. Hampeng Jurry
71. Mr. Disie
72. Rev. K.N. Shimray
73. Mr. S. Noksa
74. Shailendra Subba
75. Mr. Ningchang Chamroy
76. Rev. Timothy Phaomei
77. Mr. Ilow Eung
78. Mr. John Kape
79. Imna Imsong
80. Rev. Dr. W. Pongsing

81. Mr. P. Bumo
82. Miss H. Mongshai
83. Mr. M. Khumong
84. Miss Tsela Rengma
85. Mr. R.T. Bate
86. Miss Bensele Kath
87. Mrs. Ghosihito W. Sumi
88. Mr. Z. Keago
89. Mr. K. Rusutho
90. Rev. Thsuwachu S. Nyami
91. Mr. Tivisie
92. Mr. Yansenthu
93. Mr. M.M. Batelo
94. Miss Seilorhu
95. Rev. T. Kachusie
96. Abatu
97. Rev. Mp. Namthuirei
98. Mr. Imchawati Kichu
99. Miss Aram Pamei
100. Mr. Alemrenba
101. Miss Bethel Nuh
102. Miss Susan Waten
103. Miss Imtimenla Pongen
104. Miss Temsumenla Pongen
105. Miss Kenesa Kath
106. Miss H. Asang Phom
107. Mr. Chekrovei Cho-o
108. Mr. V. Yepthomi
109. Mrs. P. Mongshai
110. Mr. Kroduo Pao
111. Mr. Lodiho Thapo
112. Rev. Pusazo Chuzho

Dated, Dimapur, Nagaland
10 March 1995

Index

C

Y

Z